PERSPECTIVES
IN
CURRICULUM STUDIES

Perspectives *in* Curriculum Studies

Margaret N. Endeley & Martha A. Zama

Spears Books
Denver, Colorado

Spears Books
An Imprint of Spears Media Press LLC
7830 W. Alameda Ave, Suite 103-247
Denver, CO 80226
United States of America

First Published in the United States of America in 2021 by Spears Books
www.spearsmedia.com
info@spearsmedia.com
Information on this title: www.spearsmedia.com/perspectives-in-curriculum-studies

ISBN: 9781942876823 (Paperback)
ISBN: 9781942876830 (eBook)

Spears Media Press has no responsibility for the persistence or accuracy of urls for external or third-party internet websites referred to in this publication, and does not guarantee that any content on such websites is, or will remain, accurate or appropriate.

Designed and typeset by Spears Media Press LLC
Cover designed by Doh Kambem

Distributed globally by African Books Collective (ABC)
www.africanbookscollective.com

To our families for their unending support

About the Authors

Martha M. A. Zama, PhD obtained a Bachelor of Science in Education/ Zoology and Master of Education in Curriculum and Methodology degrees from the University of Nigeria Nsukka, and a PhD in Curriculum Studies and Teaching from the University of Buea. After 15 years of secondary school teaching in Nigeria and Cameroon, she moved to the Ministry of Higher Education in Cameroon serving primarily as a member of the university administration, and an adjunct lecturer in teacher education establishments and departments at the universities of Buea and Bamenda, spanning various periods. For 23 years, she taught courses in Curriculum and Pedagogy at both undergraduate and graduate levels and co-supervised several M. Ed dissertations. Commitment and passion for teaching opened her up to several opportunities as a participant and resource person in local, and national curriculum and teaching workshops, conferences, and commissions. Notably, she served as national vice-president of the scientific committee during the development of the 2018 Cameroon primary school curriculum. She is now retired from administrative duties but continues to work as an independent scholar.

Margaret Nalova Endeley is an Associate Professor of Curriculum Studies and Teaching in the Faculty of Education, University of Buea, Cameroon. Her passion for teaching has paid off with 27 years of a rich teaching career. She has taught across levels, from secondary to Higher Education. She has a diploma in English Modern Letters from the Higher Teacher's Training College annex in Bambili; a Bachelor's degree in English Modern Letters from the University of Yaoundé; a Master's degree and a PhD in Curriculum Studies and Teaching from the University of Buea, Cameroon. Her research interest areas include teacher education, pedagogy, inclusive education and more recently peace education. She has published extensively and presently she is Vice dean of Studies and Students' Affairs in the Faculty of Education. She is a mother of three adult children.

Brief Contents

CONTENTS

2

Curriculum Theory   21

11

Curriculum Implementation and Change 153

12

Curriculum Evaluation   175

Illustrations

Tables

Foreword

Perspectives in Curriculum Studies is a colossal piece of work in curriculum studies made up of sixteen chapters presented in five sections. The authors have presented the curriculum field from the perspectives of major curriculum domains: *Curriculum theory, Curriculum foundations, Curriculum planning, Curriculum design, Curriculum development, Curriculum implementation* and *Curriculum evaluation*. Their exhaustive presentation of the curriculum development process strategically follows its logical progression. The book also fulfils one of its major goals which is to serve as a textbook for graduate students, as the authors succinctly integrate the ideas and views of various authors in curriculum studies whose works are timely and timeless with cross-cultural philosophies and theories of child development and learning processes, and their personal experiences in curriculum work. Thus, they also offer curriculum planners a broader and more relevant base for curriculum work.

Breaking new grounds, *Perspectives in Curriculum Studies* addresses the long-standing challenges from colonialism that enslaved the African mind-set through the absence of curriculum and pedagogic responsiveness. The exigent thrust of this book towards addressing Africentric vision in the education enterprise, especially in the 21st century with its enormous sociopolitical and health challenges, underscores the need for a dynamic curriculum that addresses relevance, equity in higher order learning, inclusion and above all quality. This work resonates with the anti-colonialist, Julius Nyerere's vision for education in Africa focusing on self-reliance, lifelong learning, and education for liberation. I believe like Nyerere, these authors are reminding us that we must move away from colonial practices that dominate formal education. These practices continue to perpetuate western norms in contradistinction to what will enrich and enhance the African mind.

The scope of this insightful volume is far reaching as it clearly captures the desires of the 2030 agenda on the 17 sustainable development goals (SDG) by providing a new pathway in curriculum studies through the authors' proposed model for curriculum-making called the **Hybrid model**. Given the centrality of education in these current times, the volume is very timely particularly as concerns the stand-alone SDG 4 addressing *inclusive and equitable quality education and promote lifelong learning opportunities for all* that cuts across all the SDGs. On this account, education faces the challenges to address this through its curriculum. This book therefore supports the need for developing a curriculum framework for the SDGs that *allows for a high degree of flexibility through the non-prescriptive nature of its content*. The authors are reminding us of our responsibilities to step up to these challenges that are reiterated in the Continental Education Strategy (CESA,16-25). The book further captures two of seven aspirations set forth in Agenda 2063 of the African Union. I find these authors speaking to aspirations 5 and 6 which set as a goal: (5) *An Africa with a strong cultural identity, common heritage, values, and ethics*; (6) *An Africa whose development is people-driven, relying on the potential of African people, especially its women and youth, and caring for children.* This thoughtful Africentric curriculum textbook rich in content, orientation and style certainly responds to these aspirations in intent and content.

Consequently, in writing this book, the authors seek to reinvigorate a qualitative system of education and training based on promoting contents and practices with African core values. The well-researched volume provides valuable resources for developing education stakeholders most especially curriculum specialists, teacher educators, teachers, and education researchers. I hail their industry.

Therese M. S. Tchombe, PhD
Emeritus Professor and Honorary Dean, UNESCO Chair for Special needs Education,
University of Buea

Preface

Perspectives in Curriculum Studies is a product born out of need. The scarcity of curriculum textbooks relevant to local contexts made it imperative for us to embark on this project. Among the challenges facing education in Africa today, irrelevant curricula, poor quality of teaching and teacher education are frequently cited. While in the broadest sense, education is the process of equipping people with knowledge, skills and values that would enable them fit into their respective roles in society, curriculum is the road map for that process as well as its substance. One obvious reaction of education authorities to the problems of education quality is to revisit the curricula. In the case of *Perspectives in Curriculum Studies* this "revisit" has been inspired by many years of our teaching experiences at various levels in the formal education system in Cameroon, Central Africa.

Although education occurs in formal, informal, and non-formal settings, curricula are associated almost exclusively with schooling and transmission of academic knowledge thus marginalising indigenous African knowledge systems and world views, whose ultimate goal of education is preparation for life in the community. Effective re-construction of African school curricula would mean nurturing a generation of curriculum workers (classroom teachers, curriculum experts, education inspectors and superintendents etc.) who are well grounded in curriculum principles and issues as well as in African educational foundations, to enable them to establish an African identity in school curricula. Because the curriculum field in Africa is still largely underdeveloped with few books on curriculum planning and design, there is a need for curriculum textbooks like ours (*Perspectives in Curriculum Studies*) to direct curriculum development and renewal efforts that can transform nations.

Consequently, this book is intended to serve as a textbook for graduate courses in Curriculum Studies and related disciplines in Education. It will also benefit classroom teachers, teacher trainers, instructional designers, researchers, decision makers in Education and anyone interested in advancing knowledge in the theory and practice of Curriculum. Knowledge from this book is largely normative and less analytical with the belief that the starting point for good practices is an in-depth understanding of the standard practices in the field of curriculum which will translate into proper implementation and better quality. While we emphasise standard curriculum principles which can also be applied in other parts of the world, peculiarities of the African context are highlighted, illustrated, and considered where necessary. We believe that foundations of education in Africa must be factored in because inappropriate conceptions and practice will be detrimental to education access, equity, relevance, and lifelong learning. It is hoped that the reader of this text will not only get acquainted with curriculum terminology, but will be able to apply, analyse and evaluate with competence and confidence the concepts and principles articulated in this book; with the goal of contributing effectively to decision-making towards the creation, implementation, and maintenance of appropriate curricula that would address quality and relevance for educational systems, particularly in developing countries.

The book is organised into sixteen chapters lodged in five parts. Part 1 introduces the Curriculum field, part 2 deals with Foundations of the Curriculum, part 3 is on the Curriculum development process while part 4 focuses on Instructional design and part 5 ends the book with Global perspectives of Curriculum development.

Reader friendly features of the book include graphic illustrations, a comprehensive glossary, references, and subject index.

Acknowledgements

We are most grateful to Professor Leke Tambo, Professor in Curriculum Studies and Teaching and our revered teacher and mentor for inspiring us to rise up to the challenge of contributing to curriculum discourse. We equally appreciate Professor Emeritus Therese Tchombe, UNESCO Chair for Special Needs Education in the University of Buea, for not only being a role model to us but taking time off her busy schedule to review the book and for accepting to write the foreword. Special thanks also go to Joyce Ashuntantang, Professor of English at the University of Hartford, Connecticut, USA; Nelson Ngoh, Professor of Science Education and Director of Graduate Programmes in Science Education, University of Bridgeport, Connecticut, USA and Dr Azah Vera Ndifor, our former student who now works as an independent researcher in Toronto, Canada, for reading through the manuscripts and providing invaluable feedback that contributed to improving the quality of the work. We wish to acknowledge the moral support of our families who bore the brunt of our 'absence' during the compilation of this text.

Part One

The Curriculum Field

With John Franklin Bobbit's publication in 1918 titled 'The curriculum', the curriculum field emerged in the early twentieth century as a major outgrowth of the academic discipline of Education. Being a relatively young field, many of its sub-fields appear indistinct and some theories are still in their formative stages. The concept of curriculum itself still appears fragmentary, elusive, and confusing to many. This part of the book which consists of two chapters, introduces the reader to the curriculum field attempting to clarify its major concepts and notions in chapter one. Chapter two prepares the reader for the next part of the book by presenting various orientations to curriculum theory and theorising as a precursor to curriculum practice.

1

Basic Concepts in Curriculum Studies

Though the curriculum field is relatively young, the term curriculum is not new in educational discourse for the simple reason that its existence was recognised long before curriculum morphed into a separate discipline. Even with this, an absolute agreement on the meaning of curriculum has not yet been reached by educationists, thereby creating discrepancies as to the correct definition of the concept. Curriculum definitions are often perceived as debatable, problematic, and even confusing. Apparently, the term has a long history that may have affected its conceptualisation at various points in time, despite its constant use in education literature and the development of study areas in the field of curriculum. Reflections on various conceptions of the term curriculum and its related concepts will be presented in this chapter. Such reflections will clarify common understandings of the components of an appropriate curriculum as well as give meaning to the different orientations of growing domains of the curriculum as a field of study.

Defining the term 'Curriculum'

The word curriculum is derived from one or both of the Latin words *currus* and *currere*. The former is a noun meaning a racecourse, and the latter is the infinitive verb form which means to run. Literally then, this may be translated as 'to run through a racecourse'. Applied to education and particularly to schooling, this would loosely mean going through the educational route provided by a school for its students through its schedule of activities. However, different perspectives abound in the definition of this word curriculum, describing it as subjects, or a plan, a product, a process, learning outcomes and learning experiences among others. The major perspectives and related definitions are discussed below, ending with an operational definition by the present authors.

Curriculum as Subjects

Subjects studied in school are listed as the curriculum. This common viewpoint has been the traditional way of describing the curriculum; as subjects or a collective history of standardised knowledge. Such a conceptualisation is narrow, failing to take into account all other facets of the teaching-learning process that take place within and outside the classroom. Examples of definitions that fall within this category are:

The content pupils are expected to learn (Smith and Orlovsky,1978).

Curriculum can be understood as a process of selecting courses of study or content. (Beauchamp, 1977).

Curriculum as a Plan

A curriculum can also be considered as a plan for the systematic implementation of educational content, instructional methods, and assessment strategies, or a systematic outline or blueprint. This sense of the term offers a broader scope. Macro-plans such as syllabuses and micro-plans such as course outlines and lesson plans could be called curriculum plans in addition to lists of subjects taught and learnt in school. Some definitions of the curriculum with this orientation are:

- Ralph Tyler (1957): The curriculum is all the learning of students which is planned by and directed by the school to attain its educational goals.
- Hilda Taba (1962): All curricula, no matter what their design, are composed of certain elements. A curriculum usually contains a statement of aims and of specific objectives; it indicates some selection and organisation of content; it either implies or manifests certain patterns of learning and teaching, whether because the objectives demand them or because the content organisation requires them. Finally, it includes a program of evaluation of the outcomes.
- David G. Armstrong (1989): Curriculum is a master plan for selecting content and organising learning experiences for the purpose of changing and developing learners' behaviours and insights.
- J. Galen Saylor, William M. Alexander, and Arthur J. Lewis (1974): We define curriculum as a plan for providing sets of learning opportunities to achieve broad goals and related specific objectives for an identifiable population served by a single school centre for persons to be educated.
- Peter Oliva (1982): Curriculum is a plan or programme for all experiences which the learner encounters under the direction of the school.

Curriculum as Experience

This curriculum perspective includes the planned and operational curriculum, such as the activities in the classroom, as well as the events in the school environment that are directly or indirectly linked to the planned study program. This means that the relationship between plans and experiences is intertwined, where "plans" refer to planned curricula in advance and "experiences" refer to unplanned happenings in classrooms. Although preparation is a precursor to action, it is important to remember that unplanned activities frequently take place in classroom environments. Therefore, the actual curricula which are implemented in classrooms consist of a combination of plans and experiences. The most accepted definitions of the curriculum fall within this category. Below are some of them:

- Franklin Bobbit (1918): Curriculum is that series of things which children and youth must do and experience by way of developing abilities to do the things well that make up the affairs of adult life; and to be in all respects what adults should be.

- Caswell and Campbell (1935): Curriculum is composed of all of the experiences children have under the guidance of the teacher.
- James Duncan and Jack Frymier (1967): A set of events, either proposed, occurring, or having occurred, which has the potential for reconstructing human experience.
- Glen Hass (1987): The curriculum is all of the experiences that individual learners have in a program of education whose purpose is to achieve broad goals and related specific objectives, which is planned in terms of a framework of theory and research or past and present professional practice.
- Ronald Doll (1970): The curriculum is now generally considered to be all of the experiences that learners have under the auspices of the school.
- Daniel Tanner and Laurel Tanner (1995): The curriculum is the reconstruction of knowledge and experience that enables the learner to grow in exercising intelligent control of subsequent knowledge and experience

Curriculum as a Product

This perspective focuses on the objectives or intended outcomes of the curriculum. It looks at what the capabilities of the student are before and after instruction. Definitions that fit this category are:

- Mauritz Johnson (1967): Curriculum is a structured series of intended learning outcomes. Curriculum prescribes (or at least anticipates) the results of instruction. It does not prescribe the means to be used in achieving the results.
- Bell (1971): The offering of socially valued knowledge, skills, and attitudes made available to students through a variety of arrangements during the time they are at school, college, or university.
- James Popham and Eva Baker (1970) define a curriculum as the planned learning outcomes for which the school is responsible.

The narrower definitions see curriculum only as a plan, programme, course of study or a package that can bring about learning while the broader definitions see curriculum as a process. The process includes the philosophical viewpoint and the continuous effort of making curriculum to serve the needs of society. It is a process that determines the knowledge, values, attitudes, and experiences that students acquire inside and outside the school. Putting together all perspectives, curriculum is underpinned by three major interacting factors: the learner, knowledge and society.

Classification of definitions based on the nature of the Curriculum

The definitions presented in the preceding section including many others have been classified in the literature as either *prescriptive* or *descriptive* (Glatthorn et al, 2019). Prescriptive definitions state what ought to happen, and usually take the form of a plan, an intended program, or expert opinion about what needs to take place in the course of study. Descriptive definitions on the other hand, present the situation as it is in real classrooms. In other words, it is the experiences of learners that matter. Examples of the definitions of the Prescriptive curriculum are shown on Table 1.1 while those of the descriptive definitions are found on Table 1.2.

Table 1.1. Prescriptive Definitions of Curriculum

Date	Author	Definition
1902	John Dewey	Curriculum is a continuous reconstruction, moving from the child's present experience out into that represented by the organized bodies of truth that we call studies . . . the various studies . . . are themselves experience— they are that of the race. (pp. 11–12)
1918	Franklin Bobbitt	Curriculum is the entire range of experiences, both directed and undirected, concerned in unfolding the abilities of the individual. (p. 43)
1927	Harold O. Rugg	The curriculum is a succession of experiences and enterprises having a maximum lifelikeness for the learner . . . giving the learner that development most helpful in meeting and controlling life situations. (p. 8)
1935	Hollis Caswell in Caswell & Campbell	The curriculum is composed of all the experiences children have under the guidance of teachers. Thus, curriculum considered as a field of study represents no strictly limited body of content, but rather a process or procedure. (pp. 66, 70)
1957	Ralph Tyler	The curriculum is all the learning experiences planned and directed by the school to attain its educational goals. (p. 79)
1967	Robert Gagne	Curriculum is a sequence of content units arranged in such a way that the learning of each unit may be accomplished as a single task, provided the capabilities described by specified prior units (in the sequence) have already been mastered by the learners. (p. 23)

Table 1.2. Descriptive Definitions of Curriculum

Date	Author	Definition
1935	Hollis Caswell & Doak Campbell	All the experiences children have under the guidance of teachers.
1941	Thomas Hopkins	Those learnings each child selects, accepts, and incorporates into himself to act with, on, and upon, in subsequent experiences.
1960	W. B. Ragan	All experiences of the child for which the school accepts responsibility.
1987	Glen Hass	The set of actual experiences and perceptions of the experiences that each individual learner has of his or her program of education.
1995	Daniel Tanner & Laurel Tanner	The reconstruction of knowledge and experience that enables the learner to grow in exercising intelligent control of subsequent knowledge and experience.

Date	Author	Definition
2006	D. F. Brown	All student school experiences relating to the improvement of skills and strategies in thinking critically and creatively, solving problems, working collaboratively with others, communicating well, writing more effectively, reading more analytically, and conducting research to solve problems.
2009	E. Silva	An emphasis on what students can do with knowledge, rather than what units of knowledge they have, is the essence of 21st-century skills.

Source: Glatthorn, Boschee and Whitehead (2008, p 4-5)

A working definition of curriculum for this book has been constructed around several perspectives. Thus, curriculum comprises all the planned and unplanned content and activities implemented in the classroom as well as other school-related activities outside the classroom which directly or indirectly enrich learners' experiences. This definition considers formal studies, informal classroom and school activities and non-formal activities carried out under the auspices of the school as components of a curriculum.

Components of a Curriculum

Four main components constitute a curriculum plan. These four components of the curriculum are highly interrelated.

1. Curriculum Aims, Goals and Objectives

Aims, goals, and objectives refer to the intended learning outcomes determined by the curriculum planners. The curriculum aims, goals and objectives spell out what is expected to be achieved. They clearly define the purpose of education in terms of what a school offers and this drives the rest of the components of the curriculum.

2. Curriculum Content or Subject Matter

Subject matter or content states what topics are to be included in the curriculum. It consists of knowledge to be acquired in school. Content is an element or a medium through which the objectives are realised. In organising the learning contents, the elements of balance, articulation, sequence, integration, and continuity must be respected to form sound content.

3. Curriculum Experiences

Curriculum experiences include the instructional strategies used to transmit organised knowledge. Instructional activities, methods and materials are at the core of curriculum experiences. They convert the curriculum content to learning experiences and produce learning outcomes.

4. Curriculum Evaluation

Curriculum evaluation is a critical element of an effective curriculum. It identifies the quality, effectiveness of the program, process, and product of the curriculum using a variety of assessment instruments and strategies.

For purposes of planning for instruction, curriculum plans can be subdivided into programs, courses, units, and lessons.

Program

A program of study is a set of learning experiences offered to learners over a long period of formal education. Often ending with the award of a certificate, a program consists of many courses that take several years to complete. At the University of Buea, for example, the program of study leading to the award of the degree B.Ed. Curriculum Studies and Teaching (CST) in History implies that the student takes required courses in the departments of Curriculum studies and teaching, and History as well as compulsory university wide courses for three years. At the primary school level, pupils are often required to go through all the programs in the school. The secondary school offers more flexibility as students go higher. Some students may study programmes in science and others in the arts at the second cycle of secondary school.

Programs are usually described inside curriculum framework documents outlining program goals and objectives, and policy statements on time allocations among other requirements.

Course

A course is a subset of a program. It consists of a set of organised learning experiences with a given title. Course assessment may end with the award of a grade. A course may last for a year, a semester, a term, or a quarter. At university level, courses have grade numbers or numerical descriptions. For example, Econs 101 means that it is an introductory course for first year students offered by the Department of Economics. That course may be taken by students of different programs.

Courses in primary and secondary schools typically last for a year. It should be noted that at the primary and secondary school levels, course titles are often the same as program titles. For example, English language is a course for primary one pupils, and it is also the title of one program in the primary school curriculum.

Unit

Units are subsets of courses. In other words, a course can be divided into units. Units are usually developed by teachers around a single overall concept, though they sometimes omit them during instructional planning. Each unit may last for one to four weeks. For example, in an undergraduate course titled *General pedagogy*, there can be a unit on *Effective teaching*.

- Topics under that unit would include
- perspectives of the concept of effective teaching.
- elements of effective teaching behaviour.
- characteristics and competencies of effective teachers and
- promoting effective teaching.

Lesson

It is a set of related learning experiences typically lasting between 15 mins and one hour in primary and secondary schools. Lessons may have extended durations depending on the activities to be undertaken. At the level of tertiary education lesson periods are relatively longer. Lessons outline specific objectives to be attained.

Types of Curriculum

As noted earlier, the term curriculum has been subjected to varied interpretations some of which give a narrower or wider meaning to the concept. Such variations affect classification schemes used in curriculum typology. Narrow definitions of the term curriculum give rise to fewer curriculum types and vice versa. Classification schemes are influenced by contexts of curriculum practice and eras of curriculum theorising. American writers in the early years of the curriculum field suggested five curriculum types namely: *ideological, formal, derived, operational* and *experiential*. In the past few decades, the *names overt, societal, hidden, null, supported, recommended, phantom, concomitant, rhetorical, curriculum in use, received, internal and electronic* are more commonly cited as types of curriculum operating in American schools (see Goodlad, 1979; Glatthorn et al, 2019; Wilson, 2020).

The literature presents a plethora of types of curriculum with synonymous and sometimes confusing appellations. To bring to a common understanding the diverse terms used in describing curriculum types, Marzooghi (2016), collected the names and descriptions of over 215 types of curricula stated by scholars in various academic texts. He analysed and grouped them into sixteen categories as shown on table 1.3.

Table 1.3. Categories of Curriculum Types

Category	Types
1. Theoretical-oriented	Behavioristic, cognitivist, humanistic, constructivist, democratic, community-service, descriptive, eclectic, inclusive, inert, spiritual, modernistic, post-modernistic, post-formal, monoculture, multicultural, normative, mono-realistic, pluralistic, progressive, scientific, society-centered, student-centered, subject-centered, transformative, trans active, transmission, transpersonal, transcendental, developmental, deliberative, service-learning, positivistic and emancipatory.
2. Social-oriented and curriculum-development system	Place-based, school-based, space-based, in content, site-based, centralized, semi-centralized, decentralized, institutional, adapted, contact, cross-cultural, localized, globalized, localized, internationalized, national, local, societal, traditional, big, in- between and state-mandated
3. Racial-oriented and gender-oriented	Feministic-based, male-oriented, sex-based, differentiated, segregated and race-based.
4. Subject-centered and learning levels	Scientific broad-field, knowledge-based, disciplinary, inter-disciplinary, multi-disciplinary, trans-disciplinary, integrated, fused, enabled, multi-vocational, professional, separate subject-matter, skill-based, technical, core, vocational, linear, helix, spiral, spider web, hierarchical, staircase, sequenced, balanced and parallel

Category	Types
5. Methodic and process-based	Activity-based, action-based, inquiry-based, problem-based, innovative, collaborative.
6. Schooling level	Pre-school, elementary, secondary, postsecondary, higher education, early childhood, further, complementary
7. Formal/Intended	Approved, common, explicit, generic, ideal, phantom, overt, planned, prescriptive, public, visible, exiled, written and internal.
8. Implemented and based on teacher contribution:	Operational, actual, applied, adopted, delivered, instructional, taught, experiential, live, teacher-based, teacher-proof, adapted, enacted
9. Learned and learner-based	Achieved, experienced, narrative, personalized, student-oriented, student-proof, individualized.
10. Evaluation-oriented	Assessed, evaluated, tested, measured, appraised, outcome-based, unmeasured
11. Implicit	Tacit, concomitant, correspondence, embodied, ignored, invisible, real implicit, unintended, unintended-implicit, adjusted, adaptive, thematic, overuse, mindless, informal
12. Hidden	Unwritten, unspoken, unstudied, covert, neglected-hidden, sterilized-hidden, resistance, clandestine, universalistic, particularistic, pre-planned hidden
13. Non-formal	Un- schooling, homeschool, extra, extracurricular, media, outside
14. Emergent	Incidental, expressive, exposed, bouncy, un-preplanned
15. Null	Absent, empty, in-absentia, distorted, intended-distorted, intended-null, intended-omitted, intended-sterilized, lost, missed, neglected, omitted, omitted-hidden, intended sterilized, unintended, distorted, unintended omitted, unintended null, unintended sterilized, intended neglected
16. Digital	Electronic, web-based, online, offline, internet-based, intranet-based, computer-based, digital implicit, digital hidden, digital omitted, digital sterilized, digital neglected, digital distorted

Source: Marzooghi (2016 p. 168-169)

This proliferation of types of curriculum observed in the literature is partly because of the use of a variety of adjectives to describe the curriculum. Indiscriminate and widespread use of adjectives to determine curriculum types leads not only to unnecessary repetition but to somewhat cumbersome appellations that are not quite useful to curriculum workers. Perhaps it is for this reason that some scholars prefer to talk about attributes of a curriculum instead of types (see Tambo, 2003p. 105-106) and in doing so present them in a somewhat non exhaustive manner.

Curriculum typology does not present a precise number of curriculum types but considers descriptors of curriculum and venues or variations in curriculum (Schubert, 2010), depending on one's conception of curriculum and context of practice. Some curriculum types are planned and visible and those that are not, termed by Ornstein and Hunkins (2018 p. 202) as shadows within the curriculum do exist because curriculum is a human endeavour. However, seven major curriculum types (both substantive and shadows) will be identified and described here, and their relationships shown in figure 1.1.

The Written Curriculum

This is perhaps the most well recognised type of curriculum. The written curriculum consists of explicitly stated learning opportunities offered to learners in any given school system. Such statements are guided by laws, decrees and government texts relating to curriculum policy. Documents that clearly state the written curriculum are curriculum guides or frameworks, syllabuses, schemes of work, timetables, textbooks, and course manuals.

The written curriculum is also known as the *intended* curriculum because it grows out of carefully formulated and articulated goals and objectives and well thought out specifications for execution and attainment of educational expectations. Anyone interested in knowing what the curriculum of any school is, can easily visualise learning opportunities displayed on one or all the aforementioned documents. This open nature of the written curriculum has also earned it the name *overt* curriculum. Its other appellations include *formal, explicit, official*, and *recommended* curriculum.

Functions of the Written Curriculum

Control is a major function of the written curriculum. Pedagogic inspectors and head teachers charged with monitoring curriculum implementation have a duty to ensure that curriculum goals and design specifications of the written curriculum are followed as intended by curriculum designers. However, education authorities and classroom teachers in Cameroon seem to perceive this function differently. While the former see control as a management responsibility, teachers see instructional supervision as a fault-finding activity that creates anxiety and poor interpersonal relations between pedagogic inspectors and teachers (Titanji and Yuoh, 2010) instead of one that encourages teachers to discuss ways of addressing challenges of executing the written curriculum (Ojong, 2019). Nevertheless, control activities sometimes reveal a disparity between the written curriculum and what goes on in the classroom. Reasons for wide disparities range from inadequate human, material, and financial resources to inability of classroom teachers to adapt the written curriculum to local realities.

Other functions of the written curriculum are mediation and standardisation (Glatthorn et al, 2008). Curriculum documents get to implementers in forms that need to be exploited and translated into the instructional process. The written curriculum therefore mediates between what experts recommend being taught in schools and what teachers interpret as that which can be taught. The standardising function describes the compromise that inspectors or head teachers and classroom teachers arrive at to ensure comparable standards among schools for any given level.

The Taught Curriculum

Also known as the *operational* curriculum, the *actual* and the *delivered* curriculum, the taught curriculum is one that 'an observer sees in action as the teacher teaches' (Glatthorn et al, 2019 p. 37). It describes all knowledge, skills and attitudes that a teacher deliberately makes the learner to acquire. Since it is understood that in practice, teachers do teach in and out of prescribed syllabuses, the taught curriculum for the same class or grade taught by two different teachers is not necessarily identical. The taught curriculum is therefore determined solely by the classroom teacher. Distribution of time to an activity or choice of teaching strategies suggests that a teacher's personal philosophy of instruction influences the taught curriculum, among other factors.

The relationship between the taught curriculum and the written curriculum is a direct one because teachers get directives on what they are to teach from prescribed syllabuses and textbooks. That notwithstanding, the taught curriculum is hardly equivalent to the written curriculum as has been observed earlier in this section. Some writers hold that the written curriculum has only a moderate effect on the taught curriculum. They argue that most experienced teachers rely on their assessment of what has worked in the past and what is required in examinations is given greater attention. It is the duty of educational authorities to emphasise continuously to classroom teachers the absurdity of placing the cart before the horse. The taught curriculum and examinations should derive from the written curriculum and not the reverse.

Functions of the taught curriculum

The major function of the taught curriculum is accountability. Record of workbooks popularly called "cahiers de textes" (the French equivalent of logbooks) in Cameroon schools contain records of what teachers teach daily. From these records, monitors of curriculum implementation can easily map out those content areas that are often neglected by teachers and redress the situation. Pedagogic inspectors expect the written and taught curriculum to be almost identical emphasising that teachers should teach all and only what is prescribed in syllabuses. Other schools of thought argue that academic freedom requires teachers to teach outside of prescribed syllabuses if such knowledge does not lead away from curriculum goals and objectives. Proper curriculum alignment implies that both taught and written curriculum must work towards curriculum standards and wide disparities between them may not be helpful to the system.

The Tested Curriculum

Curriculum goals and objectives are of little or no use if there is no established pattern of finding out whether they are being achieved or not. The tested curriculum describes all the learning experiences learners are tested on. Continuous assessments and final examinations are strategies commonly employed to measure and evaluate learner achievement of the curriculum. By differentiating teaching syllabuses from examination syllabuses, curriculum developers attach importance to the tested curriculum. Unfortunately, this has been misconstrued to the extent that some teachers have replaced teaching syllabuses with examination syllabuses and model answers to past questions.

The tested curriculum has a direct relationship with the taught and invariably the written curriculum. It derives from what students have been taught from what has been prescribed and described in official documents. Yet, from our personal experiences it is not uncommon to hear students in African schools complaining that teachers set tests and examinations on content they did not teach. In practice, therefore, the tested curriculum may not always reflect the taught curriculum.

Functions of the tested curriculum

The sole function of the tested curriculum is evaluation. It emerges as a system of processes and tools that are used to determine the extent to which students are acquiring or have acquired knowledge and skill. To the casual observer, the tested curriculum gives an idea of how far the written curriculum has been executed.

The Co-Curriculum

Non-academic activities that fall outside the realm of the written curriculum although these activities are official and recommended constitute the co-curriculum. Co-curricular activities include school sports, school clubs, and national day activities in which students participate. These activities usually take place out of the regular classroom and sometimes out of school premises and timetables. It is for this reason that some educators refer to them as extra-curricular activities giving prominence to the prefix 'extra'. Given the important role these activities play in the all-round development of a learner, co-curriculum is a better term than extracurricular activities, a term that denotes 'outside of something'. Etymologically, co-curriculum would mean a curriculum existing side by side with the written curriculum. In other words, the co-curriculum complements the written curriculum even if it takes place outside of classrooms.

Functions of the co-curriculum

Co-curricular activities enhance holistic development of a learner. An educated person is a product of physical, social, emotional, and intellectual development. Specifically, co-curricular activities are designed to accomplish the following:

- Enhancing the self-esteem of learners. For example, a student who is poor in mathematics but has good artistic skills and whose paintings make it to exhibitions during school open door days, is unlikely to have a low sense of self despite dismal performance in mathematics.
- Improve students' career opportunities. Through extra-curricular activities, students can showcase their talents and have opportunities to be spotted for future career development. Many outstanding professional footballers and music stars had humble beginnings in school co-curricular activities.
- Physical development. Sports, games, dance, and related activities enhance the development of body parts and smooth functioning of the human biological system. A healthy mind functions best in a healthy body.
- Social development. Co-curricular activities give room for social interaction of learners from diverse backgrounds. During such interactions, learners develop social skills such as tolerance, healthy competition, cooperation, and collaboration.

The Hidden Curriculum

It is the kind of curriculum that is neither stated anywhere nor intended by curriculum planners though its existence and worth are undeniable. An American educator Philip Jackson first coined and used the term hidden curriculum in 1968 when he published the book titled *Life in the classrooms* (Jackson, 1968). He did so after observing that schools were enforcing some desirable student behaviours like turning up on time, quietly waiting for your turn and being courteous among others, though these expectations were not stated in books. He stated that such behaviour resulted from the hidden curriculum. The hidden curriculum goes by other names such as the *unintended, latent, invisible, informal, implicit,* and *covert* curriculum.

On the other hand, a critical theorist Paolo Freire (1972) who published his famous book, *Pedagogy of the Oppressed* in Portuguese in the same year as Jackson, argued that schools oppressed powerless individuals. When Freire stated that, 'the oppressed, having internalised the image of the oppressor and adopted his guidelines, are fearful of freedom', he was alluding to the fact that schools indirectly teach undesirable behaviour patterns in learners through the differential use of power and power structure. By-products of schooling can therefore birth both desirable and undesirable behaviour patterns. Pupils and students often exhibit new forms of behaviour because of exposure to school activities. These behavioural outcomes point to the existence of invisible but influential learning experiences in the school life of learners. Learners do not only learn what teachers teach. They imitate and model situations. They construct meaning from personal and collective experiences in the social milieu of the school environment. All of this constitutes the hidden curriculum.

Since it is never deliberately planned, it is important for educators to identify the sources of the hidden curriculum to give it appropriate attention. Longstreet and Shane (1993 p.46) define the hidden curriculum as "the kind of learnings children derive from the very nature and organization of the public school as well as the behaviours and attitudes of teachers and administrators". From Longstreet and Shane's definition, two sources of the hidden curriculum emerge: Organisation structure of a school and the behaviour of 'significant others.' School culture can be added as a third source of the hidden curriculum.

Organisational structure of a school has constant and changing factors. The hierarchical nature of the school administration is constant. The line of authority, power structure and school regulations are clear to everyone. So, the patterns of power distribution and the way authority is exercised are learnt unconsciously by students. Organisational variables such as class size, seating arrangements, graded or non-graded classes, availability and accessibility to libraries, laboratories, playgrounds also impact the hidden curriculum in many ways. Schools with better libraries and more extensive playgrounds may produce students with better predispositions to a reading culture and recreational activities. On the other hand, students in large classes where classroom space and learning resources are limited, survival instincts tend to foster aggressive and selfish attitudes among learners.

The attitudes of teachers towards students and students towards their peers are social variables that also give rise to the hidden curriculum. Relationships that endear warm and relaxed or tense and anxious social climates provide lessons on mutual trust, respect, fear and many other emotions and values. When teacher-student relationships are cordial, students share in decision making and there are extensive opportunities for them to participate actively in the learning process without unnecessary fear and anxiety. Bullying is an increasingly present phenomenon in the school milieu today. Unhealthy relationships among fellow students are a culprit.

Guardians and parents exert pressure on learners in a way that causes the hidden curriculum to emerge. Through approval or disapproval of school decisions, they send unintended right and wrong messages to their children concerning the importance of the issue in question. It is obvious that financial and moral support from parents and other members of the community go a long way to improve the functioning of a school and overall success and attainment of curriculum goals. If the hidden curriculum strains or fosters the relationship between home and school community, this weakens or strengthens the written curriculum.

School culture describes the way of life of members of a school as a cultural system. Answers to questions such as: *Does student discipline reflect bias? Does the physical appearance of teachers command respect? Do students have opportunities to be heard? Who decides on how collective funds are spent? Are there reports on how collected money is spent? Is late coming frowned at?* can paint a vivid picture of a school culture. Arguably, school culture is a predictor of issues relating to punctuality, fairness, honesty, beauty, neatness and more.

Functions of the Hidden Curriculum

The hidden curriculum greatly influences character building. Although it is unintended, the hidden curriculum cannot be ignored by curriculum planners and implementers. It influences the intended curriculum by either reinforcing its goals and objectives or pulling it away from their full realisation. The hidden curriculum may therefore be seen to have advantages and disadvantages, or positive and negative effects. No matter how this is visualised this curriculum type is largely responsible for attitudes and values that students exhibit in and out of school and in later life after schooling.

The outcry of many African countries today is corruption and mismanagement of public funds, unpatriotic acts, civil disobedience, lethargy in public service and many other unproductive behaviours exhibited by public servants who are school graduates. The question that begs to be asked and answered is whether school curricula do not include Civics and Ethics, Economics, and other social sciences. The written curriculum is just part of a school curriculum albeit a major part. The hidden curriculum is another. School culture may indeed be a microcosm of the culture of the larger society. Schools have a huge responsibility to shape the character of students to fit societal expectations. Curriculum planners must see the hidden curriculum as a mirror of societal values and organise learning environments in ways that this unseen curriculum that emerges can promote desirable values.

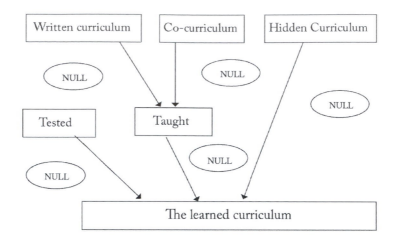

FIGURE 1.1. Relationships of the major Curriculum Types

The Learned Curriculum

It is also called the *received* curriculum and the *bottom-line* curriculum. For many people, the learned curriculum is the real measure of curriculum because it represents what a learner internalizes or acquires from exposure to school. It is a combination of knowledge, attitudes, and skills that the learner acquires from the written, taught, tested, co-curriculum and hidden curriculum. If the written curriculum represents what learners are supposed to learn, the learned curriculum is what learners succeed in learning. It is not everything that is stipulated in the written curriculum that learners learn. They do not learn all of it because not all of it is taught in the first place and even when all of it is taught, the nature of the learning process does not guarantee that every learner absorbs or makes meaning from what is taught. The learned curriculum is not uniform for all learners of the same class or school level.

It is the duty of classroom teachers to close this gap among learners. Factors affecting learning should be arranged in such a way that the quantity and quality of learning increases. Such concerns have caused instructional designers to produce theory-oriented types of curricula reflected in appellations like humanistic curricula, constructivist curricula etc.

Null Curriculum

This is a term that was introduced by Eisner (1994) to describe the content that is deliberately or unintentionally left out of school learning but recognised as being ignored by the students and the community. These are often controversial topics and subject matter.

Curriculum Domains

Curriculum domains are the knowledge bases in the field of curriculum studies. These domains are highly interrelated yet constitute sub-fields on their own.

Curriculum Theory

It may also be defined as a set of related statements or a coherent and systematic body of ideas used to give meaning to school curriculum by pointing up the relationship among its elements, directing its development, use and evaluation while analysing problems to guide people on deciding on appropriate justifiable actions. Curriculum theory helps us name the problem and its elements, factors relating to the problem, resources necessary for handling the problem and strategies to solve the problem. Theory thus provides us with a way of viewing the matter, of thinking and talking about it and relating it to other issues.

Curriculum Foundations

Foundations are the ideas that influence the minds of curriculum developers. These forces are beliefs and orientations as well as conceptions of learning and the needs of society. These affect the content and structure of the curriculum. Foundation of curriculum is rooted with the foundation of education. The four main foundations of the curriculum include the historical, philosophical, psychological, and sociological foundations.

Curriculum Development

Curriculum development, also referred to as curriculum construction or engineering, is defined as a planned, purposeful, progressive, and systematic process to create positive improvements in the educational system. Curriculum development incorporates three distinct phases: Planning, implementation, and evaluation of the curriculum. Curriculum development is not limited to teachers, learners and production of plans for schooling but plays a vital role in enhancing societal development.

Curriculum Planning

Curriculum planning refers to making decisions about what to learn, why, and how to organise the teaching and learning process, taking into account existing curriculum requirements and the resources available (UNESCO-IBE, 2019). It is the first part of the curriculum development process. At the general level, it often results in the definition of a broad curriculum framework, as well as a syllabus for each subject to be used as reference by individual schools. At the school level, it involves creating course and assessment plans for different subjects. At the classroom level, it involves creating more detailed plans for learning units, individual lessons, and lesson sequences.

Curriculum Implementation

It is the process of interaction between the curriculum developers and teachers, ranging from field trials to professional development and teaching. The final stage of implementation takes place within the school and the teacher occupies a central position.

All the activities associated with teaching and learning including evaluation fall under implementation. Implementation also deals with how change is managed.

Curriculum Design

Curriculum design refers to the ways in which curriculum components are positioned in a curriculum plan to form a pattern. The three major curriculum design patterns are subject-centred, learner centred and society (problem) centred. Design is the technical part of curriculum planning. Curriculum design has two components: the structure of the curriculum, and its content. While the structure reflects a pattern, the organisation of the content and activities within this pattern all fall within the domain of curriculum design.

Curriculum Evaluation

Curriculum Evaluation is the process of collecting, analysing, and interpreting data to find out the extent to which curriculum goals and objectives have been attained. Evaluation helps us judge the worth of a programme. Results from curriculum evaluation form the basis for curriculum renewal or revision. Evaluation is the last stage of the curriculum development process.

Curriculum Change

Curriculum change incorporates the concepts of innovation, reform, development, renewal, and improvement of a curriculum. It is the process of altering some practices in the system and bringing in new ones. Curriculum change is based on results of curriculum evaluation and as a response to societal changes. For example, there's been a great deal of curriculum change in African schools' curricula from the colonial era to the present day.

Curriculum and Instruction

Curriculum and instruction are central ingredients of the schooling process. Whereas curriculum describes the content and learning activities that enrich learners' educational experiences in school, instruction can be defined as "the intentional facilitation of learning towards identified goals" (Smith and Ragan, 2005 p. 2). Although each one, curriculum and instruction can be studied and analysed separately, they cannot function in mutual isolation. The term instruction cannot be eliminated from curriculum theory and practice. Designing a curriculum without taking into consideration instruction can lead to disastrous results. To understand and get a clearer picture of the relationship between these two concepts, a distinction will first be made between them.

Distinguishing Curriculum from Instruction

Foshay and Foshay (1986) distinguish curriculum from instruction by stating that curricularists are concerned with the problem of worthwhile knowledge and instructional designers with technical delivery of instruction. In other words, these authors maintain that the curriculum answers the question *what learning experiences should we offer learners in a school?* Whereas instruction answers the question *how should learning experiences be offered to learners in a school?* Curriculum is therefore the package of school experiences and instruction is the delivery of the package. It is practically difficult to separate the delivery mechanism from the structure of the package. Wiles and Bondi (2011 p.1) express the same views by describing curriculum as "a goal or set of values which are activated through a development process culminating in classroom experiences for students."

Models of Relationship between Curriculum and Instruction

Most authors see curriculum and instruction as separate entities that are closely related. They opine that separating curriculum from instruction is artificial. Both words are sometimes pronounced like one word curriculumandinstruction. Some have gone as far as suggesting the creation of two new words *instriculum* and *curstruction* to depict the intimate nature of the relationship between these two terms (Yates, 2000; Srivastava, 2005p.119).

Four models of the relationship between curriculum and instruction identified by Oliva (2008) will be described here.

Curriculum-Instruction Dualism (The Dualistic Model)

Curriculum and instruction co- exist in a school system but operate independently. Views of curriculum as defined courses of study support the dualistic model. They see curriculum purely as subject matter devoid of methods of transmitting the subject matter. Accordingly, curriculum is a plan whose implementation varies depending upon context. A gulf is evident between the master plan on the one hand and classroom practice on the other hand. It is often the case when curriculum planners and instructors ignore each other. This relationship between curriculum and instruction is depicted in figure 1.2.

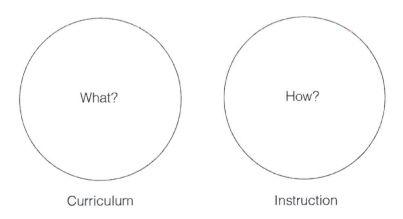

FIGURE 1.2. The dualistic model

Interlocking Model

According to advocates of this model, curriculum and instruction are integrated in each other. They argue that curriculum and instruction have many commonalities. Curriculum is seen as a dynamic mix of knowledge (content) and experiences (methods) for learners. It is an instructional plan or better still an instructional system. These two are represented diagrammatically as a Venn diagram shown in figure 1.3 .

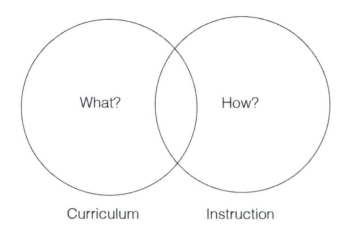

FIGURE 1.3. The interlocking model

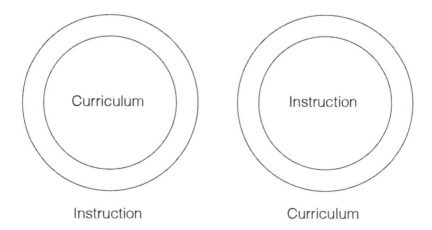

FIGURE 1.4. The concentric model

Concentric Model

In this model, the relationship between curriculum and instruction is hierarchical. One is superordinate and the other subordinate. The relationship can be represented in two ways as shown on figure 1.4. Wiles and Bondi (2011p. 157) hold that traditionally, instruction has always been perceived as a subset of curriculum.

Cyclical Model

Curriculum and instruction are processes that alternate with each other. This model stresses the importance of feedback from the two entities during curriculum practice. It is argued that continuous adaptations and improvements occur after each process. Instructional decisions are made after curriculum decisions which are in turn modified after instructional decisions. This relationship between curriculum and instruction is depicted in figure 1.5.

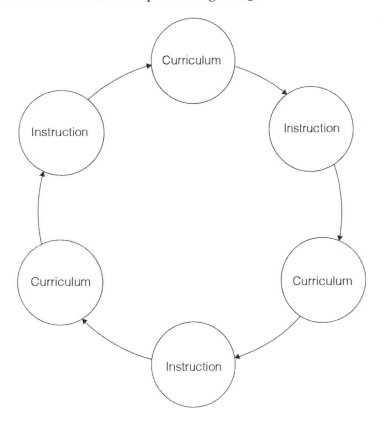

FIGURE 1.5. The cyclical model

Discussions in subsequent chapters will reflect some or all of these intimate relationships between curriculum and instruction.

2

Curriculum Theory

The quest for meaningful explanations to natural and social phenomena has led people to make propositions that are universally acceptable. This is the foundation of theory building and its most prominent function. Theory establishes relationships among variables to offer plausible explanations to observed phenomena. Almost every high school graduate the world over is familiar with the theory of evolution and the theory of demand and supply. The former offers an explanation as to the origin of life on earth while the latter explains the fluctuation of goods in an economic system. Theory was at first readily associated with the natural sciences, but the humanities and social sciences have built up theories that direct and enrich their knowledge bases. In this chapter, the domain of contemporary curriculum theory will be presented and discussed.

The Nature and Functions of Theory

One of the most widely used definitions of theory in the social sciences states that, "a theory is a set of interrelated constructs (concepts), definitions, and propositions that present a systematic view of phenomena by specifying relations among variables, with the purpose of explaining and predicting phenomena" (Kerlinger, 1986 p. 9). There are other definitions of theory which point to "thoros" or 'theorein', the Greek origin of the word which means 'to look at'. This implies that theory at times stresses the mental model of perceived reality. It means that theory may be abstract and may not necessarily be accepted by all. Theory may be accepted or challenged to ascertain its veracity. It may remain speculation to some. Theories make assumptions and generalizations. They indicate relationships among concepts in each field of study.

Theory may also be defined as a set of related statements that are arranged to give functional meaning to a series of events. This may take the form of definitions, assumptions, hypotheses, generalizations, laws, and theorems. Apart from exposing the nature of theory, some definitions of the word suggest the functions of theory.

- "A theory is a set of related constructs, definitions, and propositions that present a systematic view of phenomena by specifying relations among variables with the purpose of explaining and predicting the phenomena" (Kerlinger, 1986).
- "A theory is a coherent group of general propositions used as principles of explanations for a class of phenomena" (Webster's dictionary, 2006).

These two definitions suggest explanation and prediction as functions of theory. Other functions of theory include description and control. A theory provides a framework for explaining observations by suggesting reasons for the relationship.

Curriculum Theory and Theorising

Curriculum theories if there are any, do not stand out as theories unrelated to other disciplines in the enlarged field of education. Long before curriculum became an academic discipline, the term curriculum had featured on educational texts because curriculum practice existed in school settings. In the early twentieth century when the curriculum field emerged as a distinct discipline in education with Franklin Bobbitt's publication (Bobbit, 1918), the dominant focus was on curriculum development. Curriculum theory is a relatively new domain in curriculum studies, although some form of curriculum theorising was present in earlier educational texts. Much of curriculum discourse is regarded as curriculum theorising. Whereas theory is a noun denoting the existence of a complete and definite entity, an end- product, theorising is a verb denoting ongoing reflections.

Curriculum theory is 'a set of propositions, observations, facts, beliefs, policies, and procedures proposed or followed as a basis for curriculum action' (Hewitt (2006 p. 133). Syomwenei (2020 p.327) also defines curriculum theory as 'a sub-theory in education that explains and describes curriculum phenomena'. Curriculum phenomena in this definition encompasses the elements of curriculum such as the objectives, content, learning experiences and evaluation. From these definitions and others put together, curriculum theory can be considered as a set of coherent and consistent principles found in a set of statements that guide curriculum construction, maintenance, and legislation. These statements within a theory must be related in such a way as to produce great meaning to the individual parts to extend its meaning to general events. Curriculum theory gives meaning to a school curriculum by pointing the relationship among its elements and by directing its development, its use and evaluation.

Thus, theory serves as a springboard for prescribing and directing curriculum-related practical activity. In this sense, theory is similar to philosophy in that it is not directly thought of as open to empirical validation. The fact that this approach is not called curriculum philosophy may be due to the fact that the people who engage in it are not usually trained philosophers, despite the fact that much of it is a form of philosophising.

Theorising strives to enlarge vision, present new possibilities to bring about deeper understanding of curriculum phenomena (Huenecke, 1982). Theorising is a process that may lead to development of theory. There is some disagreement among theorisers regarding the goal of theorising. Among the few who give serious consideration to this issue, there appears to be three major camps in this problem. One group by far the most significant regards theory as a guiding framework for applied curriculum development, research, as well as a tool for assessing curriculum creation.

A second "camp" of younger theorists adheres to a more traditional understanding of scientific theory. This group attempted to identify and describe the variables in curriculum as well as their relationships. This theory's purpose is primarily conceptual, and research would be used to empirically validate curriculum variables and relationships rather than to test the efficiency and effectiveness of a curriculum prescription.

A third group of people sees theorising as a creative intellectual task that should not be used as a basis for prescription or as an empirically testable set of principles and relationships. The goal of these individuals is to create and critique conceptual schema in the hope that new ways of talking about curriculum will emerge in the future that are far more fruitful than current orientations. At the moment, they would argue that the state of the art requires a much more playful, free-floating process.

Functions of Curriculum Theory

About the function of curriculum theory, Huebner (1975) identified six kinds of languages used in curriculum theory: (1) descriptive, (2) explanatory, (3) controlling, (4) legitimizing, (5) prescriptive, and (6) affiliative. From this analysis, curriculum theory varies with the intentions of theorists, as witnessed by their use of language. Other writers have identified and stated the functions of curriculum theory.

The most stated functions of curriculum theory are *description*, *explanation*, *prediction*, and *guidance*. Curriculum theory contributes to understanding of phenomena under consideration by providing clear and useful descriptions and explanations. In performing its guidance function, curriculum theory directs the work of teachers, administrators, policy makers, curriculum developers and designers. It also resolves curriculum problems, helps researchers to analyse data and provides clear directions for curriculum research. It clarifies underlying values of decision makers. Theory gives grounding to the curriculum. It backs up curriculum practice, it conceptualises and gives meaning to the curriculum. Curriculum theory helps us name a curriculum problem and its elements, factors relating to the problem, resources necessary for handling the problem and strategies to solve the problem. Theory thus provides us with a way of viewing the matter, of thinking and talking about it and relating it to other issues. Curriculum theory gives meaning to practice and justifies practice. It helps us answer questions such as *why is curriculum A better than curriculum B? What kind of curriculum is appropriate for a developing country?* Thus, curriculum theory has a moral dimension.

The set of ideas that make up curriculum theory generally include ideas about the purpose, content, and structure of education, specifically the student, the subject, the learning environment, the teacher, or other resource. Curriculum theory is used to explain why a practice was or was not a good idea. Thus, theory becomes a springboard for prescribing and guiding practical activity in relation to curriculum. Theory in this sense functions like a philosophy.

Normative and Critical Role of Curriculum Theory

There are two ways to look at curriculum theory's normative function. One refers to the rules or principles that govern the creation and implementation of the curriculum, and the other refers to the purpose of education. In the first sense of the word, the normative view calls for curriculum review to achieve a better curriculum. This is technical as it guides teachers on what to do. Therefore, curriculum theory plays a vital role in evaluating how to come up with better expectations. The critical role focuses on analysing the assumptions, strengths and weaknesses of existing curricula, and the ways that the concept of the curriculum is used. As analysts, the curriculum worker needs to examine the benefits and limitations of existing curricula and how they are applied. It is important to base criticism on laws or norms. Thus, the normative and critical functions of curriculum theory overlap.

Curriculum Theory Building

The purpose of curriculum as a field is to advance knowledge about curriculums and curriculum systems. This is done through curriculum theory-building activities, namely:

1. The establishment of descriptive and prescriptive definitions of technical terms: the definition and usage of such technical words such as curriculum, design, implementation, assessment, etc., must be clear, consistent, and regularly used.
2. Classification of Existing Knowledge: knowledge classification such as descriptive, predictive and critical, is important for theory. It is a base for philosophy. The lack of curriculum theory classification has contributed to differences or the contradictory usage of technical words. While some classification of curriculum information has been carried out, there is still a lack of systematic classification.
3. Carrying out inferential and Predictive Research: In the job of a theoriser, this is very important. To arrive at meanings, explanations, classification schemes etc., a study must be conducted. This research may contribute to the development of sub-theories such as planning, execution, and assessment of curriculum design. Progress in curriculum theory has typically been slow. Few experts in the curriculum field have reacted to thoughtful curriculum work.
4. Sub-theory development and development and use of models: Another activity for the curriculum theorist is model building and the theorist can use models in a variety of ways. Models can be used to show a person's perspective on curriculum design. They are useful for depicting curriculum planning and implementation procedures. Models can be created to demonstrate the relationships between curriculum design, curriculum engineering processes, and evaluation processes.

Landmark events and prominent Scholars in Curriculum Theory Building

Philosophers and educators were visibly burdened by education concerns towards the end of the nineteenth century. Many have expressed their perspectives on elements relating to curriculum theory at different points in time. This section looks at a summary of some contributions made by various scholars.

Herbert Spencer

In analysing what should be taught and learned, he published his essay entitled 'What Knowledge is of most worth?' in 1859. In other words, what is worth knowing and experiencing? He believed that this question needed to be answered before any curriculum was chosen or any instruction commenced.

To him, the main goal was to teach subjects that would contribute to successful living. He believed education should focus more on the future preparation of children. He advocated for math, sciences, and citizenship.

John Dewey

Dewey was a pragmatist and believed that school and society were related. In a hands-on method or learning through doing, human beings learn. This has become known as progressive schooling. Dewey claimed that truth must be observed and, thus, in order to understand, students need to engage with their surroundings. He believed in child-centred education that places the focus of learning on the child's needs and interests. In the laboratory school that he opened in 1896, he tested these theories.

Franklin Bobbit

Franklin Bobbit published the first definitive work on the general curriculum in 1918. He was the first expert in the discipline of Education to establish a curriculum posture on curriculum development issues. He believed that education should prepare one for adult life that consists of specific activities. These activities could be identified in the world by way of abilities, attitudes, habits, appreciations, and forms of knowledge that are needed in society. These will make up the objectives of the curriculum and the curriculum itself will be that series of experiences which children and youth must have to attain those objectives.

Bobbit believed in a program that had both general education and specialised/vocational education (to provide children with the skills they need to prepare for their roles as adult citizens). Based on evaluations of their intellectual abilities that defined their ultimate destinies, this specialisation should be achieved. Together with other scholars like W.W. Charters, Ross Finney, David Snedden, they formed the Social Efficiency Movement (Bobbit, 1918) which believed that the purpose of education was to prepare the youth for specific workforce and citizenship roles which they would perform on reaching adulthood. Bobbit was one of the first Americans to advance the case for the identification of objectives.

Werrett Wallace Charters

Charters was very much in agreement with Bobbit. He came up with an activity-analysis approach to curriculum construction in 1923. This included a description of individual roles in every social interaction. Such specifications have been converted into program goals. Both were committed to the use of science methods in addressing problems in the curriculum. His most valuable contribution to the field of curriculum creation came in the form of his curriculum building approach to activity-analysis. For him, a scientific approach to the development of curricula included defining tasks as a basis for choosing educational targets. It is noteworthy that Ralph Tyler and Hilda Taba were inspired by his approach.

However, by the early 1920s, there was a shift in education thought towards a child-centred curriculum with the advent of the progressivists. To prepare students for adult life, emphasis was diverted from the curriculum to the desires and needs of children in school - the child-centred movement. Because the desires and needs of children arose from their everyday experience, a pre-planned curriculum without the participation of the children in the planning became a significant weakness to the implementation of a new educational program.

The child-centred and society-centred reform movements jointly wrote the 26th yearbook of the National Society for the Study of Education, and the conflict between the child-centred and society-centred groups of curriculum specialists was brought into focus in two volumes. Despite the differences of opinion, various scholars were able to contribute to the book and this came very close to being considered as a statement of curriculum theory at the time.

William Kilpatrick

Kilpatrick was the proponent of the project method influenced by Dewey in his 1925 publication, *Foundations of Method*. He proposed replacing it with a child-centred approach to get away from rote memorisation and rigid curriculum. He thought school should serve both an educational function, an intellectual one and a social one as well. It should not only be a mastery of content but also focus on the social development of the child so the curriculum should come from real life and not compartmentalized subject matter. So, he advocated for an integrated curriculum that emphasised maximum student participation. He came up with what is called the project method which has the following procedure:

- Identify the purpose for education
- Come up with a plan
- Execute the plan
- Assess and judge students and curriculum

Harold Rugg

Rugg published his first major work, *The Child-Centred School* in 1928, which described the historical and contemporary foundations of child-centred education. This work had a significant impact on progressive educators and is still an excellent explanation and critique of the subject. He believed that the curriculum should develop the whole child. He saw formal education as having a central role to play in American society's restructuring. In the curriculum, he stressed social studies and the need for the teacher to prepare the lesson in advance. Rugg is credited with remaking the curriculum for social studies and providing the first collection of social studies textbooks for colleges. He also sought to advance inclusive education in the Deweyan style and encouraged a scientific approach to developing the curriculum.

Hollis Caswell

In his book entitled *Curriculum Development* published in 1935, he asserted that subject matter is developed around the interest of the learners and their social functions. So, the curriculum is made up of a set of experiences. Learners must encounter what they learn. Caswell believes that curriculum, instruction, and learning are interrelated.

He also set a performance model for leadership in curriculum development. He focused on teacher involvement in curriculum decisions, organisational structures for planning groups and procedure for defining the meaning of curriculum, determining objectives, selecting content, determining design, and measuring outcomes.

Specific theoretical curriculum problems arose from the discussions, namely: the theory of the design-child-centred, society-centred or interactive, the structured arrangement of school subjects. However, only in the 1950s did the technical dimensions of curriculum theory-building begin to penetrate literature.

Regarding later developments, at about the mid-19th century, perspectives on curriculum theory continued to appear in literature. The first formal and large-scale discussion of curriculum theory took place in the University of Chicago in 1947. Each author was given complete freedom to present his topic individually. These papers were published in a monograph in 1950. The aim of the discussion was to identify key issues in curriculum development, point out the relationships existing and suggest approaches to resolve these issues. This is where the Tyler's Rationale was developed. Tyler's rationale was guided by four questions as follows:

1. What educational purposes should the school seek to attain?
2. How can learning experiences be selected which are likely to be useful in attaining these objectives?
3. How can learning experiences be organised for effective instruction?
4. How can the effectiveness of learning experiences be evaluated?

Ralph Tyler

He agreed that the curriculum should revolve around the needs and desires of the students and the fact that students should play an active role in the process of teaching and learning and evaluate not only the students but the curriculum. His model was intended to be a guide for curriculum growth. He described the different phases of curriculum development in 1949 in his book, *Basic principles of curriculum and instruction*, which is the first model for curriculum development. The following questions direct it:

1. What should the educational objectives of the curriculum be?
2. What learning experiences should be developed to enable students to achieve the objectives?
3. How should the learning experience be organized to increase their cumulative effect.
4. How should the effectiveness of the curriculum be evaluated?

Hilda Taba

In 1962 Taba published a book entitled *Curriculum Development Theory and Practice* in which she outlined four principles that seem to articulate her vision of curriculum theory and curriculum development. They are:

1. Social processes, including human socialisation, are not linear and cannot be modelled using linear planning. In other words, learning and personality development cannot be viewed as

one-way processes of establishing educational goals and deriving specific objectives from a proclaimed or imagined ideal of education.

2. Curriculum and program reconstruction is a long-term process that will take years to complete.

3. Social institutions, including school curricula and programs, can be reorganised more effectively if, instead of the common method of administrative reorganisation—from top to bottom—a well-founded and coordinated system of development from bottom to top is used.

4. The development of new curricula and programs is more effective when it is based on democratic principles and a well-founded distribution of work. The emphasis is on competence-based collaboration rather than administration.

Influenced by Tyler's Rationale, Hilda Taba developed a model of learning. Taba believed that there was a specific order to develop a curriculum. This model is used to help students improve their critical thinking skills. She believed that teachers are aware of the needs of their students. As a result, they should design unique teaching-learning scenarios for their students. They should use an inductive approach to teaching, i.e., from specific to general, rather than the traditional deductive approach, which begins with the general and works its way down to the specifics. Taba advocates the "Down-Top model," also known as the Grassroots approach.

Taba contended that curriculum development should be a sequential and logical process, and she advocated for greater information input at all stages of curriculum development. She also claimed that all curricula are made up of basic elements. The central concept of this model is that students are at the forefront of the curriculum. She believed that after the content standards had been established and implemented, there should be a process for evaluating student achievement of content. The main idea behind this model is that teachers must be involved in the development of curriculum. Taba's grassroot model has seven steps, which are listed below, and advocates for teachers to play a significant role.

Taba proposes that curriculum should be designed according to the following seven steps:

1. Diagnosis of needs.
2. Formulation of objectives
3. Selection of content
4. Organisation of content
5. Selection of activities/experiences
6. Organisation of learning activities experiences.
7. Determining what to evaluate and the ways and means of doing it.

George Beauchamp

From this discussion, the first edition of the book *Curriculum Theory* written by Beauchamp appeared in 1961 and a second edition was published in 1968. This was the first book to present an organised statement of status and dimensions of curriculum theory about a structure and the relationships among the elements. In 1963, a National Conference of the Association for Supervision and Curriculum Development led to the contribution about the dialogue to curriculum theory.

From then on, curriculum theorising grew. The following are some contributors and contributions by various scholars to curriculum theory:

He studied the scientist's strategy in the construction of curriculum theory. As in all other scientific studies, the use of technical terms, the study and classification of knowledge and conjecture, and the use of predictive science have been carefully and systematically established. This would raise the number of concrete generalisations, laws and concepts that would both clarify the phenomenon of the curriculum. Beauchamp reviewed advances made in study and writing on curriculum theory between 1960 and 1965. A synthesis of this led to six curriculum components being established as a field of study, namely: foundational influences, subject matter, curriculum design, curriculum engineering, evaluation, and research theory-building.

Thomas Faix

In 1964 Faix came up with a paper entitled structural-functional analysis to curriculum phenomena, "Toward a Science of Curriculum: Structural-Functional Analysis as a Conceptual System for Theory and Research," in which he believed that curriculum functions determined whether the structure should be maintained or changed, and this revolve around the following kinds of questions:

- General questions about curriculum phenomena
- Questions about curriculum system
- Questions about units of analysis and elements
- Questions about the structure of a curriculum system
- Questions about curriculum processes
- General questions about structural-functional analysis procedures

James B. MacDonald

MacDonald also made a significant contribution to the use of models in his paper "Curriculum Theory: Problems and A Prospectus" in 1965 during a meeting of professors of curriculum by identifying four systems dominant in school namely:

- Curriculum
- Instruction
- Teaching
- Learning

He illustrated the interaction of the four systems and analysed the curriculum system which he said is made up of elements such as input, process, output, and feedback.

Mauritz Johnson

Johnson published an article in 1965 entitled "Definition and Models in Curriculum Theory," in which he distinguished between curriculum and the process of curriculum development. Johnson depicted curriculum as a structured series of learning outcomes and to him curricula relates more to intentions than outcomes. To Johnson, experiences that pupils have under the guidance of a school become part of the domain of instruction. He came up with a six-point understanding for a curriculum as follows:

- A curriculum is a structured series of intended learning outcomes
- Selection is an essential aspect of curriculum formulation
- Structure is an essential characteristic of curriculum
- Curriculum guides instruction
- Curriculum evaluation involves validation of both selection and structure
- Curriculum is the criterion for instructional evaluation

Elizabeth Steiner Maccia

Marcia in her paper entitled "Curriculum Theory and Policy" in 1965 examined four types of curriculum theory as follows:

- Event theory/curriculum theory – having to do with instruction
- Valuational curriculum theory – seeking the value of instructional content
- Formal curriculum theory – the structure of the curriculum content
- Praxiological curriculum theory- suitable means for reaching curriculum goals

Othanel Smith

Smith presented a paper on the role of philosophy in the development of scientific curriculum theory in 1965 where he identified the essence of philosophy in the development of curriculum theory as follows:

1. Formulate and justify educational purposes
2. Select and organize knowledge
3. Deal with verbal traps

He further noted that there were some lapses in the development of curriculum theory. One of these was the failure to recognize the interrelationships between objectives and content in a school programme and the criteria for selecting these were not clear. He attributed these to the language used in curriculum theorising.

John Goodlad and Maurice Richter

In their paper "The Development of a Conceptual system for Dealing with Problems of Curriculum and Instruction" in 1966, they deliberated on the development of a conceptual system for dealing with problems of curriculum and instruction and used the Tyler rationale as the primary main point of departure. Nevertheless, they operationalised its structures significantly. Although it was more general than a theory, they thought such a conceptual system was still a good basis for the construction of the theory. Decisions about educational aims would lead to general behavioural objectives and then to the identification of behavioural and substantive elements.

Elliot Eisner

By openly challenging the importance of observable goals advocated by academics like Franklin Bobbitt and Ralph Tyler, Eisner in his paper, "Franklin Bobbit and the Science of Curriculum

Making" in 1967, moved the curriculum landscape. Noting that goals were useful in some cases, Eisner argued that the use of behavioural goals alone acted as a constraint on the curriculum through its inability to account for the meaning and desires of students. In articulating the importance of qualitative research in education, Eisner was instrumental, particularly at a time when positivist-oriented researchers frequently regarded it unfavourably. By voicing his possible achievements, Eisner inspired several academics to rethink the merits of qualitative study to educational research.

He states that three levels of curricula are always present in any learning environment namely:

Explicit Curriculum. This is what the school advertises that it does (the items on its "education menu").

Hidden Curriculum (unofficial curriculum). This is the "hidden" curriculum that is learned because of such things as a school's structure, the peer group, social interactions, cultural capital, and poor/excellent teachers.

Null Curriculum (absent curriculum). This is what schools do not teach. These include under-taught subjects (e.g., art, intellectual processes, things that are the first to go in times of economic hardship).

Jack R. Frymeir

In his paper "Around and Around the Curriculum Bush or Quest of Curriculum" in 1967, he took the position that the curriculum consists of three basic elements namely: actors, artifacts, and operations. Actors are persons directly involved with the curriculum, artifacts are the content of the curriculum including design problems, while operations are the processes involving the interaction of actions and artifacts. A typical unit of study in a curriculum should have:

- That which is planned
- That which occurs
- The evaluation

Dwayne Huebner

Huebner in his 1968 paper "The Tasks of the Curriculum Theorist," provided an analysis of theoretical statements. He observed that theorists categorize language in terms of its various uses. As a result, he discovers six types of language in use:

1. descriptive,
2. explanatory,
3. controlling,
4. legitimizing,
5. prescriptive,
6. affiliative.

His approach has focused on language systems and how language shapes the process of developing conceptual models and/or facilitating it. Based on this analysis, it is observed that "the curriculum theorist" varies according to theorists' intentions, as evidenced by the use of language at any given time and place.

Arno A. Bellack

He published a paper in 1969 entitled "History of Curriculum Thought and Practice" where he looked at the historical evolution of curriculum thought and practice while Kliebard examined the curriculum field from the beginning and concluded that the basic problem of the curriculum field is self-identification and that a dialogue was necessary.

George Posner

Like Johnson, Posner in a paper entitled "Education: Its Components and Constructs" in 1972 analysed the components of education and stated that curriculum, instruction, and learning outcomes need clarification and that for purposes of theory and research, curriculum must be conceived to be product-oriented, prior to instruction, and descriptive.

The above contributions to curriculum theory are inexhaustive. However, all these viewpoints, arguments and contributions have helped in defining the field of curriculum theory and its components.

Curriculum Theory Camps

Curriculum theorising has been and still is undertaken by all persons interested in curriculum work ranging from classroom teachers, academics, teacher trainers to curriculum experts. These different categories of persons have different personal philosophies and therefore it is not surprising that curriculum theory has many orientations to what should constitute a worthwhile curriculum. As Schubert (1986) pointed out, curriculum theory is philosophy. Due to divisions on the focus of curriculum theory, textbooks writers have grouped the multiplicity of theorists and theories into categories to ease identification and description of their ideas. Marsh and Willis (2007) identify and describe three main groups of theorisers: prescriptive, descriptive, and critical –exploratory.

Prescriptive theory

Theorisers in the prescriptive category attempt to create structural frameworks called models, which can be used for curriculum development. This is aimed at improving school practice. The works of Ralph Tyler, D. K. Wheeler and Franklin Bobbit fall in this category of prescriptive theory. These authors see their theories or contributions as the best way of design that leads to the creation of best possible curricula. When prescriptive theory is transformed into practice, it takes the form of recommendations that state what ought to be taught in schools. Teachers' guides, textbooks, and some texts from educational authorities constitute prescriptions.

Descriptive theory

The descriptive category examines how curriculum development takes place in school settings. Descriptive curriculum theorists approach research from the perspective of natural scientists by using an inductive approach to theory development. They are concerned with meaning and choice.

Their approach is practical inquiry: mapping out procedures for curriculum development. Prominent names in this group are Joseph Schwabb, and Alfred Reid.

Critical theory

The critical-exploratory theorisers attempt to understand deficiencies in the practice of curriculum development. They understand the curriculum in terms of what has been, what is and what might be. They attempt to expose unhealthy social relationships that schooling is thought to promote. They examine ways in which school curricula encourage the perpetuation of inequalities experienced by the downtrodden. They criticise the status quo and create intellectual tasks for curriculum policy makers. Apple, Pinar, Mauritz Johnson are prominent critical theorists.

Other categorisation schemes of curriculum theory and theorising found in the literature are presented on table 2.1.

Table 2.1. Categories of Curriculum theories

Glatthorn et al, 2008	Huenecke (1982)	Maccia (1965)	Schubert (1986)
Structure-oriented (descriptive)	Structural	Event	Descriptive
Value-oriented (critical)	Generic	Formal	Prescriptive
Content-oriented (prescriptive)	Substantive	Valuational	Critical theory
Process-oriented (descriptive and prescriptive)		praxiological	Personal theorising

Curriculum Camps and Their Orientations

Since curriculum workers use different curriculum theories alongside their personal philosophies to determine how curriculum work should be approached, curriculum studies literature presents various camps, calling them orientations (Miller and Seller 1990), meta- orientations (Ornstein & Hunkins, 2018) and ideologies (Schiro (2013). These are presented on table 2.2.

Curriculum Ideologies

Schiro (2013) described four ideologies or philosophies that advocate different purposes of schooling and different methods of achieving the respective purposes. Each of the four visions of curriculum embodies distinct beliefs about the types of knowledge that should be taught in school, the inherent nature of children, what school learning consists of, how teachers should instruct children and how children should be assessed. Each has its own value system. Each ideology has a long history and has been known by a variety of names. These philosophies often cause disagreement among curriculum workers about the nature of the curriculum they should adopt. These ideologies have been given different appellations by different scholars (see table 2.2). The implications of these conceptions on curriculum features are summarised on tables 2.3 and 2.4, respectively.

Table 2.2. Different Appellations of Curriculum conceptions

Ornstein& Hunkins, (2018) Meta- orienta- tions	Schiro (2013 Ideologies	Miller and Seller (1990) Orientations	Mc Neil (2006) Prevailing conceptions	Schubert (1996) Orientations
• Behavioural • Managerial • Systems • Academic • Humanistic • Post modern	• Social efficiency • Academic scholar • learner centred • reconstruc-tionist	• Transmission • Transaction • Transforma-tion	• Academic • systemic • Humanist • Social recon-structionist	• Intellectual traditionalists • Social behaviourists • Experiential-ists • Critical recon-structionist

The Scholar Academic Ideology

Some writers also term this philosophy the Intellectual Traditionalist (Schubert, 1996). It suggests that culture, which has been organised into academic disciplines found in universities and education, has accumulated over the years, and should help students learn this essential knowledge to acculturate the individual. Edward Hirsch, one of its key supporters, claimed that acculturating children is the main objective of schooling. This ideology believes in preserving cultural heritage. They believe that the academic, intellectual and knowledge world are the same. An academic discipline is seen as a hierarchical society of truth inquirers (teachers, scholars, and students), so education tries to apply these disciplines to young people. The goal of Scholar-Academics' education is to expand their fields by bringing young people into them. This includes making a discipline's youth, participants by first moving them as students into it and then moving them from the bottom of the hierarchy to the top.

The extension of a discipline is achieved by the transfer to students of their expertise and ways of thought. Progressives and experientialists have criticised that this perspective does not take theories of learning, motivation, knowledge, or school and community into account. They also say that the view encourages democratic principles as it adopts an authoritative stance on what a given society's general knowledge is.

Social Efficiency

The social efficiency also known as the social behaviourist posits that the purpose of schooling is to meet societal needs. The goal is to train youths in the skills they need in the workplace and at home to live productive lives. Curriculum developers and educators who adopted the Social Efficiency ideology view the curriculum as an instrument that prepares students to be contributing members of society and support the thought that schools are places where students are prepared for a meaningful adult life. Educators must select methods that will help learners acquire the behaviours prescribed by their curriculum. Learners may require a lot of practice to gain a mastery of skills. They believe in applying the scientific procedure of cause and effect where learning experiences become stimuli, which leads to the desired effects. So, the curriculum developer's priority is to determine the needs of society – their client. The things that will fulfil these needs are called the terminal objectives of the curriculum. The developer must then find the most efficient way of producing a product, the educated person who meets the terminal objectives of the curriculum and thus fulfils the needs of society.

The Learner-Centred ideology

The learner-centred or experientialist ideology pays attention to the needs and concerns of individuals. The experiential perspective is typical of the twentieth century. The birth of progressive education and the experiential perspective coincided with the social reform movement of the early twentieth century and John Dewey, the main proponent was an American philosopher and psychologist. They believe that people grow naturally according to their innate natures. Students' needs and interests are the source of content for the curriculum and are considered as curriculum outcomes: so, the growth of learners is the main theme in this philosophy. The experiential perspective posits that curriculum should take a holistic approach in educating students by considering all their experiences. It therefore supports a learner-centred curriculum in which students engage with the world and create meaning for themselves. This philosophy has been criticised for making immense demands on everyone seeking to make realistic decisions on the curriculum, because it implies that the curriculum is the same as the very living method.

The Social Reconstruction Ideology

This ideology also known as the critical reconstructionist ideology is sensitive to societal needs and the injustices done to the disadvantaged. They view current society as unhealthy, and the purpose of education is to facilitate the construction of a new and more just society that offers maximum satisfaction to all by eliminating undesirable cultural aspects. In this reconstruction process, educators and schools are active agents of this transformation. Developers of social reconstruction conclude that the social process by which society is to be rebuilt is the schooling of the masses. In the curriculum, these developers firmly believe in the capacity of education to educate students to understand the essence of their community in such a way that they can create a vision of a better society and then act to bring that vision into being.

Influences on Curriculum Purposes and Design

Table 2.3. A Comparison of the Ideologies' Views Regarding Knowledge

Knowledge	Scholar Academic	Social Efficiency	Learner Centered	Social Reconstruction
The nature of knowledge is . . .	didactic statements	capabilities for action	personal meanings	intelligence and a moral stance
Knowledge gives the ability . . .	to understand	to do	to actualize oneself	to interpret, act on, and reconstruct society
The source of knowledge is . . .	objective reality as interpreted by the academic disciplines	normative objective reality as socially interpreted	individuals' personal creative response to experience	individuals' interpretation of society's past, present, and future
Knowledge derives its authority from . . .	the academic disciplines	its ability to perpetuate society through skills provided to its members	the meaning it has to its possessor	individuals' visions of the future good society
The truth of knowledge is verified by . . .	finding the degree to which it reflects the essence of an academic discipline	seeing if it corresponds to society's view of the nature of empirical reality	the personal insights of its possessor	individuals' beliefs in its ability to improve society

Source: Sage

Table 2.4. Curriculum features of McNeil's categorization of curriculum orientations

Conception	Curriculum design	Purpose
Humanistic	Self- directed learning Teacher as facilitator	Goals are personal growth, integrity, and autonomy Provide learner with intrinsically rewarding experience
Social reconstructionist	Teacher and student take active roles in curriculum development Focus on collaboration with the community and resources	Instrument for effecting social reform
Systemic	Outcomes based programs Prescribed goals with standards Assessments evaluate progress	Aligns goals, standards, programs with instructional materials and assessments for learning outcomes
Academic	Matching subject matter concepts and pedagogy	Students have opportunity to experience research and learn what counts as knowledge. Inquiry driven.

Source: McNeil (2006). Contemporary curriculum in thought and action.

Part Two

Foundations of the Curriculum

Factors that underpin the design and development of a curriculum are called its foundations. Without adequate consideration of these factors, a curriculum crumbles like a building without support. Conventionally, four foundations are cited, described, and used in the curriculum process. They are philosophical, historical, psychological, and sociological. Each of these is presented and examined from both western and African perspectives in separate chapters that make up the second part of this book.

3

Historical Foundations of the Curriculum

Curriculum history is concerned with the processes of describing, analysing, and interpreting previous curriculum thought and practice. It is possible to better understand the present by studying the past, as well as to benefit from insights and approaches to problems that are relevant to similar circumstances today. Educators are then better positioned to analyse current conditions and chart future courses of action as a result of their study of history. Historical roots of the curriculum typically concentrate on how at various points in time, as a result of changes in society, theories of academics evolved and shaped the curriculum and how these ideas have been modified or developed. The history of the curriculum is a valuable tool for the curriculum developer/teacher as it gives them a greater awareness over time of curriculum changes. In decision-making, such context knowledge is helpful for the curriculum worker. In literature, however, there are different approaches to curriculum history, and in different countries the historical basis of the curriculum is different. Curriculum as a field of study began in the United States of America, and a lot of important contributions from activities that took place in America influenced curricula around the world. Thus, the methodology of Glatthorn, Boschee and Whitehead (2008), who examine the history of the curriculum in America within eight separate periods, will be discussed as well as a history of the curriculum in Africa. Knowledge of the history of the curriculum in Africa is an important foundation for understanding the wave of curriculum reforms sweeping across Africa since independence.

Historical foundations of the curriculum in the United States of America

Academic Scientism 1890–1916

Both academic and scientific philosophy influenced this period. Academically, colleges made a systematic effort to improve the basic education curriculum. It was led by Charles Eliot of Harvard University. He contributed to the primary, secondary and higher education curriculum and claimed that for all students, a sound curriculum was best. There was also an effort to focus newly established science knowledge on the mission of the school and curriculum material. Science guided the curriculum and could inform educational thinkers and be applied to solve problems and so it merited to be given priority in the curriculum because the main purpose of education was to solve real world problems. This required an understanding of the physical world as well as the social world. Scientific knowledge of the child offered valuable insights into the curriculum and the teaching techniques. Major supporters of Academic Scientism included Stanley Hall, who provided leadership for the child-centric education movement. He believed in evolutionary social change in which the school would support the child's gradual change, particularly by providing individualized activities for the gifted child. Another proponent who led the progressive movement was Francis W. Parker. He promoted child-centred or natural approaches that build on what the child knows. During this time, two important reports were published. The Committee of Ten was named by the National Education Association to make recommendations for the High School Curriculum and the Elementary Curriculum Committee of Fifteen. The Committee of Ten proposed the offering of four programs to high school students: classical, Latin-scientific, modern languages, and English. On their part, the Committee of Fifteen suggested a concentration on grammar, literature, geography and history that was necessary for the training of the mind. Thus, English grammar, geography, natural science, hygiene, general history, physical culture, vocal music, and drawing were subjects taught from the first to the 8th year. Up to the sixth year, handwriting, mathematics and arithmetic and spelling were taught, Latin in the 8th year and boys' natural training and girls' sewing, algebra and its history in the 7th and 8th years. The recommendations of the Fifteen Committee made the curriculum subject-centred.

Progressive Functionalism 1917–1940

John Dewey dominated this time. The emphasis was on the child, on progressive viewpoints and on functionalists. Their opinions were completely different, but influenced both the curriculum and teaching. The child and the child-centred curriculum that started with identifying the interest of the child and connecting material to these interests became the focus of the progressive movement. In order to actively develop the child, the arts were emphasized while subjects such as mathematics and grammar that were less enticing to the child were de-emphasised.

Here, functionalism referred to the philosophy of social efficiency in which the components of the program were derived from an interpretation of an adult's expectations in society. By studying and evaluating tasks carried out in society by adults, education could be made more effective. John Dewey and Franklin Bobbit were among the supporters of progressive functionalism. Dewey concentrated on the interaction between schools and society and thought that democracy was perfect.

It was important to accommodate diversity and so he stressed experience because he believed in the school's social existence. In order to make learning meaningful, such interactions were made up of appropriate and worthwhile activities that were diverse or democratic and strengthened initiative in the child. Such opinions were expressed in his book *Democracy and Education*, published in 1916, and in 1938, *Experience and Education*.

On the other hand, Bobbit proposed a scientific curriculum for each social or vocational class in which a list of skills and personality elements for the child's training would be included. Also, to calculate these talents, a scale had to be drawn up. Based on the skill of the learner, the amount of training had to be calculated and these amounts would be specified in terms of the measurement scales. So, while both scholars' ideas influenced the curriculum, they were very different. While

Bobbit was more interested in aligning practices with performance, Dewey looked at the starting point of the program as the child's growth.

During this time, *The Cardinal Principles of Secondary Education* (1918) and *The Basis of Curriculum Making* were the two major publications (1927). Some guidelines referred to as the Cardinal Principles of Secondary Education were made by the Commission on the Reorganization of Secondary Education, appointed by the National Education Association. They included: health, command of fundamental processes (reading, writing, arithmetic, oral and written expression) worthy of home membership, vocation, citizenship, dignified use of leisure time and ethical character. The 26th Year Book had to bring together the divergent views of these pioneering leaders in Curriculum Development.

From these perspectives three programmes emerged: constants (required courses) curriculum variables (specialised subjects based on student goals) and free elective subjects (based on other interests of the student). The American High School was geared to serving the needs of the youth and not just to abide by the dictates of college (University) as seen during the academic scientism period.

Developmental Conformism (1941-1956)

During this period, the emphasis was on the growth of children and teenagers. Dewey had been concerned with the development of the child prior to this age, and during this time the emphasis was on the growth phases for children and youth. The research conducted by Havighurst (1972) described developmental tasks at different stages of development. A good accomplishment of these duties has led to the child's happiness and vice versa. The following stages were graded according to these tasks: early childhood, middle childhood, and adolescence.

The prevailing educational view, based on the conceptualisation of the developmental tasks of Havighurst, was that education should help children adhere to established social norms. There was also the view that, after that point, the program had to concentrate on practical skills that would make the student functional. Schools were required to create core curricula with an integrated nature, focused on the learners' common needs. Consequently, the literature of this time concentrated on making education more important. Ralph Tyler and Hollis Caswell were other significant prominent scholars during this time.

In planning the syllabus for the graduate course he was teaching at the University of Chicago, Tyler noted that "what educational purpose should the school seek to achieve?" was the first question to be answered when developing a curriculum.

By looking at information about the learners themselves, contemporary society and recommendations from subject specialists, this question which referred to educational goals could be addressed. The second question was, "how to select learning experiences that are likely to be helpful in achieving these experiences." The third question was, "How can learning experiences be organised for effective instruction?" and the final question was, "How can the effectiveness of learning experiences be evaluated.

On his part, Caswell developed study materials and bibliographies to assist teachers with child development and curriculum outcomes, engaging teachers in curriculum development, and identifying key factors such as child interests, social context, and subject matter that influenced the curriculum. During this period, Jean Piaget's 1950 book, *The Psychology of Intelligence* was popular among publications where he described developmental stages as he saw it. Four of these processes range from infancy to puberty. They include the sensory-motor stage which begins from birth to 2 years, the preoperational stage which goes up to about 7 years; the concrete operational stage, between the ages of 7 and 11 years and the Formal operational stage where adolescence begins.

Scholarly Structuralism (1957-1967)

Academic scholars led the creation of specific curricula during this time, and several major disciplines were developed for both the basic and secondary levels. This was the time when Jerome Bruner's and Joseph Schwab's ideas had a big impact. Bruner claimed that the school curricula had to enhance the transition of learning and that educators had to take much of the limited time because the time available was limited. To him there was so much knowledge available that the student could not learn everything. As a way of delineating what students had to learn, the structure of the discipline was a kind of curriculum scope.

Scholars who were more familiar with curriculum theory were also concerned with the discipline's structure. Schwab, however, believed in numerous valid approaches to understanding the world because disciplines had different systems, so he was more concerned with the curriculum process, which he felt would draw from several areas and perspectives of knowledge.

The "Conant Report" by James Bryant Conant in 1959 and PSSC Physics by "The Physical Science Study Committee" (PSSC) curriculum project in 1961 were two major publications during this time. Compulsory completion of 4 years of English, 3 years of social studies, 1 year of mathematics and 1 year of science was recommended by the Conant Report, while talented students were expected to take an additional 3 years of mathematics, 4 years of one foreign language and 2 more years of science.

As part of their social studies requirement, students were all expected to take classes in American Problems where they were forced to have open conversations on even controversial topics. As its main teaching method for physics, the Physical Science Committee made use of discovery and inquiry. This attempt was a constructive step towards regulating the method of instruction.

Romantic Radicalism (1968-1974)

It was a period characterised by experimentation in child–centred education so as to develop programs. In three ways, this experiment was carried out in alternative schools, open classes, and elective programs.

Alternative schools were like traditional schools, but the concept was considered to be for experimental purposes. Teachers practically ran the school. Teachers served as the principal, drafted the curriculum, provided support services in the place of traditional school specialists.

The program responded to the students' needs and interests and they were able to choose their own activities. It had a learner-centred orientation, therefore. Evaluations took the form of teachers' anecdotal reports focused on self-assessments of the students. The peculiarity of alternative schools was that students were elected to the alternative school rather than assigned to attend it.

A rich learning environment with stimulating educational opportunities and activities to make learning attractive was emphasised in the open classroom. Children could switch and participate in discussions from group to group. There was no concern at all about the disorder this could cause. Therefore, to learn, students need self-discipline. The open classroom was limited to the primary schools, but an effort by the high school to initiate the open classroom was the elective programs. Students were allowed to choose from a variety of short-term courses instead of taking a general course. Such courses were organised differently from the regular elective courses.

During this period, influential leaders included Carl Rogers and John Holk. Carl Rogers, a counselling psychologist, was able to clearly explain what was meant by open school advocates. Holt claimed that what the school needed most were teachers who could provide learners with a stimulating learning atmosphere and a positive learning experience.

During this time, major publications included Charles Silberman's *Crisis in the Classroom* (1970), which generated awareness of open education. He introduced educators who were outstanding in this book. A social studies course of study (MACOS) was also established at the Fifth and Six Graders Education Development Center, which was a curriculum project. It strengthened the students' exploration skills, which were important in the study of social sciences.

Privalistic Conservatism (1975-1989)

This era ushered in the school's conservative stance. The school's primary function was to express culture and to prepare students for their role in a technological society. It was important to scrutinise and closely track the program for effectiveness. This age was marked by many patterns. School performance and school improvement have been among these phenomena. This was based on research conducted to recognise elements that make a school a productive school in order to create a school improvement plan. One of the influential scholars in this analysis was Pinky and Smith (1983).

In order to better serve the interests of American youth, another development was an emphasis on a more academically rigorous curriculum. State laws and district policies that institute additional graduation standards could make this possible. The emphasis on a comprehensive curriculum has also given rise to an interest in critical thinking. This was necessary for the technologically focused knowledge age which the Educational Commission of the States (1982) concluded was the "basics of tomorrow." This included abilities for assessment and interpretation, critical thinking, abilities for problem solving, synthesis, creativity, decision-making and communication skills.

Another theme that was given some significance was accountability. In implementing the prescribed curriculum, teachers had to be held more responsible. The curriculum taught had to reflect the written curriculum and the goals had to be reflected in the tested curriculum. During this period, the voucher system was also another trend. Parents were expected to have a say in how their children should be taught and could employ trained teachers with the support of state funds. For the good of the people, this was to provide opportunities funded by tax revenue. Some states supported this voucher option proposal, which also had a negative side.

Multicultural education was another theme and various states had different systems for multicultural education. Some states, such as Tennessee, integrated Black History Culture into their social studies curriculum, while others, such as Indiana, concentrated on world culture. It was not compulsory for all of these levels, however, even in teacher education programs.

The National Education Goals 2000, which was the result of the first Education Summit that brought together all of the 50 governors of the nation in 1989 under President George Bush to look at issues affecting the future of America, was another trend during this time. The six goals for this summit were as follows:

In America, all kids can start school ready to learn.

1. The graduation rate for high schools will rise to at least 90%.
2. American students can leave grades 4 and 12 with demonstrated competence in difficult subjects such as English, mathematics, science, history and geography, and every American school can ensure that all students learn to use their minds well so that they can be prepared in our modern economy for responsible citizenship, more learning, and productive jobs.
3. In mathematics and science achievement, United States students will be the first in the world.
4. Each American adult will be literate and have the knowledge and skills required to compete and exercise the rights and responsibilities of citizenship in a global economy.
5. Each American school will be free from drugs and violence and will provide a learning-friendly, disciplined atmosphere.

In 1994, international languages, civics, democracy, economics, and acts were added to Goal 3 as topics to be studied with the passage of Goal 2000 legislation in the American Congress, while two more targets were added to make a total of eight goals. They were as follows:

1. The leading force of the nation will have access to programs for the continuous development of its technical skills and the ability to gain the expertise and skills required for the next century to teach and train all American students.
2. Each school will foster collaborations that improve parental involvement and participation in fostering children's social, emotional, and academic development. However, a criticism of these objectives showed that it was a dream that did not emanate from the grassroots, so there was no consensus.

This period's major scholars included Benjamin Bloom, John Goodlad and James Banks. A very important contributor to the curriculum and his theory of master learning was Bloom's Taxonomy of Educational Objectives.

Goodlad was an influential educator who seemed to have had a strong vision of helping schools meet their objectives. He evaluated the content of the balanced curriculum and found that only basic skills were emphasised in academic areas such as English, mathematics, social sciences, and science. Critical thinking and problem-solving abilities were absent from them.

In a multicultural background, James Banks was one of the advocates of multi-cultural education and the ability to assess schools as coral structures. This key concern was educational equity and to him a multicultural world needed a complete change in policies, attitudes of teachers, materials, methods of evaluation, teaching methods and therapy.

A nation at risk "High School: A Report on Secondary Education in America" and "Multi-ethnic Education: Theory and Practice" were two influential publications during this period. In 1983, the National Commission on Excellence in Education created a country at risk. It was a study that highlighted risk factors and made clear recommendations. It was very well diffused on television and radio and became the subject of discussion amongst stakeholders notably parents and legislators, yet it had very little impact on schools.

Technological Constructivism (1990-1999)

This age followed the 1980s, when there was a fight to improve public education after the Nation at Risk Study and there was proof that education had not changed much. So, there was the Charter Schools campaign. The goal was to: increase learning opportunities and access to quality education for all students; create options within the public school system for parents and students; establish a system of accountability for public education outcomes; promote creative teaching practices; create new career opportunities for teachers; facilitate involvement by the community and parents in public education.

Research on the effect of charter schools, however, has shown that it has not accomplished its aim of revamping the former educational system. Outside the regular public school governance system, so many states have switched to separate state level charter boards or other charter authorities.

During this period, technology had a key role to play. Education did not have to depend exclusively on the textbook or printing. With the advent of the machine that could link to many libraries in the world from the most remote places, as well as the use of phones, other modes of communication arose. These innovations also made the exchange of knowledge possible between large groups. The technology literacy challenge of President Clinton pushed the nation into a digital opportunity state with the goal of linking every classroom and library to the internet, expanding access to modern interactive computers, making high-quality educational software an integral part of the curriculum, and encouraging teachers to effectively incorporate technology into their teaching. Therefore, the 1990s gave a boost to the innovations used in today's classrooms.

During this time, three figures clearly stood out: Elliot E Eisner, whose works fall within the arts, education, curriculum studies and qualitative research methodology; Robert J. Marzano, who has been widely acclaimed for transforming research and theory into classroom practice; and Joseph, S. Renzulli, whose research focuses on discovering and cultivating young people's creativity and talents.

This age was influenced by two publications: "Classrooms that work" by Patricia Cunningham and Richard Allington was a positive guide containing realistic concepts, programmes and organisational techniques. Victoria Bernhardt's book on *Data Analysis for Comprehensive Schoolwide Improvement* has had a positive effect on state leaders, school system administrators and teachers. It then played a major role in the nationwide school improvement process as it helped these authorities deal with data that helped them to move forward.

As it was going to direct learning, teaching quality and assessment, research was to be the basis of all these objectives.

Regarding the model of school vouchers, the government provided tax-financed certificates to parents to pay school tuition for their children, whether public or private. This offered parents the option of institutions or approaches to education. While the scheme of vouchers was somewhat controversial, it was beneficial to the disadvantaged.

Home schooling progressed from a point where individuals knew little or nothing about it to a point where, amid many criticisms, it became common. There have been a number of improvements to home-schooling recently with the knowledge of school choice. In 50 nations, home schooling is officially legal. Home education has many benefits, including teaching a specific set of values, principles, and worldview, achieving more academically than in schools, individualizing the curriculum, strengthening family relationships between children and parents, providing children and youth with a safer atmosphere.

Modern Conservation (21st Century)

During this time, the need to equip students with 21st century skills was recognised, including the global problem of literacy-solving, innovation and creativity. This contributed to the 2002 introduction of the "No Child Left Behind (NCLB) Act" However, as the Act was constantly subject to scrutiny, no agreement was reached. As a result, the National Governors Association's proposals for modifications give the application of the Act a bit of autonomy. Global education, school vouchers, home-schooling and p-16 education were other developments in education during this time.

Americans saw the need for global literacy after the terrorist attack on September 11 in America, which they conceptualized as having cultural literacy, scientific literacy, and multiple literacy. This culminated in the recognition of education's fundamental and institutional goals. Each child was to be ready for school by the age of six with key objectives; each child must be able to read by the age of six; each child was to be fluent in algebra by the age of 13; each learner was to complete a comprehensive core curriculum by the age of 17 and complete the first two years of college by the age of 21.

Structural goals were also defined as follows in order to achieve the core objectives: beginning universal public education at age 3; smoothing transitions from one stage of education to the next; shifting from a carriage-unit system to a skill-based system; providing more flexible learning opportunities for teenage learners and moving the agreed endpoint of public education from grade 12 to grade 14.

The 1990s was also a decade of 12 educational standards in which all states had adopted academic standards that could direct teacher training except the state of Loera. This ushered in a model that matched classroom activities to state expectations. The relation between what is being studied in high school and college (university) has now also been made. This was going to help boost college performance.

The big leaders of the time were Linda Darling-Hammond and Carol Anne Tomlinson. Darling-Hammond, a Professor of Education, was very instrumental in educational policy and practice issues, including evaluation of school reforms, professional development research in education, and she worked in numerous key roles, including executive director of the National Commission on Teaching and the Future of America, member of the National Commission on Teaching and the Future of America National Board for Professional Teaching Standards and chain of the Interstate New Teacher Assessment and support Consortium (INTASC) Committee Faculty Sponsor for Stanford's Teacher Education Program (STEP) and authored several books that directed the course of Education.

There were several releases during this time in America. The "No Child Left Behind Act (2002) was popular among them, which looked at improving the achievement of students; aligning the brain's leading standards, specifically how children learn." Another publication during this time was Charlotte Dancelson's *Enhancing Student Achievement* (2002), which concentrated on developing teaching strategies as well as Michael Fullan's *Leading in A Culture of Change* (2001). In this fast-changing world, the emphasis is on efficient leadership, which is important in any organisation.

The ideas discussed above have influenced curriculum practices around the world in various ways. These influences were introduced in Africa by colonial masters and the use of western-oriented textbooks even after independence. However, before colonisation Africa had its own form of education. The next section discusses the origin and evolution of curriculum in Africa.

Historical Foundations of the Curriculum in Africa

Pre-colonial period

Much of the education that took place in precolonial Africa was aimed at responding to the demands of society as a whole by educating its members, either in groups or individually. It was like a 'school of life' geared towards producing an honest, respectable, skilled and cooperative individual who fitted into social life. African education was a means for survival, and it connected young people to social networks (Gwanfogbe, 2011).

African indigenous education was more within the family, which was an important framework for the provision and development of information. Education did not have a standardised curriculum, which resulted in considerable knowledge and skills being lost in most cases when the custodians of those knowledge and skills died or were no longer lucid. This means the curriculum was not written but only tacitly organised. It was not divided into distinct disciplines like history, geography, economics or biology even though these disciplines were implicit in educational ideas and practices.

Parents, especially mothers were first teachers beginning with language training to sanitary and aesthetic education. Siblings, older relatives and community members were teachers too. Learning processes and pedagogies emphasised observation, imitation, and participation. Learning experiences were provided through games, storytelling, proverbs, folklore and hands-on activities. Assessment and evaluation were progressive. Terminal evaluation often culminated in a kind of certification by admission to initiation rites and ceremonies marking graduation. Fafunwa (1974) and many others have argued that African indigenous education was functional because curriculum though informal, was developed to attend to the realities of the community, and it was needs-based.

Colonial era

Kwabena (2006) reports that the production of curricula in British West Africa can be related to the educational activities of early European merchants and missionaries who, in the late 15th and early 16th centuries, visited the continent. They came from all over Europe, and all participated in the growth of colonial education in Africa by the Portuguese, Dutch, French, Spaniards, Italians, British, and Germans. To achieve their business goals, European merchants founded schools. On the other hand, missionaries set up Christian schools to spread the gospel, again with the aid of the Africans.

Schooling was a medium by which Western values were transmitted by their colonisers to the African continent with the introduction of formal education. As Adedeji (1990) cited, McGregor claimed that the implementation of formal education in Africa was initially prompted by the desire to provide upright and honest Christian clerks, merchants, interpreters, and chiefs with "moral". It was also intended to create Africans who could speak the colonial powers' language. Elements of the African culture like dance and music were removed from the curriculum.

Indigenous knowledge that had existed on the African continent since time immemorial was de-emphasised. In exchange for the colonial government's funding, the missionaries had to follow certain conditions. The disregard of vernacular language in the school curriculum or as a means of instruction was one such circumstance (Awoniyi 1975). Formal education in Africa thus adhered to Western education and, during the colonial period, gained prominence. Formal education varied because of its non-vocational nature, focusing on the development of reading and writing skills instead of learning on the job.

Evangelism was the philosophy that influenced colonial missionary education and its curriculum: through the act of creation, humankind originated from Heaven, and human destiny was to return to God. A human being could accomplish the gift of divine elevation only through education, which would eventually place him or her in union with God (Gutek 1988). The colonial curriculum was also influenced by the theory of essentialism (Oliva 2004), on the basis of which those principles and concepts were universal to all humanity and essential for the growth and promotion of civil society. These core values had been present in the civilizations of the past, and contributed significantly to public welfare (MacDonald 1965).

In the latter part of the 18th century, when the British gradually took over Ghana, Sierra Leone, Gambia, and Nigeria, British educational planners planned and introduced curricula fashioned after the European model for West African colleges (Szostak 2003). In all public schools, the content of the curriculum has shifted to concentrate more on British subjects, concepts, and interests. In all public schools in areas formerly under the administration of other European nations, the English language became the medium of instruction.

Even though these West African territories were taken over by the British colonial government, missionaries remained in possession of their own parochial institutions. Because of Germany's defeat in the First World War, only German missionaries lost control of their schools (Guggisberg 1922). The new British curriculum thus emphasised courses that would train West Africans to speak English and to pursue jobs in the British West African colonies as clerks, teachers, missionaries, or law enforcement officers (Rado 1972; Ocholla 2000).

Since they had little to contribute to the creation of a civilised and modern society as established by the colonists and missionaries, African cultural and social practices were not considered necessary. What Bestor (1955) identified as the presumed intentions of the curriculum planners, who were naturally all British, were reflected in the curriculum content.

The content of the colonial school curriculum was composed of algebra, religion, and reading or the "three Rs" for 300 years. Biblical themes and all reading materials were based on foreign ideas. Religion was based on the Bible, mathematics was made up of topics based on foreign words and definitions such as " pounds", "shillings", "pence", and "miles" and geography was based on England or Europe's hills, rivers, capes, and bays (Judd 1917). These were all ideas in Africa that aroused no sense of imagination. Memorisation, which was not learning at all, was the only way to understand what was taught (Dewey 1933; Wright 1981).

The historical subjects were European and not West African. Topics in the study of nature in Europe were plants, insects, animals, trees and birds. Singing was about British culture, all subjects from Europe were chosen in the humanities and music was all about English themes, principles, ideas, or beliefs or tales. The study of the works of Shakespeare, Chaucer, Elliot, or Dickens applied to poetry and literature. The topics at the heart of the curriculum were intended to turn the African to serve the needs of a colonial government and a new African society in his own setting.

The colonial school curriculum tended to emphasise foreign interests and ambitions from the late 15th century to the early 19th century (Wright 1981). The regular argument put forward by the colonial government was that in African history, geography, languages, music, art, politics, or agriculture, there were no local materials created by people of experience and authority that could be used in the local schools.

By 1914, a typical school curriculum in a West African public school was made up of the following subjects: (1) Colloquial English (2) Arithmetic (3) English Reading (4) Writing (5) Hygiene (6) Plain Needlework for girls (7) Hand and Eye: Industrial Training to include Drawing or Nature Study and Agricultural Training (8) Object Lessons in Nature Study and Elementary Hand and Eye Training in Infant Classes. The list of optional subjects included the following: (1) Vernacular Reading (2) Singing (3) Geography (4) History (5) Grammar (6) Drill and Physical Exercises (Hilliard 1957: 79) (7) Book-keeping (8) Shorthand (9) Mensuration. (10) Algebra (11) Kindergarten. Clearly absent from the public school curriculum was religion, although it remained a strong component in the parochial schools.

The way West Africans were forced to memorise information by colonial schoolteachers gave the impression that rote learning was successful. Rote learning is no learning, as we know today. Although the British colonial government and the missionaries worked closely together to lay the foundations of a modern West African curriculum, the curriculum they adopted was not compatible with local interests to a very large extent. The net result was that African scholars of European history, geography, plants, or animals were produced by the colonial educational system.

Postcolonial era

During the postcolonial or early independence era, Jansen (1989) reports that commitment to curricula in the immediate aftermath of independence, took at least two major forms. On the one hand, there was a desperate struggle to define suitable content. On the other hand, there was an opportunity to criticise the colonial curriculum severely and repeatedly. These concerns were, however, shadowed by another priority in the first phase of independence: education expansion.

At the 1961 Ababa Conference, it was observed that educational content in Africa did not correspond to African conditions and recommended that educational content for African authorities be revised and reformed to reflect African environment, child development, cultural heritage and demands of technological advancement and economic development (Greenough, 1961)

There was a general perception of the irrelevance of the Western curriculum model in an African setting, for example, that the implementation of such projects at local level was extremely difficult.

Recently, independent states have taken some radical positions about the West and adopted some socialist education. The curriculum trends in 1960s and 70s were very divergent and geared towards "Education with Production" This was practiced in Angola, Botswana, Mozambique, Zimbabwe and Guinea Bissau, in one form or another. African countries since then are engaging in curriculum reform activities to make curricula more responsive to their context. A detailed account of the evolution of the curriculum in Africa is found in chapter 15.

Credible and sustainable curriculum reforms will require the active engagement of all education stakeholders and especially the input of curriculum scholars. There is evidence of Curriculum studies as a discipline in African universities but regrettably, Lesley le Grange paints the picture of a field that is largely underdeveloped in all 53 countries. He mentions the paucity of curriculum scholars, very little research and theory consequently little writing on curriculum planning and design; few conferences on curriculum development in the continent and that very few African scholars publish in international journals (Le Grange, 2011). He states further that their scope of publication is limited to

- Historical studies of curriculum change,
- literature reviews of curriculum reconstruction,
- case studies of curriculum innovations and
- Comparative studies.

His observations are a challenge for African scholars to enhance scholarship in the field, which is one of the objectives of this book.

4

Philosophical Foundations of the Curriculum

Although philosophy has wide and varied meanings, etymologically, philosophy means the love of wisdom because the word philosophy comes from a mixture of two Greek words: "philos" which means "love" and "sophi" which means "wisdom. Wisdom describes knowledge of a person or a group of people's actions and how they function and think. Philosophy is the belief system of an individual, stemming from an effort to find a solution to problems in society. In this broad and general sense, philosophy is the way people seek to understand themselves and the world. When considered as an academic discipline, philosophy studies the nature of knowledge, reality and existence with distinct branches such as axiology, epistemology and ethics. In relation to education, philosophy would mean one's beliefs on why, what, and how education should be carried out. Education and philosophy are strongly interrelated and interdependent. Education clearly responds to philosophy because education without philosophy would have no direction.

Philosophical foundations of a curriculum are those philosophical components that have an impact on the choices made about the school's goals and content. Therefore, educational philosophy is very useful in the field of curriculum design. It is the starting point of decision-making of every curriculum and also the basis for all subsequent curriculum decisions. It is the driving factor for many curriculum choices. In this chapter, major world philosophies will be presented and discussed in relation to education, followed by presentation and discussion of educational philosophies. The chapter ends with reflections on perspectives and possibilities of African philosophies in relation to education.

Four world philosophies

Philosophy has been cited as a screen for the determination of the curriculum's objectives (Tyler, 1949), selection, organisation, and implementation of learning experiences. Philosophy helps one to answer questions like: "What are schools for?" Which subjects are of value?", "How can the material be learned by students? Philosophy in relation to education consists of what you believe about education, the collection of ideals that govern your professional practices. Four major universal philosophies that have shaped education namely, Idealism, Realism, Pragmatism and Existentialism will be discussed in this section.

Idealism

The oldest system of philosophy known to humankind is Idealism. In the East, its roots go back to ancient India, and to Plato in the West. Its basic viewpoint stresses the human spirit as the most important element in life. Idealism sets out the argument that reality is a conceptual construct as we view it. This implies that the presence of things outside the domain of the intellect cannot be interpreted. There are many views of idealism, but the main outlook is that the truest truth is ideas and knowledge. There are many things that change in the world, but ideas and wisdom are long lasting. Idealists claim that lives can be transformed by ideas. A person's most important part is the mind. It should be nurtured and grown. It is the driving factor for many curriculum choices.

Implications of Idealism to Education

Idealist education aims at preserving, enriching, and transmitting culture, which enables an individual to become much more rational, acquire and apply practical knowledge and skills to a democratic society. Literature, history, philosophy, and religion will be emphasised by a program inspired by idealism. Through discussion, the teacher must encourage thought while the teacher helps refine the ideas. Methods for teaching can be both overt and indirect. They will include lecture, discussion, questioning, deductive and inductive teaching, all of which are meant to trigger latent concepts in the mind. Through modelling, reality is established. The function of the school, therefore, is a place where ideas are tested, introduced, and restructured. It is a miniature society which, in preparation for democratic living, gives the child experience.

Realism

Realism is one of the oldest philosophies of Western culture, like idealism, which dates back to ancient Greece at least. Realism was founded by Aristotle, who lived from 384 to 322 B.C. (Amaele, 2002). Aristotle's philosophy was categorised as classical realism. He held in his classical work that ideas do not make sense if they fail to explicitly relate to material things, even if they are essential in themselves. There are many advocates and interpretations of realism, such as classical realism, religious realism, scientific realism, and others, but the common elements are the emphasis here.

Independently of the human mind, the matters, or objects we see around us exist. This is contrary to the position of the idealists who claimed that there are objects or matters only when man's mind acknowledges his existence. Realists usually think that human beings at birth have no inborn, or innate, thoughts in their minds. The mind is a blank slate, "tabula rasa," All that the mind can then contain comes from experience. The only source of input into the human mind is experience.

Implications of Realism on Education

Realists agree that the education curriculum should be realistic and useful. Realism-based schooling enhances the child's physical and mental powers. It improves and trains the child's senses. This prepares the baby for real life. This offers an interpretation of the material world by investigation. It is an analysis of science and methods of science. It transmits culture and develops human existence, and in order to guarantee survival and good life, there is a need to know the environment.

The program stresses the subject matter of the physical world. Natural science, physical science, health culture, physical activity, math, geography, history, and astronomy are the key subjects. Methods of teaching include demonstration, observation, and experiment.

Pragmatism

The term pragmatism is derived from the word 'Pragma' in Greek, meaning activity or job completed. Pragmatism developed as a school of thought in the 19th century with the work of C.S. Peirce, William James, and John Dewey, who are usually referred to as the 'classical' pragmatists. They have shared themes that are scientific in the broadest sense, despite holding differing opinions on a number of different topics, although they deny much of the psychological image that is related to empiricism. Practicability and utility are of great significance to this philosophy. Pragmatists assume that in its measurable practical results lies the truth or sense of a concept or a proposition.

Pragmatism helps one to discover the processes and do things that work best to help us achieve desirable goals. There are no set or ultimate ideals, no ultimate priorities, no absolute reality. It believes that only those theories that work in practical situations are valid and that the scientific method is important. Pragmatists believe that as people pass through life, education should be an ever-evolving process of reviewing, reconstructing, and incorporating their experiences.

Schools should not be simply learning institutions for pragmatists; they are social institutions for training students for democratic living. The classroom, as a miniature community, gives teachers and students opportunities to participate in constructive learning, critical thinking and problem solving. The Pragmatists, instead of stressing awareness of traditions and cultural heritage, recommend content and activities that are important to the desires, needs and problems of the students. The curriculum should be interdisciplinary rather than compartmentalised into subjects or disciplines, integrated and action oriented.

However, with such an approach, pragmatism may compromise the acquisition of content or discipline knowledge. Regarding the curriculum development Pragmatists have prescribed certain principles: There is the principle of utility which states that only subjects, activities and experiences which are useful to the present needs of the child and also meet the future expectations of adult life should be included in the curriculum. According to the principle of interest, only those activities and experiences where the child takes interest should be included in the curriculum. The child's activity, vocation and experience are another principle of the pragmatic curriculum. These three should all be interwoven with each other. The curriculum should consist of such varieties that promote independent ideas, and freedom to develop social and purposeful attitudes and curricula should include subjects and activities, because of the holistic nature of knowledge.

Implications of Pragmatism on Education

Pragmatic methods for learning through personal experience are recommended by pragmatic practitioners on the basis of the theory. Pragmatic learning is designed to prepare children for life, and therefore methods of experimentation, projects, lab work, discussion, play are recommended. The teacher is an initiative and innovative guide. He needs to improve democratic values, know the interest of students and be a good leader in the group.

Existentialism

Existentialism deals with the problems of one's existence. Its main ideas stem from the philosophers of existence, such as Soren Kierkegaard, F. W. Nietzche, Martin Buber, Karl Jaspers and Jean-Paul Sartre. Existentialists say that a good education underlines the individuality of a person. It emphasises that everyone is responsible for defining his or her own destiny. It emphasises the individual's unique nature against a group. Existentialists criticise schools that undermine their individuality and view students as part of a group to serve society's needs.

The existentialist program responds to the individual's needs and interests. Humanities and the arts are especially useful when it comes to drawing the attention of students to the questions, challenges, dilemmas and problems facing humanity. They are also an alternative way for students, through drama, drawing and creative writing, to express their choices in a creative way. But existentialism was criticised for disregarding community and society's needs. The existentialist teacher respects the student's personal liberty and choice. He/she is open-minded and reflective and creates an environment for learning, which promotes reflection, inquiry and dialogue. Under standardised tests, flexible tests are not encouraged. The teacher helps students to define their own essence, exposing them to different paths in their life and creating an environment for their own choice.

Implications of Existentialism on Education

The subject matter takes second place at the existentialist classroom to help students understand and appreciate themselves as unique persons that fully take responsibility for their thoughts, feelings and actions. Although many existentialist educators provide some curricular structure, existentialism, more than other educational philosophies, affords students freedom in their choice of subject matter. Humanities are often emphasised in an existentialist curriculum. They are explored to give students experiences which can contribute to their creativity and self-expression. Existentialist methods concentrate on the person. Learning is autonomous, self-directed, and includes a lot of personal communication with the teacher, who has an open and honest relationship to each student.

Philosophies of Education

Educational philosophy deals with philosophical questions about the nature, goals and major issues of education. It utilises the parent discipline of philosophy guided by developmental psychology, cognitive science, sociology, and other relevant subjects. As a branch of practical philosophy, philosophy of education has many theoretical orientations. Theories of education deal with educational components such as curriculum, teaching and learning. They are rooted in one or more of the world philosophies which have been discussed in the preceding sections. Also called philosophies of education, the most well-known of the theories of education will be presented and discussed in this section. They are Perennialism, Essentialism, Progressivism, Reconstructionism and Constructivism.

Perennialism

Idealism and realism are the roots of perennialism. Robert Hutchins and Mortimer Adler are its leading supporters. Idealism is influenced by the perennialists who argue that the goal of education is to help students to understand and assimilate universal and sustainable ideas and values. The objective of education for perennialists is to ensure students get an insight into the great ideas of Western civilisation. Perennialists believe that ideas that have lasted for centuries should be the focus of education, because ideas are still relevant today. The aim is to teach ideas that remain eternal, to search for permanent truths that will not change, because the natural and human worlds are not changed. The goal of a perennialist educator is to teach students to think rationally and develop minds that can think critically. Humans are rational beings, and their minds need to be developed.

Implications of Perennialism in Education

A constantly organised classroom is expected to be a well-disciplined environment that develops a lifelong student's search for the truth. Perennialists think that education must be made to enable students to understand and appreciate the great literary and artistic works, the laws and principles written by the best thinkers of history, which have stood the test of time and have never been outdated. These ideas have the potential at any time to solve problems. In a worthwhile education, therefore, cultivation of the intellect is the greatest priority. Perennialist classrooms also focus on teachers to achieve these objectives. Teachers don't care about the interests or experiences of the students. They recommend schools to spend more time teaching concepts and explaining how significant they are for students. Recitation and lecture are common methods of instruction. There is no difference between students, and everyone learns the same thing at the same speed. One form of such curriculum is the "three Rs."

Essentialism

Essentials believe that a core of knowledge needs to be transmitted to students in a disciplined and systematic way. James D. Koerner (1959), H. G. Rickover (1959), Paul Copperman (1978) and Theodore Sizer are all advocates of essentialism (1985). Educational critics believe that children should be careful and rigorous in learning traditional basic subjects. They maintain that the core of our culture is that schools are obliged to transmit to students in a disciplined and systematic way.

It should focus on the education of students to read, write, speak and compute clearly and logically. Although the philosophy of education is similar in certain respects to perennialism, contrary to perennialists, essentialists accept the idea of changing the core curriculum. Schooling should be practical and ready to make students worthy members of society. The objective of students is to instil the essentials of academic knowledge, which are the main things, in order to adopt a back-to-basic approach. Schools should emphasise on intellectual and moral standards in this conservative perspective.

Implications of Essentialism on Education

Knowledge, skills, and academic rigour are central to the curriculum. In other words, education requires subjects and values which all those going to school must study and that the school must provide knowledge to build and develop a good character. Essentialist education is largely focused on students. It stresses that the teacher is the ultimate authority. Essentialists will usually teach subjects like Reading, Writing, Literature, Foreign Languages, History, Mathematics, Science, Art, and Music. The teacher's role is to instil respect for authority, perseverance, duty, consideration, and practicality.

Progressivism

The idea that education should be centred on children rather than focusing on the teacher or content is based on progressive thinking. In the 1920s and 1930s, John Dewey's writing (1859-1952) contributed greatly to the spread of gradual ideas. One of its principles was to improve the school's way of life by experiencing freedom and democracy in schools. Progressivists believe that education should not focus on the content or teacher, but should focus on the whole child. This philosophy emphasises that students should test ideas experimentally.

The progressive philosophy of education says that educators should educate children to think rather than rely on rote memorisation. Learning is rooted in the concerns of learners who experience the world. It is active, not passive. The learner is a solver and thinker of problems who makes sense in the physical and cultural context through his/her individual experience. The progressive philosophy also argues that the current knowledge may not be true in the future. Therefore, the best way to prepare students for an unknown future is to equip them with problem-solving strategies that will enable them to discover meaningful knowledge at various stages of their lives.

Implications of Progressivism on Education

The teacher serves as the guide or resource person in a progressively oriented classroom whose primary responsibility is to facilitate learning for students. Progressive people improve their learning experiences and use practical projects which enable students to learn by taking an active part in activities which use their knowledge. Professors provide experiences to enable students to learn. The progressive teacher is committed to offering students experiences that as much as possible replicate real experiences. Students can cooperate in groups and often solve the problems identified as important by the group, not by the teacher. Progressive educators use the scientific method so that students can systematically and directly study matter and events. The most prominent progressive methods are research and methods of teaching based on problems.

Constructivism

Constructivism is a learning philosophy based on the belief that through experience, people build an understanding and knowledge of the world. It is based on the basis that many people form or build up knowledge from what they have done, seen or heard. Each of us produces our own "rules" and "mental patterns" that our experiences use to make sense. Consequently, learning is simply the process of adapting our mental patterns to fit new experiences.

Implications for the Classroom

Students will best learn when actively engaged in learning experiences than when they are passively receiving information. Learning is inherently a social process because it is connected into a society as students and teachers work together to build knowledge. Since knowledge cannot be imparted directly to students, the aim of teaching is to offer experiences which will facilitate knowledge building. Teachers need to understand the mental models that students use to understand the world and the assumptions they make in support of those models in order to teach them correctly. The purpose of learning is to build an individual's own meaning, not just for learners to memorise and regenerate responses. Education is interdisciplinary, so evaluation should provide students with the information about the quality of their learning. This is a valuable way of measuring learning. Strategies like problem-based learning, cooperative learning, project-based learning, experimentation are typical constructivist activities.

Reconstructionism/Critical Theory

Social reconstruction is a philosophy that requires addressing social issues and seeking to create a better society and democracy worldwide. Curricula highlighting social reform as the goal of education are the main focus of Reconstructionist educators. In the reaction to the realities of World War II Theodore Brameld (1904-1987) who was the founder of social re-constructionism-recognised the potential to either kill people through technology and human cruelty or the ability to build a beneficial society through technology and human compassion. This simply means that human beings had the potential to either improve or destroy their society.

George Counts (1889-1974) acknowledged that education is the way to prepare people to build this new social system. Critical theorists believe that systems should be changed to overcome oppression and improve human conditions, as do social re-constructionists. The Brazilian, Paulo Freire (1921-1997) had a lifetime of poverty that brought him to the field of education and literacy as a means to social transformation. In his opinion, people should learn to resist oppression and not suffer or oppress others. To this, the development of awareness to overcome domination and oppression requires dialogue, critical awareness and instead of 'teaching banking,' in which the educator deposits information in the heads of students, Freire sees teaching and learning as an investigation process in which the child needs to invent and reinvent the world.

Implications of Reconstructionism in the Classroom

For social re-constructionists and critical theorists, curriculum focuses on student experience and taking social action on real problems, such as violence, hunger, international terrorism, inflation, and inequality. Strategies for dealing with controversial issues (particularly in social studies and literature), inquiry, dialogue, and multiple perspectives are the focus. Community-based learning and bringing the world into the classroom are also strategies. A teacher in the Reconstructionist classroom engages the students on the moral concerns. Students select their goals and social priorities individually and then, with the teachers' guidance, prepare an action plan to bring about change.

There is no single philosophy behind a good curriculum. A good curriculum makes use of a combination of philosophy to make a full individual, who not only knows, but can contribute significantly to his/her immediate society's development. Therefore, learning philosophy is critical to guide educational outcomes for the curriculum designer.

Perspectives on African Philosophies

The advent of post-colonial education in Africa stimulated thought in looking for educational philosophy that would lay more emphasis on African cultures. African philosophy of education incorporates the ideals of African communalism, which refers to the tendencies among Africans to attach strong allegiance to their communities characterised by collective cooperation and ownership of resources by members of a community (Heinz, 2006). Two African philosophies which reflect these values are *Ubuntu* and *Ujamaa*.

Ubuntu

Ubuntu can best be described as humanism from an African perspective as proposed by the former president of Zambia, Kenneth Kaunda. It is Africa's vision of social relations. It is a social and humanistic ethic. The word Ubuntu is derived from the aphorism of 'Nguni' (isiZulu): 'Umuntu Ngumuntu Ngabantu', which can be translated as "a person is a person because of or through others" (Moloketi, 2009; Tutu, 2004). It is otherwise stated as "I am because we are" or "I am human because I belong." Various words representing key values have been used to describe the presence of ubuntu. Some of these are sympathy, compassion, benevolence, solidarity, hospitality, generosity, sharing, openness, affirming, available, kindness, caring, harmony, interdependence, obedience, collectivity and consensus. These social qualities have the potential to strengthen the moral fabric of the community.

Ubuntu is guided by three maxims: The first maxim states that to be human is to affirm one's humanity by recognising the humanity of others and, on that basis, to establish respectful human relations with others. The second maxim states that if one is faced with a decisive choice between wealth and the preservation of the life of another human being, then one should opt for the preservation of life. The third maxim, deeply embedded in the traditional African political philosophy, says that the King owed his status, including all the powers associated with it, to the will of the people under him (Samkange and Samkange, 1980).

The Ubuntu ideology integrates all facets of daily life in Africa, and is a term embraced by people of Bantu descent from all ethnic groups in Southern, Central, West, and East Africa (Rwelamila, Talukhaba & Ngowi, 1999). The philosophy of Ubuntu believes in group solidarity, which is central to the survival of African communities (Mbigi & Maree, 2005). An African is not an isolated individual, but a person living in a community. It is only through such community solidarity that issues like hunger, isolation, deprivation, poverty, and any emerging challenges can be overcome, because of the community's brotherly and sisterly concern, cooperation, care, and sharing. The philosophy implies that an African should be able to empower the community around them and help it improve.

Applicability of Ubuntu Philosophy

Socially, Ubuntu as a philosophy is attributable to African blacks, particularly sub-Saharan Africa. However, its application is now global (Wichtner-Zoia, 2012). Cooperation and collaboration are key principles in community work. Desmond Tutu claims that Ubuntu symbolises the backbone of African spirituality. He asserts that while western countries have given the world an economic standpoint like capitalism. the social ethic of Ubuntu has been Africa's biggest contribution to the world.

Educational Implications of Ubuntu

Values enhanced by Ubuntu can be promoted in the affective domain of a school's program. Concepts such as compassion, benevolence, solidarity, hospitality and generosity can be taught directly in subjects related to social studies such as moral education, citizenship, religion and human rights and can be modelled and reinforced in the classroom. These values can also be enhanced by teaching methods such as cooperative learning, peer teaching and role-play/dramatization. Teachers must make a conscious effort to promote these values both in Africa and beyond.

Ujamaa

Julius Nyerere identified four flaws in Tanzanian education that were also present in many African countries. First, colonialist schooling was elitist in nature, structured to serve the desires and needs of a limited percentage of the population, and thus failed to create an egalitarian society. Secondly, education for the most part uprooted its recipients from their native cultures, resulting in a lack of connection between them and society. Thirdly, education appears to focus heavily on book-based knowledge, emphasising knowledge gained by theory rather than life experiences. Finally, education does not mix school learning and work. Based on this observation. Nyerere proposed the philosophy of *Ujamaa*, a Kiswahili word meaning familyhood or brotherhood (Cornelli, 2012) which he considers the basis of African socialism.

Nyerere portrayed Ujamaa (his type of socialism) as a mentality that was needed to ensure that people were concerned about each other's well-being. This mentality was referred to as "brotherhood" or "familyhood" by him. As a result, Nyerere believed that caring for one another and the attitude of brotherhood or familyhood were inextricably linked. He claimed that people would only really care about one another if they saw each other as brothers and sisters or members of the same family.

Therefore, Nyerere was convinced that if by living and working together, traditional societies were able to overcome the difficulties of their time like hunger, sickness, uncertainties of weather and depredation by wild animals, then the contemporary generation of Africans could also overcome their development challenges by living together and working for the common good. Nyerere maintained that in traditional Africa everybody was a worker, meaning that it was obvious to everyone in the community that everybody contributed his/her portion towards the production of its wealth. Since everyone contributed to the wealth of the community, there were no lazy people who took advantage of the hospitality of society, giving nothing in return. As a result, Nyerere asserted that in traditional society laziness was a disgrace. In traditional African society, wealth was shared. No one could amass wealth for the sole purpose of acquiring power and prestige.

Educational Implications of Ujamaa

Education must foster the social goals of living together and working together for the common good and prepare young people for work. Such an educational philosophy calls for the teaching and modelling of values of communalism; critical thinking and problem-solving techniques to enhance skills for the world of work and group work/cooperative learning, peer-teaching as teaching strategies to enhance socialism. After independence, many countries in Africa revised their curricula to incorporate some of these values which were not enhanced by western education.

5

Psychological Foundations of the Curriculum

Psychology, widely known and defined as the scientific study of the mind and behaviour (American Psychological Association, 2015), greatly impacts the design, delivery, and assessment of school learning experiences. This academic discipline has revealed how humans grow and develop, how they learn, and what they need to learn successfully. As the consumer of curriculum, the learner is a central focus in the processes of curriculum development and instruction. Just as a fashion designer cannot produce a customized outfit without making some physical measurements of the client, curriculum workers find knowledge of learner characteristics and learning theories indispensable for arriving at curriculum decisions.

Knowledge of psychology facilitates the creation of appropriate programs, courses, lessons, syllabuses, textbooks, and support materials used in school. Specifically, the nature of the learner and the learning process inform the formulation of goals and objectives, organisation of curriculum content, selection of instructional methods, materials, activities, and assessment strategies (Snowman and Biehler, 2006; Print, 2020) to enhance the quality of curriculum systems. Principles of human growth and development and learning theories as well as their implications and applications to curriculum and instruction will be dealt with, in subsequent sections of this chapter. Special attention is given to African developmental theories and learning processes in relation to curriculum work.

Human Growth and Development

Development may be defined as the pattern of biological, cognitive, and socioemotional changes that begin at conception and continues through the lifespan, involving growth and decay or dying (Santrock, 2011 p.29). Learners develop physically, mentally, morally, socially, and otherwise as they age and move to the end of their life spans. Developmental psychologists like Sigmund Freud, Eric Erickson, Lawrence Kolberg, Jean Piaget, Frobel, and others have provided educators with huge insights on how human behaviour changes over time, primarily influenced by nature and nurture. Other developmental influences on human behaviour hinge on continuity and discontinuity of activities, and early and later life experiences of an individual (Santrock, 2011 p. 31-32).

Understanding developmental patterns clarifies available alternatives from which curriculum and instructional designers make their choices. To get a clearer picture of what these patterns are, a summary of developmental theories and their highlights are presented on Table 5.1.

The table indicates that developmental theories birthed principles of growth and development which have been assumed valid and universal. These principles guide descriptions of general characteristics of learners. Notable principles of growth and development are i) growth and development occur in stages, ii) development is sequential, iii) maturation and readiness, and iv) individual similarities and differences. Growth and development principles inform curriculum planners on developmentally appropriate curricula in several ways.

Table 5.1. Human Developmental Theorists, Theories, and Principles

Name of theorist	Theory	Highlights
Sigmund Freud	Psychosexual theory (personality development)	Ego and super ego; Emotional nature of unconscious motivation.
Eric Erickson	Psychosocial development	eight stages of human life cycle; each stage presents a crisis to be resolved
Lawrence Kohlberg,	Moral development	six stages of moral reasoning in three levels;
Jean Piaget	Cognitive development	four stages of mental development; assimilation; accommodation and equilibration
Arnold Gesell	Physical development	Maturation, sequential development

Growth and Development Stages

Humans grow and develop in somewhat distinct stages even though the rate and pace may differ slightly among individuals of the same chronological age. Each developmental stage has its characteristics. This implies that curriculum goals and objectives should be feasible and attainable given learners' levels of development. For example, Piagetian stages of mental development that have dominated the stage for over eight decades, offer guidance as to intellectual experiences that could be selected and offered to learners in elementary school classes. For maximum benefit to be derived, the content scope of school subjects and learning expectations should reflect the capabilities of the child at each of the developmental stages.

Sequential Development

Growth and development are known to be sequential with three principles of biological sequence identified and described in the literature; Cephalocaudal development, which is development that begins from head to tail, proximodistal that begins from centre to the periphery and mass, to specific which sees mass movements displayed before specific actions. The principles of biological sequential development imply that learning experiences requiring physical activities must take development sequences into consideration. For example, designers of early childhood school curricula must sequence learning activities in physical education, writing, initiation to mathematics and science bearing in mind these developmental sequences. This creates awareness of, and distinction between learning objectives that are feasible and those that are not at a point in time in the life of a learner.

Maturation and Readiness

School failure sometimes results from learners' unpreparedness to engage in learning activities. Unpreparedness can be physical or mental. Until physical structures are mature or ready, no amount of practice is enough to establish a skill. It would be futile to spend time and energy teaching a skill before maturation of physical structures needed for that skill to be performed. Maturation is an essential condition for learning. It is the ability to do certain tasks at certain stages of development; tasks that could not be done previously.

An application of the principle of maturation in curriculum planning is in the timing of training. Many early childhood education programs demand children of less than five who are learning to form letters, to begin on sand trays using their fingers instead of pens and pencils and paper because maturation is needed for hand-eye coordination and fine motor movements for effective use of complex writing instruments. Maturation and readiness in essence, precedes learning.

Individual Differences

No two human beings are identical irrespective of their genetic makeup and upbringing. Even identical twins differ in many respects, confirming the interplay of nature and nurture in producing human behaviour. In a classroom consisting of many children of approximately the same chronological ages and physical characteristics, there are still differences among them. Students have different levels of motivation, different attitudes towards teaching and learning and different responses to the learning environment. Educators can identify fast and slow learners, introverts, and extroverts, tall and short, gender differences, differences in interest and capabilities, differences in learning styles etc.

Here are some of the ways that curriculum and instructional designers have applied this principle of individual differences for the benefit of the learner.

- Curriculum goals and objectives are made to reflect the needs of all learners bearing in mind individual differences. Well formulated curriculum goals should be inclusive. If, for example, a curriculum goal states that, "to prepare individuals for self-reliance," this means that both persons with abilities and disabilities pursuing this curriculum will be provided with diverse learning opportunities to promote self-reliance.
- There is a wide range of subjects included in the curriculum content of school programs to cater for general and individual needs and interests of learners. Subjects that cater for demonstrated talents are included especially in learner centred curriculum designs. In subject centred designs, some of these subjects commonly called electives, are made optional.
- Special programmes (e. g. compensatory education and special education), courses and modules have been created for learners with special needs in many instances. In a strict modular system of curriculum design, gifted learners as well as learners with physical and

learning disabilities may be required to complete different blocks of content at different times.

▪ Variety is a key guideline when selecting and providing learning experiences to respect the principle of individual differences. A variety of teaching methods, activities and materials are employed in curriculum and instructional materials to accommodate the variety of learners that exist in any instructional situation.

▪ In grouping of learners for instruction, classroom teachers do not lose sight of individual differences. To create groups that promote rather than hinder effective learning, the merits, and demerits of heterogenous and homogenous grouping must be weighed. Heterogeneous grouping is often preferred over homogenous grouping so that individuals can benefit from individual differences of learning teams.

Learning Theories and the Curriculum

From descriptions of the learning process in psychological literature, it is widely understood that humans learn through a variety of ways such as conditioning, imitation, performing mental functions, information processing, actively constructing meaning with the help of physical and social environment, among others. Though classroom learning is often misconceived as a receptive process, learning theories have proven the contrary. Learning theories reveal that learner personality, culture, locus of control, motivation, instructional methods and materials, prior knowledge and lots of other factors exert considerable influences on the learning process. Subsequent paragraphs will examine and identify four schools of thought in relation to the classroom learning ecosystem, with focus on implications for curriculum work.

The Classroom Learning Ecosystem

In any classroom setting, there is a learning ecosystem comprising the learner, the teacher, the environmental setting, and the curriculum as represented in figure 5.1. Each factor exerts influence on the other. For dynamic equilibrium to be maintained in the learning ecosystem, each of the four factors must relate appropriately to one another. The kind of learning that will occur, its quality and quantity will to a large extent be determined by classroom processes in the learning ecosystem.

Schools of thought that explain learning processes are discussed here under four subheadings: behaviourism, cognitivism, constructivism and humanism.

Behaviourism

Behavioural psychology flourished in the 20th century when James Watson, its founder, published a paper wherein he argued that psychology should be the study of observable behaviour rather than mental life which is covert. His ideas gained support from other psychologists and behaviourism began and grew. Behaviourism is based on three beliefs: i) learning is a change in behaviour ii) environmental stimuli shape behaviour and iii) the closeness in time for an event cause the formation of a bond between them (Tchombe, 2011). These tenets summarise the concept of conditioning. New behaviour is learned through conditioning. Learning therefore occurs as people continually respond to stimuli in their environment just as people do in habit formation. Differences in explanations of how conditioning occurs led to the distinction between pure behaviourism and neo-behaviourism as shown in table 5.2.

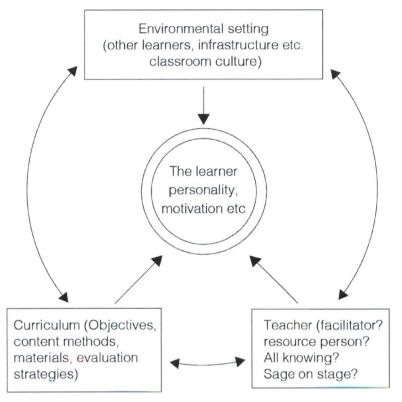

FIGURE 5.1. A Classroom Learning Ecosystem

Table 5.2. Behavioural Theorists and Principles

	Pure Behaviourism	Neo-behaviourism
Proponents	Ivan Pavlov, Edward Thorndike JB Waston	BF Skinner, Tolman
Theory	Classical conditioning	Operant/instrumental conditioning
Major features	Responses elicited S-R (stimulus response)	Responses emitted S-O-R Stimulus operation-response
Laws/ principles	Law of exercise, law of effect, law of readiness	negative and positive reinforcement.

Behaviourists carried out a series of experiments with animals, recording their results from which they observed that behaviour resulted from the stimuli these animals were subjected to. After several experiments, Thorndike, a pure behaviourist, put forward three laws: Law of exercise, law of effect and law of readiness. The law of exercise stated that connections between stimuli and responses are strengthened by practice and weakened when practice diminished. The law of effect states that the strength of a response increases or decreases when results are satisfying while the law of readiness implies that learning is dependent on a learner's preparedness to act.

The neo-behaviourists differ from the behaviourists in that animals involved in their experiments had to do something for responses to be observed. In other words, responses were emitted and not just elicited. Skinner used rats and pigeons in his experiments. He noticed that in some cases the animal had to do something as a response. He called such responses "operants". Operants are respondent behaviour that skinner described as "emitted" responses as opposed to Thorndike and Pavlov's elicited responses. Operant behaviour, he noted, must receive reinforcement for it to occur and continue to occur. Positive reinforcement is one whose introduction increases the occurrence of a response. A negative reinforcer is the withdrawal of a stimulus to encourage the occurrence of a response. Their principle of reinforcement was somehow like Thorndike's law of effect but with more illuminating details such as positive reinforcement, negative reinforcement, and punishment.

Although these experiments were done with rats and pigeons, the results are applicable to humans. Human behaviour is variable depending on environmental circumstances. Defined from a behaviourist perspective, learning is a change in human disposition or capability that persists over a period of time and is not simply ascribed to processes of growth (Gagne, 1970). Conversely, teaching can be thought of as the arrangement of learning experiences to promote habit formation. Together, the work of behaviourists and neo-behaviourists birthed some principles of learning with far reaching implications for curriculum design, classroom teaching and learning.

Applications in Curriculum and instruction

- Behaviourist principles are used when creating new programmes. Based on the law of effect and principle of positive reinforcement, curriculum designers sequence topics in syllabuses, textbooks, and school timetables in such a way that students find learning enjoyable and will want to continue to learn. Hatred or love for subject matter comes with feelings.
- Behaviourists rely on step-by-step methods. Learning content and methods can be broken down into small units and steps. Each step or unit is orderly arranged and reinforced appropriately to produce desired results.
- The importance of planning the learning environment: To get from learners, responses that make up desirable behaviour, teachers should build associations among ideas and elements in the learning ecosystem. This leads to habit formation. Formation of attitudes and habits is promoted by conditioning.
- In the classroom, Skinner's principles of reinforcement imply that learners' behaviour can be shaped through prescribed tasks using selective reinforcement. Use of praise, material, and self-esteem rewards or even verbal encouragement act as positive reinforcers by

strengthening desirable behaviour. Reinforcement and punishment play a great role in the learning process.

- Behaviourist teachers use teaching methods like lectures, drill, and practice. These methods are justified by Thorndike's law of exercise. Drill and practice are suitable for learning motor skills. Thorndike's law implies learning by making repetitive responses. This kind of learning is appropriate for the acquisition of facts.

Critics of behavioural learning theory have highlighted the following limitations.

- Instruction based on behaviourism does not enhance problem solving or creative thinking skills in the learner. It is largely rote learning. The learner is only prepared for recall of basic facts, automatic responses or performing tasks. The learner is thought to be passive. A passive stance cannot account for complex learning behaviour.
- Behaviourism emphasises very much on factors external to the learner and does not consider internal factors like genetics which equally has a significant role in learning. <ul>
1. Theories of behaviourism are based on experiments carried out on animals and this may not be directly applicable to human beings.
2. People may respond differently to the stimuli they receive from the environment. This makes it difficult to predict what the learning outcome (response) will be for various learners.

Cognitivism

Cognitivism derives from the word "cognition" which literally means learning through mental processes, senses, and experience. As a sharp reaction to behaviourists who believed the human mind was a black box that could not be studied, cognitive psychologists came forcefully in the 1960s and showed that learning also resulted from mental processes not necessarily reflected in overt behaviour. Cognitivists felt that an individual's thought processes (internal factors) contribute to outward manifestation of behaviour. Behaviour is therefore not limited to factors in the environment. To them, learner factors that cannot be seen constitute the mind.

Diverse approaches to cognitive psychology have led to different branches namely: cognitive development, social cognitivism, cognitive constructivism, and information processing. These branches of cognitive psychology have numerous proponents. However, only the contributions of Albert Bandura, Jerome Bruner, Jean Piaget, Miller and Atkinson and Shiffrin will be highlighted in this section.

Social cognitive theory

Bandura's social cognitive theory also called observational learning is often seen as a bridge between behaviourism and cognitivism. The principles of attention, retention, motor reproduction and motivation in learning are prominent in his theory. His famous bobo doll experiments on aggressive behaviour revealed that humans learn by imitation (modelling). He also believed that a person could master a situation and produce positive outcomes. This personal factor called self-efficacy is influenced by thoughts and expectations for success.

Teachers as curriculum implementers need to demonstrate and teach new behaviours. Peers, mentors, role models in the community and teachers themselves do act as role models. In addition, teachers must get learners to monitor, manage and regulate their own behaviour rather than let it be controlled externally. Learners need to talk positively to themselves to reach their full potential.

Bruner's theory of instruction (cognitive constructivism)

The theory of instruction put forward by Jerome Bruner in 1966 is anchored on four major principles. Predisposition of the learner towards learning, the structure of knowledge, sequencing, and the nature and pacing of rewards and punishment. According to Bruner (1966), instruction must be concerned with experiences and contexts that make the student willing and able to learn. Curiosity and uncertainty increase students' desire to learn. Prior knowledge is very important too. The structure of subject matter greatly eases acquisition and retention implying that curriculum and instruction must be organised according to the structure of subject matter such that content can easily be grasped. The order of presentation of curriculum content to learners should therefore consider the structure of knowledge. Bruner's concept of the spiral curriculum allows for logical progression of curriculum content to facilitate understanding and assimilation. Both visual and verbal representations of any subject matter are possible because Bruner holds that any domain of knowledge can be represented in three ways: iconic, enactive, and symbolic modes of representation.

Bruner's principles of learning undoubtedly inform the design of curriculum and instruction. The principles of continuity and sequence articulated in many curriculum texts as vertical and horizontal considerations of curriculum design are offshoots of Bruner's spiral curriculum. Curriculum elements must be arranged in a way that continuous repetition in a meaningful order brings about intended learning outcomes.

Cognitive development theory

Jean Piaget was a Swiss psychologist who studied human cognitive development by observing his own children. He drew the following major conclusions.
1. Human cognitive development occurs in four defined stages:
    i.   Sensorimotor stage (0-2yrs)
    ii.   Pre-operational stage (3-7yrs)
    iii. Concrete operations (7-11yrs iv) Formal operations (11yrs plus). At the sensorimotor stage, a child acquires knowledge through sensory experiences and develops object permanence which means things continue to exist even if they cannot be seen. At the preoperational stage, the child learns to use words and symbols to represent objects. Children also tend to be egocentric at this stage. At the stage of concrete operations, children begin logical thought. They can conserve quantities. The formal operational stage begins the ability to think about abstract concepts.
2. There are building blocks of intelligent behaviour named schemata. A schema represents a way of organising knowledge mentally.
3. Learning occurs through assimilation, accommodation, and equilibration. These processes are an interplay of biological maturation and environmental experiences of children as

they re-organise schemata. They are adaptation mechanisms and processes by which the child develops into an individual who can think. Assimilation occurs when a person uses or changes new information to fit into prior knowledge. Accommodation occurs when there is a change in prior knowledge to accept information from the environment. Equilibration drives the learning process because a child is constantly trying to achieve balance during assimilation and accommodation.

Information processing theories

Information processing theories began and flourished in the 1960s as a branch of cognitive developmental psychology, when the computer was invented. Psychologists noticed that the computer mimics the human brain. Humans receive and process information from their environment. They take information in, manipulate it and store for future use. Storage is done in the memory. Prominent theories and theorists here include multi-stage theory of memory by Atkinson and Shiffrin in 1968, Information processing theory by Miller in 1956, Dual coding theory by Paivio in 1971, Cognitive load theory by Sweller in 1988.

Miller's theory brought forth two important concepts: chunking and short-term memory. The short-term memory as its name suggests can hold information for a limited duration. Information that can be held in the short-term memory is done in meaningful bits called chunks. A chunk can be digits, words, faces etc., each chunk ranges from five to nine units. In other words, each chunk is seven plus or minus two.

Implications of Cognitivism on curriculum, and instruction

From a cognitivist perspective, learning is a change in learners' understanding of things around them. Learners actively construct new ideas based on past knowledge. New knowledge is acquired in the form of abstract representations in the minds of learners. Learners discover knowledge for themselves in the process. And this provokes an inner desire to learn more, leading to long-lasting learning. This implies that school should be a place where learners do not fear to ask questions or are not afraid of being wrong.

Curriculum developers apply cognitivist principles in some of the following ways:

- Cognitive stages of development imply hierarchical organisation of the structural framework of a curriculum. This means levels of schooling (nursery, primary and secondary school classes or grades) and corresponding learning experiences are related to stages of mental development.
- Complex concepts and subject matter can be transformed into mental operations appropriate to the level of the learner and their prior knowledge. For example, in primary mathematics schemes of work, introducing the notions of addition, subtraction, multiplication and division to the learner at the same time is not profitable.
- Curriculum organisation. There is declarative knowledge and procedural knowledge as well as different modes of knowledge representation. These are useful concepts in arranging curriculum content. Curriculum designers and teachers must specify the ways by which

knowledge should be presented for learners to easily grasp.

- Organisation of subject matter should promote acquisition and retention of new information. Continuity and sequence are curriculum design principles borne out of Bruner's ideas of a spiral curriculum. Bruner's structure of subject content and Ausubel's "advance organisers" are relevant in this area.
- Chunking, analogies, mnemonics, and other cognitive strategies borne from information processing theories also promote acquisition and retention of new information.
- Learners' attention span and issues of retention should be considered when allocating learning time to learning content on school timetables.
- Teachers are role models whose behaviour is reflected in the hidden curriculum.
- Instructional methods and activities that challenge learners to think and not just memorise facts stem from cognitivism. Learners' thought processes are important in understanding how they arrive at answers to questions. Cognitivist constructivists justify learner-centred teaching strategies and methods such as indirect teaching, discovery and problem solving because children are thought to learn best when they actively construct knowledge and seek solutions (Santrock, 2011).
- Choice of assessment strategies and tools used in instructional evaluation should not be haphazard. In assessment and evaluation, prior learning should be considered when judging a learner's performance.
- Categorisation and development of instructional objectives. Bloom's cognitive domain of educational objectives describes a hierarchy of thinking skills required to demonstrate learning.

Constructivism

Strictly speaking, constructivism is a combination of learning theory and epistemology. In relation to learning, there is an overlap between constructivism, cognitivism and social learning giving rise to sub-branches like *cognitive constructivism* and *social constructivism*. Generally, constructivist learning theories hold that learners' understanding, and knowledge of the world is based on how they make meaning of their life experiences. Prominent constructivists include Jean Piaget, Jerome Bruner, John Dewey, Maria Montessori, and Lev Vygotsky. Since the theories of Piaget and Bruner have been examined under cognitivism, attention here will focus on social constructivism.

In the classic titled, *Mind in Society*, Lev Vygotsky, a Russian psychologist propounded the theory of sociocultural learning. The theory holds that individuals construct knowledge through social interactions. It is through social interactions that individuals develop higher thinking skills (Vygotsky, 1978). Three prominent themes in the theory are:

1. More knowledgeable others (MKO)

As individuals interact with different persons in social settings, they get exposed to different ideas and shades of opinions from more knowledgeable persons in the domains of exposure. It is through this process that a learner constructs knowledge first at an interpersonal level and then at the intrapersonal level. MKOs are not necessarily older persons or teachers. They may be peers or younger people provided they possess a higher ability in respect to a particular task, process, or concept. They are people who act as scaffolds to support learners as they go through the zone of proximal development (ZPD).

2. Zone of proximal development

The ZPD is "the distance between the actual development level as determined by individual problem solving and the level of potential development as determined through problem solving under adult guidance or in collaboration with more capable peers" (Vygotsky, 1978 p.86). In the ZPD, a learner and the MKO work together to promote the construction of knowledge.

3. Language and cultural tools in cognitive development

Language is an important cultural tool in thought formation. At first, a child uses language for social interaction but later, language use signifies the structure of a child's thinking.

Implications and applications of social constructivism for curriculum and instruction

Social constructivism has far reaching implications for classroom teaching and learning. Curriculum developers and instructional designers have exploited these principles in different ways that include the following:

- Constructivism supports the transaction orientation to curriculum development where the curriculum is perceived not as a tool that prescribes what students should learn, but an instrument that promotes dialogue between teacher and student leading to the construction of knowledge (Tambo, 2012 p.114).
- Active engagement of the learner in the instructional process is prominent and pertinent in social constructivism. The teacher is a resource person and not an all-knowing sage on stage. Collaboration and cooperation are not only conducive but essential strategies for learning.
- Since learning is a collaborative process, there is a need to enhance academic learning through the promotion of participatory pedagogies such as reciprocal teaching, collaborative, and cooperative learning. Social and interpersonal skills are enhanced as well.
- The realisation that language is a tool for cognition and through social interaction, learners' communication skills are enhanced, has helped to enforce language across the curriculum programs.
- Based on the importance of MKOs in the learning process, cognitive apprenticeship programs are gaining more prominence during training. such training programs use techniques like coaching and scaffolding.
- Related to social constructivism is the principle of situated cognition which holds that knowledge is situated in an activity bound to social and cultural contexts, thus supporting the use of the project and problem-based teaching methodologies.

Humanism

Humanistic psychology or phenomenology flourished in the 1960s and beyond. According to humanists, the behaviour of individuals is determined by how they perceive themselves. "Self" is the central concept in humanistic psychology. As far as learning is concerned, humanist psychologists hold that human needs and values are important influences on the learning process. Some theorists and theories are listed as follows:

Abraham Maslow   hierarchy of needs
Carl Rogers   self-actualisation
Arthur Combs   confluent education
Thomas Gordon   teacher effectiveness training.

Maslow's hierarchy of needs theory purports that humans have basic needs, psychological needs, and self- actualisation needs. See Figure 5.2.

According to this theory, humans are motivated to seek the next level of needs only when needs of the previous level have been satisfied. This implies that a pupil or student has an innate desire to grow to full potential. It is the duty of the school to provide a non-threatening and conducive environment that will satisfy learners' needs and foster learning and the realization of their personal visions.

Humanism and the curriculum

The implications of humanistic tenets are important for dynamic equilibrium of the classroom ecosystem (see figure 5.2). Students learn best in a non- threatening environment. The learning process should address learners needs. The potential for growth of an individual learner is boundless and learning should fulfil that potential. Learning is seen as a personal act. Learners should be empowered to have control over the learning process. Students should identify their own goals specific to their needs.

A student's positive self-concept exudes confidence needed for learning. Students' emotional well-being is important for learning. A teacher is a facilitator of learning, and a learner is not a passive recipient of information.

Almost all curriculum designers and practitioners give due consideration to learners' basic needs through provision of recreation periods (lunch break) on school timetables and recommend infrastructure that supports fulfilment of the need for food, water, and bowel movements.

Learner-centred curriculum designs are built on felt needs and interests of learners. Typically, activities are corporately planned by teachers and learners. And this gives learners the feeling that their contributions to a process that concerns them is highly valued. Subject matter is selected and included in the curriculum to suit the needs of learners and any demonstrated abilities and not an all-knowing sage on stage. This approach to curriculum and instruction has been labelled by many as the humanistic curriculum. Humanistic curriculum designers are oriented towards transforming learners to become the best version of themselves. Some critics however opine that humanistic principles of learning may be more readily applied to younger learners than older ones.

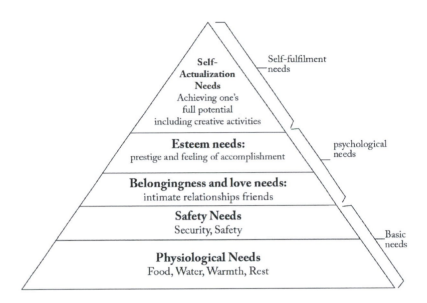

FIGURE 5.2. Maslow's Hierarchy of Human Needs

African Child Development theories, Learning Processes, and the Curriculum

As noted earlier, child development is an interplay of genetics and environment (including culture) intertwined with children's activities and experiences. In many African communities, spiritual and ancestral forces are also considered to have a significant influence on how children develop (Reynolds,1997). Since most textbooks on developmental and learning psychology are based on Western theories and research, it is challenging for educators to decide on what is appropriate and what is not for African children. Because cultural context is significant in human development and learning processes, studies of cultural and intercultural influences on human development led some scholars in the last few decades to develop theoretical frameworks for cross cultural human development. Notably among them are:

- A.B. Nsamenang. His theory, called social ontogenesis presents human development as partly determined by the social ecology in which development takes place and how African children, especially siblings and peers, learn from each other in peer cultures (Nsamenang, 1992).
- Pierre Dasen. His theoretical perspective of development includes components such as biological and cultural adaptation, ecological context, socio-political context and cosmology, religion, and values (Dasen, 2011). All these components influence observable behaviour and learning processes.
- Therese M.S. Tchombe. Her theoretical perspective of learning processes called Mediated Mutual Reciprocity (MMR) is anchored on Nsamenang's social ontogenesis theory of

development (Tchombe, 2019a).

Nsamenang's Social Ontogenesis

The fundamental idea of this theory is sociogenesis, defined as individual development related to specific observable and culturally perceived tasks but less to biological development, although the concept of social ontogenesis does not exclude nature; it assumes that nature affects social ontogenesis (Nsamenang, 2006a).

Developmental Stages in Nsamenang's West African Ontogeny

According to Nsamenang, West African ontogeny recognises three basic dimensions of personality. First, there is a spiritual self that begins at conception and ends at naming; social personality extends from naming to death (which is more acceptable in old age); and ancestral personality that follows biological death (Nsamenang 1992b p.144). These have been articulated in eight stages as presented below:

Spiritual self-hood (Prenatal): The infant is a "project in progress". The human frame shelters a spiritual selfhood. It begins at conception and ends at the naming ceremony.

Naming Ceremony (Neonatal): The first phase of social ontogenesis is the ceremony of naming, which projects the kind of socialised being the neonate should become. During the naming ceremony, names are given to the new-born based on the historical and circumstantial factors, character, and other expectations.

Social Priming (Infancy): The major developmental task of the second phase is success in *social priming*: babies are cuddled and teased to smile along with adults; parents and other caregivers offer infants food items and playthings and lure them both verbally and through nonverbal communication to return the "gifts." This is a preliminary step toward induction into the "sharing and exchange norms" that bond siblings and the entire social system together.

Social Apprenticing (Childhood): The next phase is more or less commensurate to childhood. It is the period of social learning in which the main developmental task is to recognise and rehearse the social roles of the three hierarchical spheres of life: household, network, and public. Much of the responsibility for stimulation and guidance in this early childhood development phase is assigned to pre-adolescent and adolescent children in families and neighbourhoods. The delegation of responsibility for the care and socialisation of younger children, from adults to pre-adolescents and adolescents, is an aspect of priming and the beginning of social responsibility.

Social entrée (Puberty): Secondary sex characteristics like physiological changes (breasts, curves for girls, and voice change for boys) appear. The youth may attend initiation ceremonies.

Social internment (Adolescence): Developmental tasks like social induction takes place. There is preparation and training for adulthood

Adulthood: This is the most sought-after stage which involves marriage and parenthood. Ideals and standards of family and community must be maintained, and responsibilities must be met. Seniority increases with the birth of each child.

Old age and death: The elderly are responsible for preserving the unity of the family. The person is usually a grandparent and thus an epitome of social competence. This stage is regarded as being much closer to the ancestors. Ancestral selfhood follows death and then spiritual selfhood.

Nsamenang's theory of social ontogenesis has an eco-cultural perspective based on the cultural traditions in West and Central Africa. His ideas were founded on observation and personal experience with the practices of socialisation by the Nso communities in the North- West region of Cameroon and texts of some Africans trained in philosophy and humanities (for example. Mbiti, 1990; Nsamenang and Lamb, 1995). In the African worldview, people need other people, and it is a social responsibility to individualise properly and to achieve full personality. Bame Nsamenang's justification came from the need for a human development theory that focuses on the environment in which a person is raised. He realised that the theories he studied, and the conclusions of the theorists could not be validated in his environment, and that certain theories did not reflect the scheme or stages found in his environment. He built on the ecological process for human development of Bronfenbrenner and on the implications of the ecological environment on human development.

His formulation of social ontogenesis is rooted in a widely shared view of the West African world. Human development is partly determined by the social systems and the ecology in which it takes place and by the way human beings learn and develop. Development is a transformation of the individual brought about by participation in cultural activities. Child development is seen as a process of gradual and systematic social integration. It presents the growth of social selfhood through a series of phases, each characterised by a distinctive developmental task, defined within the framework of the primarily socio-affective, developmental agenda of the culture. The theory of social ontogenesis points out how, starting early in life and through developmental stages, African children are active in the life of their families and societies, as well as in self-care and self-learning. As children are initiated and actively engaged in cultural life, they gradually and systematically identify and assume particular levels of personality, identity and being.

Educational Implications of the African Social Ontogenesis Theory

These primary strategies, embodied in traditional African child-rearing practices, have important implications for the design of culturally appropriate forms of teaching to optimise developmental opportunities for children in contemporary Africa. Teachers must understand that a learner comes to a learning environment with prior learning skills and a schema of past and/or concurrent culture that has an impact on the learning process. In order to effectively increase the skills of learners to what is necessary in a given learning program, the instructor would do well to know as much as possible about the cultural background and socialisation of the learner(s). Also, traditional African education does not divide knowledge domains such as agriculture, economics, arts, science etc. Instead, it integrates knowledge about all aspects of life into a single curriculum. As such, children are rarely instructed into what they learn, but discover it during participation. Therefore, the curriculum is arranged in sequence to fit into different stages of development that the culture perceives or recognises.

Influence of African Environment and Child development on the curriculum

Children's cultural context has been identified in the preceding sections as a major source of development because culture as a way of life of a people, shapes development beginning in the years before school and has implications for educational practice within the school years. Cultural expectations for child development and child rearing methods and practices determine what children learn, who interacts with them and how they learn (Nsamenang, 2008). In Africa, child development is enhanced through activity in a culturally constructed environment designed by adults based on what their culture considers valuable. Majority of African children learn valuable skills when they participate in domestic tasks. As family and other community members recognise their new skills, self-esteem and self-efficacy is supported. The implication of these observations is that children's participation in work activities can be incorporated in the content of education programs to promote learning. African children learn problem solving in the real world drawing on indigenous skills. Educators should exploit the cultural tool kits that children bring to school and scaffold learning to higher points. For example, developing and maintaining school gardens or farms to enhance the written and taught curriculum will enable children to grasp concepts in biology, nutrition, climate, numeracy, collective responsibility, and service.

It should be noted, however, that there is no single African childhood experience because there is great cultural diversity in the African continent.

In addition to cultural practices, adequate nutrition, good health, and warm parental care are necessary conditions for proper child development. Unfortunately, there is a burden of risks to sound child development in Africa due to low productivity and economic development, structural inequalities, political mismanagement, and conflicts (Dawes and Biersteker, 2011). Ford and Stein (2015) identified malnutrition, malaria, HIV/AIDS, and low levels of socio-emotional stimulation from maternal child interactions as risk factors for poor cognitive child development in sub-Saharan Africa, where 37 percent of children below five have suffered from severe malnutrition and are stunted (Garcia, Virata and Dunkelberg, 2008)). Physical development and indirectly, the time children start and remain in school are highly likely to be affected in the circumstances.

Influence of African culture on learning processes and learning outcomes

While upholding the assertion that culture influences cognitive learning functions, Tchombe (2011) argued that before contemporary theorists (Jean Piaget, Jerome Bruner, and Lev Vygotsky) espoused their narratives of child centred learning in participatory pedagogies based on cognitive and social constructivism, these learning processes and pedagogies existed among the Bamileke in the West region of Cameroon. In the Bamileke culture, the use of interest-driven, communicative, and mediated mutual reciprocity strategies fosters cognitive enrichment and meaningful learning (p.209-210).

The interest-driven strategy (piitfak wen) describes a child's total engagement in daily life activities that are of interest to the individual and the family. It shows learning as a process of social participation in family activities through collaboration, teamwork, and cooperation rather than a focus on instructive pedagogy that characterises rote and surface learning. This implies participatory pedagogies that are interest driven, need driven, learner centred, communal centred and sibling centred (p.213). Communication strategies (soknu-sok cwe-sah nu) among the Bamileke, take the form of storytelling, dialogues, narratives, and conversations. These create opportunities for children to express their views when requested. Noteworthy is that communicative strategies are social, cognitive, and entertaining. The mediated mutual reciprocity strategy (faksi zhi'si-hi) is a kind of giving and receiving with an expression of mutuality in the relationship.

Mediated mutual reciprocity (MMR has been developed into a sociocultural theoretical perspective of the learning process in the context of Nsamenang's West African social ontogenesis. It explains how African children face numerous challenges such as poverty, war and conflicts, health, food shortages and others, but possess cognitive and social abilities to effectively direct their actions and overcome these challenges through cultural practices that provide an enabling environment (Tchombe, 2019). Contrasting MMR with Vygotsky's sociocultural learning theory that places "more knowledgeable others" as pivotal actors at a learner's level of proximal development, Tchombe argues that the African child at that point of challenge has sustaining power that makes him or her capable of taking the lead, thus influencing the learning process. The locus of control is internal to the learner. African cultures instil in learners quite early in life, values of compassion, reciprocity, dignity, respect, harmony and humanity in the interest of maintaining the community. In addition, there are supportive structures in functional families and community, all of which build on a child's inner strength to cope with challenges. This is clearly evident in cultural practices whereby:

- the child is an active participant of social and cultural life in the family.
- children participate in daily chores that enable them to develop competencies largely depending on themselves and less on competent others (Nsamenang, 2007); enabling them to initiate, create and discover knowledge.
- children learn through engagement and not explicit instruction employing self-learning strategies in peer- controlled learning spaces.
- children are not defeated by circumstances but navigate through challenges with minimal support.
- children interact in multi-aged peer settings that foster intergenerational transfer of skills and knowledge.

Thus, MMR is anchored on three processes: mediation, mutuality and reciprocity. Mediation implies that both the child and the adults in the family are co-constructors of knowledge; Mutuality means there is active interdependence and collaboration between child and adult and reciprocity describes shared responsive connection between child and adult. The behaviours resulting from these learning processes enable the learner to initiate, negotiate and modulate their learning to suit their capabilities and also modify the behaviour of others. The learning principles that emanate from these three processes include:

1. Need-driven learning
2. Co-learning
3. Non-hierarchical learning
4. Multidirectional learning

5. Bi-directional learning
6. Multi-directional learning.

Exploiting the principles of MMR to achieve educational goals, Tchombe proposes:

- improved psychosocial support at family and community levels.
- promotion of participatory approaches to development of competencies
- use of indigenous cognitive enrichment strategies to direct children's problems
- use of assessment tools that inform educators of children's strengths to cope with adverse situations with the intention of creating orientation programs for children who need to be strengthened.

Lending support to the theoretical perspective of MMR, the present authors see its possible applications in curriculum development and instructional design particularly in the selection and creation of curriculum experiences. Its learning processes and principles stress the importance of developing curriculum experiences that mimic authentic or real-life settings. Instructional designers would therefore be encouraged to utilise instructional methods, activities and materials which engage the learner in participatory pedagogies that challenge children to action within reasonable limits. In the area of formulating curriculum goals, MMR hints against setting goals that see schooling and specifically the curriculum as a tool that equips Africans with the cultural identity of other people. MMR equally holds promise for curriculum planning and evaluation as it calls for a broader view of analysing learners during a situation analysis and suggests the ramification of diagnostic evaluation when carrying out assessment of learning outcomes.

Scholars and critics of the African school curriculum have often pointed out that there is too much emphasis on learning content and activities that promote cognitive intelligence to the exclusion of other forms of intelligence recognised and promoted in indigenous African cultures. Social responsibility intelligence is a perceptive quality of the intellect characterised by sympathetic understanding of the social world and readiness to act. This form of intelligence is expected of learners in African cultures. In informal and traditional education that characterises African cultures, much learning occurs through incidental observation, imitation, and guided participation. There is minimal rote learning, and this is particularly associated with initiation rites. Trial and error learning is limited to self-guided activity.

In a study on social responsibility intelligence, Serpell (2011) argued that in indigenous Chewa culture in Zambia, the society places emphasis on peer group cooperation (ku gwirizana ndi anzache) as an essential ingredient of socially responsible behaviour called *nzelu*. The concept of *nzelu* describes a form of intelligence and a developmental goal that is valued among parents in Zambia and other Chewa societies in Mozambique and Malawi. The intelligent and educated person in this culture is one who is socially responsible through peer group cooperation, thus putting emphasis on interactive pedagogies involving cooperative and collaborative learning. Similar views have been expressed in other African societies in West and East Africa. Empirical research in the USA also supports the contention that cooperative learning arrangements are especially effective for students from low-income African American families, reflecting the cultural theme of communalism passed down by their ancestral cultures in Africa (p. 203).

In summary, educators in Africa should not lose sight of peculiar environmental or cultural factors that may affect child development, the learning process, learning needs and learning outcomes while applying to curriculum and instruction, psychological principles that have grown out of western research. They are also challenged by the growing body of knowledge on African perspectives of child development and learning processes to apply the underlying principles when creating school programs in Africa. Regrettably, many Eurocentric and western educational practices that were common in the African colonial school persist today. There is also a need to develop more culturally inclusive theories and perspectives on child development which can be exploited by curriculum developers and educators the world over.

6

Sociological Foundations of the Curriculum

Humans are gregarious beings by nature, perpetually ready for social interaction to gain a sense of belonging and thrive. It is through social interactions that we gain knowledge and learn life skills. Society shapes people's attitudes and actions. It is common knowledge that some behaviours may be tolerated when exhibited by children but frowned at if displayed by adults. Such reactions depend on the social environment where the behaviours occur. Influence of social environment is the essence of sociology. As an academic discipline that studies the structure of human society and social interactions among its members, Sociology has provided us with documented evidence of the nature of society, its institutions and factors that influence organisation and social interactions in a group. Education is one of such factors that impacts society, and it is also impacted by society.

This chapter attempts to clarify the relationship between education and society first, then goes on to examine the implications and applications of sociological concepts and principles to curriculum work.

Education and society

For any social group to survive, her members must learn their ways. Socialisation and education are two processes through which this is achieved. Socialisation is a more general process describing acquisition of all behaviours expected of members of a society whereas education is more specific, describing the process of preparing individuals to fit into their roles as members of that society. Both socialisation and education take place in formal, non-formal and informal settings. Non-formal agents include mass media, church, youth organisations and informal agents are the family and peer groups. Formal agencies are schools and universities. Schooling is formal education. Although it is arguably not limited to formal education, the curriculum is mostly associated with schools and structured educational settings.

Schools do not exist in a vacuum. They exist and function in communities that are units of a larger society. For schools to provide meaningful experiences to learners, curriculum developers must understand the milieu in which a school operates. A learner is first a member of the larger society before belonging to the school community. Whether in school or in the larger society, the learner interacts with other people. The nature of social interactions in and out of school must be understood by educators to provide learners with appropriate experiences. By appropriate experiences, it is meant those experiences that mirror real life settings or those that shape future society.

Three main groups of sociologists are functionalists, interactionists, and critical sociologists. For the functionalists, education is the transmission of culture, maintenance of social control and promotion of change. Conflict sociologists see educational institutions as places that perpetuate inequalities. They opine that the powerful remain powerful because of the power structure and distribution in school systems. And the poor remain in a class of their own through the existence of differentiated school systems. The interactionists believe that success in school depends on the nature of interactions between teachers and learners. All three sociological orientations to education should be considered when developing curricula.

The social environments of learners exert significant influences on the acquisition of knowledge, skills, values, and attitudes. Curriculum decisions cannot afford to ignore issues relating to the social backgrounds of learners. Goals and objectives must not be far removed from the realities and expectations of the society in which the school operates. Learning content must be relevant to the needs and aspirations of contemporary society. Instructional methods and activities for operationalising the curriculum cannot be divorced from influences in the sociocultural environment. Sociological factors that directly influence decision making in the planning, implementation and evaluation of a curriculum include i) culture ii) societal problems, needs and aspirations iii) social structure iv) social diversity and change. These will be presented and discussed in subsequent paragraphs.

Culture

Every society has its unique way of life. Otherwise stated, every society has its culture. In 1871, a renowned anthropologist, E.B. Tylor defined culture as, "that complex whole which includes knowledge, beliefs, art, morals, law, customs and any other capabilities and habits acquired by man as a member of society" (Tylor, 1920). Culture can be summed up as the way of life of a people. Sociologists and anthropologists subdivide culture into the i) universals, ii) specialties and iii) alternatives. Cultural universals embrace those aspects of a culture that are accepted by all members of the society. They bind the people together, promote peace and stability. Language, norms, values, traditions, and customs are cultural universals. Specialties of culture are different domains of knowledge and practices relating to specific groups of people such as professionals within the community. Cultural universals and specialties form the core of a culture. Cultural alternatives are beliefs and practices contrary to universals, but which may be accepted with time.

Culture and the curriculum

If curriculum content is divorced from the reality of the context of education, the development of the human mind gets distorted. According to functional sociologists, the transmission of cultural heritage is the essence of education. Curriculum as a tool for attaining the educational goals of the nation must therefore be rooted in culture. From the functionalist perspective, it is imperative that curriculum planners know the cultural past of a society, its present life, and its future expectations for effective transmission to younger generations. The core of a culture embodies its most stable values and practices. It is from the cultural core that major curriculum choices relevant to the society are made. The language of instruction for example, cannot be divorced from the language used by the people where a school operates. A culture that places high value on integrity, hard work and respect as another example, will have a school culture that reflects these values. Curriculum planners should interpret the nature of a society's culture, its most stable values and incorporate these into curriculum content and instructional approaches.

Because a curriculum responds to what a society believes to be the desirable ends of education, curriculum purposes should reflect the cultural core of society. In addition, the subject matter should embrace knowledge, skills, abilities, and values inherent in the culture. Cultural values and norms determine the standard of behaviour in any society and invariably shape the expectations of behaviour standards of school and community.

Certain traditions need preservation. Curriculum content should be structured to uphold invaluable traditions and customs. Ironically, the reverse is true in some African schools today where the curriculum directly or indirectly downplays indigenous knowledge and traditions. In societies with a long tradition of schooling, the curriculum at all stages is closely related to the cultural past. The school programmes resemble what has been going on in the past. Most societies without a very long tradition of schooling had non-formal agencies of education with operational and non-formal curricula. Some practices entrenched in the so called non-formal curricula still have a place in today's schooling system. They need to be preserved.

Methods used in handling subject matter are influenced by educational history, technical inventions, and discoveries. Curriculum content and learning experiences cannot remain static in a dynamic society. Cultural alternatives play a part here as content and teaching strategies get modified over time.

Societal problems, needs and aspirations

The role that education plays in seeking solutions to societal problems depends a lot on policy, curriculum, and pedagogy. Educational policy makers provide guidelines that curriculum decision makers translate into workable solutions. Curriculum planners must understand the complex relationship between education and national needs and aspirations so that they can incorporate them into the schooling process. Curriculum development efforts and reform initiatives must rise up to the challenge for schools to meet the workforce demands of a changing society. Curriculum offerings in terms of goals and subject matter should fulfil manpower needs, improve living conditions, and promote development. This implies that the quantity and quality of school graduates are a function of the quantity and quality of learning opportunities and experiences available to learners.

Societal needs and aspirations are constantly evolving with changes in the economy and political landscape of countries. In the colonial era, African schools' curricula directly served the needs of the colonial masters. The subjects taught in school were limited and directly related to the interests of the colonial master. Colonial schools sought to extend foreign domination and exploitation of the colony. Post-independence Africa witnessed several curriculum reforms to redress the situation. Although vestiges of colonial education continue to linger, many curriculum reform efforts have attempted to address the real economic and social problems of African nations. New school subjects and pedagogical orientations are continuously being introduced to reflect the needs of the new society. Societal problems and needs are sometimes reflected in national ideologies. National ideologies are values, principles and ideals that express what a nation desires for its citizens, usually espoused by her leaders.

In Zambia for example, the ideology of humanism sprang forth shortly after independence and it was embedded in the curriculum not as a subject in schools but through educational policies (Lungwangwa, 2011). Humanism generally considered as the welfare of human beings was anchored on four principles: i) man-centredness ii) equality iii) respect for persons and iv) reciprocal obligations. At the level of primary education, the competitive selection examination system for Africans and automatic promotion for non-Africans was abolished as a response to the principle of equality. Universal and compulsory schooling from ages five to sixteen was instituted. At the secondary education level, there was diversification of secondary school syllabuses to include technical and commercial subjects and strengthening the teaching of science and mathematics in response to manpower needs.

Cameroon is another nation where ideology has influenced school curricula. Official language bilingualism, national unity and national integration as national ideologies are reflected in school curricula through the mandatory teaching, learning and assessment of English and French at all school levels. A variety of French-English bilingual education models inundate the educational system today. Even the rotatory nature of hosting co-curricular activities at national levels (FENASCO and FENASU games) is a deliberate attempt at fostering national unity and integration.

Vision 2035 is a programme outlining Cameroon's aspirations for economic emergence. It has four-fold objectives of poverty reduction, attaining the level of a middle level economy, industrialisation and enhancing national unity. Attainment of these objectives means that the education system must train skilled manpower in the areas of fisheries, animal rearing, agriculture, and forestry that are the backbone of the Cameroonian economy. It also means that to reduce poverty, school curricula should prepare school leavers not to be job seekers but job creators. Curriculum content must be relevant to identified needs. The growth and employment strategy paper and Vision 2035 undoubtedly stimulated new directions for education that are contained in the education sector report for 2015. These needs and aspirations contributed to the revisions of school curricula in primary and secondary education that took place in 2014 and 2018, respectively, which saw the introduction of subjects such as agriculture in secondary grammar schools and new subjects related to vocational and life skills, and digital literacy in primary schools.

In the economically developed world too, curriculum change has resulted from changes in the economy. In the 19th century, with a predominantly agrarian society and farm-based economy, school curricula in the United States of America consisted of the acquisition of basic skills, apprenticeship, and didactic teaching (Cristina, 2016). With the industrial revolution, the American society had a different economic system and new needs in the 20th century. So, curricula were based on the factory model, compartmentalization of knowledge and didactic teaching. The 21st century now witnesses a new post industrialised society dominated by information communication technologies and global interdependence. New curricula are responding to emerging changes in societal needs.

In addition to the rapid evolution of technologies, unprecedented problems such as climate change and new emerging diseases also call for new knowledge and novel manpower needs. The need for new knowledge in managing and eradicating new diseases and pandemics like HIV/AIDS, Ebola, MERS, SARS and recently coronavirus SARS COV 2 calls for modifications of the curriculum content of health education professions programmes. Curriculum change must also equip learners with cognitive and psychosocial competencies such as critical and creative thinking, self-efficacy, emotional intelligence and resilience to handle novel situations as they arise.

The importance of intellectual and motor skills notwithstanding, curriculum should also aim at imparting attitudes and values that equip individuals with the wherewithal to offer solutions to societal problems. Learning outcomes in the affective domain are as important as cognitive objectives. For example, the war against corruption, mismanagement of public funds and bad governance in African nations cannot be won if the content and instructional methods of school subjects like history, economics, civics, and ethics are at variance with societal expectations.

Social Structure

Social structure describes a combination of building blocks of social life. Prominent building blocks are statuses, roles, class, groups, and institutions to which people belong. Horizontal social structures are relationships and physical characteristics to which individuals belong and these enable them to form networks. The family, peer groups and religious affiliations are typical examples. Vertical structures on the other hand are social inequalities in the society which rank people. For example, social class and social status place people on different rungs of a ladder. As members of a structured society, children and adults have statuses, roles, and social networks. They are members of social institutions and groups where roles are performed according to ascribed and acquired statuses. They also experience social pressures from these structures.

Peer groups

Peer groups are social networks of children of about the same age and social status. These are usually classmates and playmates making them intimate to one another. Peer groups are a major source of the hidden curriculum. It is important that curriculum planners recognise this and capitalise on it. Capitalising on the positive influence that peer groups have on members, curriculum developers and instructional designers often suggest peer tutoring, cooperative and collaborative learning as preferred methods and strategies to attain curriculum objectives of specific subject matter. Peers may act as mentors and role models in the acquisition of attitudes and skills.

Peer culture offers students the rudiments of socialisation and democracy. Developmental psychologists have identified five types of peer statuses: popular children, average children, neglected children, rejected children and controversial children (Asher and MacDonald, 2009). Accordingly, special instructional programs may be developed for students who face socioemotional challenges from peers. Such programs help them to manage emotions, improve peer relations and promote adjustment in school.

The Home

Known as a place where a family resides, the home is both a physical structure and a psychological environment for child development. School-home linkages must be built on proper understanding of home backgrounds. Take-home assignments must consider the environment in which schoolwork is expected to be carried out. The success of some instructional methods and activities like homework and flipped classrooms depend on the educational or literacy level of parents and guardians. These and other home factors must be considered when making suggestions and recommendations on pedagogical approaches found in syllabuses. With changing dynamics of the home and lifestyles in the western world and urban areas in Africa, we are no longer certain that parents and guardians can devote enough time and energy to support the efforts of the school. It is becoming more evident that new lifestyles of less communalism and more individualism pose a challenge to instructional designers.

Socioeconomic status

Realistic curriculum goals and objectives must result from careful analysis and consideration of learners' social background and other factors. Research on relationships between learners' social class and academic achievement have produced inconsistent results. Based on some of the findings, curriculum planners and classroom teachers have tried different ways to reduce the achievement gap between children of the lower social classes and children of higher social class. While noting that gaps created by social inequalities cannot be closed by the school, schools can nevertheless reduce the effects of these gaps on achievement by improving the quality of instruction and providing relevant learning experiences. After all, for many African parents, schooling is expected to raise the social status and living standards of their children in the future.

Implications of Social structure on the curriculum

Implications of social structure for curriculum development hinges on proper understanding of learner characteristics based on social structural background and its influence on learning. The socioeconomic background of learners, for example, hint at the kind of social interactions which influence learning and schoolwork. Diagnosis of gaps, deficiencies and variations of learners' background are therefore crucial in determining what a curriculum should be. Situational analysis is the first step of both curriculum development and instructional design. It entails an assessment of learners' needs and the learning context. In addition, understanding social structure enables curriculum writers to emphasise content that is relevant to the needs of students with different roles, statuses, and networks. For example, when designing a learning unit in social studies entitled *the family,* in a context where polygamy and extended family is the norm, the concepts of stepmother, half-brother and cousins must be included in the content outline.

Social Diversity and Change

The world has almost become a global village with societies getting more diverse by the day. The phenomenon of social diversity is reflected both in the larger society and in schools and classrooms.

There are ethnic minorities, people belonging to subcultures, different religious inclinations, and people in different age brackets. Other differences in American and European classrooms include language, race, economic status, and gender orientation. Social diversity is, however, not limited to Western countries. Hardly do all members of any social group, community, or society elsewhere in the world share identical characteristics.

To ensure a socially relevant curriculum, no sub-group in a community should be neglected when deciding on what should be taught and learnt in schools. Curricula must address social pluralism. It may become necessary to have different programs, flexible curricula, and different pedagogic approaches to suit the needs of different strata of students who come to school.

Cultural diversity

Renewed interest in their own history and development has caused ethnic minorities in nations worldwide to clamour for visibility in almost all national development efforts. In the sphere of education, there are increasing trends of culturally inclusive curricula as a response to cultural diversity. In the United States of America where classrooms are increasingly witnessing a mix of Hispanics, African Americans, Caucasians and immigrants, the development of culturally responsive curricula and multi-cultural teaching strategies poses a big challenge. School districts are responding by creating multicultural curricula.

A multicultural curriculum is one that is expanded to include multicultural content. McKay (2018) suggests that this can be done effectively by:

- including a variety of perspectives on a subject.
- discussing social contexts, including issues of equity and justice and
- including activities that foster critical thinking and self-awareness.

He holds that multicultural curriculum reforms are necessary for the following reasons:

- to prepare students for diverse workplaces and multicultural environments.
- To expose biases, stereotypes, and policies that can restrict achievement.
- To ensure that content is fair, accurate, and inclusive.
- To accommodate for diverse teaching and learning styles of teachers and students.
- help students, faculty, and staff become advocates for multicultural awareness.

Multicultural education is equally relevant for Africa because the continent is immensely diverse in terms of ethnicity and race. To overcome the challenges of multiculturalism and education for the entire continent and South Africa in particular, Brown and Shumba (2011) argued for infusion of Nelson Mandela's humanistic psychology (Nsamenang, 2004) and "Madiba magic" into the African school curriculum. Mandela's humanistic psychology is a concern for people guided by reason and inspired by compassion and informed experience (p.534) while Madiba magic rests on certain pillars characterised by distinct values –a spirit of forgiveness, kindness, tolerance, chivalry and a belief in human dignity, freedom, and respect. These values guided Mandela's actions in reconciliation and his vision for a united South Africa regardless of racial or cultural differences.

The authors suggest that taking Madiba magic to school means re-thinking the curriculum of teacher education to emphasise:

- Training of culturally sensitive teachers,
- Learning to appreciate differences,
- Learning to cultivate authentic working relationships, and
- Encouraging school leaders to set a school climate that endears living together in peace and trust irrespective of cultural differences.

Perhaps a greater challenge of multicultural education lies in developing a curriculum that responds to students' diverse sociocultural values and at the same time creating a national identity based on core values and practices. Here is an example: Because of colonial heritage, Cameroon is often described as a bicultural country. She does not only have two official languages; English and French but also two systems or cultures with sometimes conflicting values, that operate side by side in educational, judicial, and administrative matters. With over 235 ethnic groups, the plurality of ethnic languages and ethnic cultures also makes Cameroon a multicultural society. This socio-political situation presents at least three alternatives to curriculum planners for consideration when deciding on curriculum structure:

1. Suppress one sub-culture and construct the curriculum based on the culture of the majority.
2. Design and implement two separate curricula in schools based on inherited English and French cultures, respectively.
3. Harmonise or blend the structure and content of curricula for schools in both French and English-speaking parts of the country.

With caution and careful analysis, curriculum reform efforts have maintained two subsystems of education in Cameroon while attempting to harmonize curriculum goals, content, and structure (see law 98/04, 1998). Efforts made to rise above the challenges of biculturalism through harmonisation have yielded more successes in the basic education sector than in the secondary and higher education sector. Failures have been attributed to misconceptions of the term harmonisation, lack of political will and reluctance to relinquish colonial heritage (Tchombe, 1999, Ngalim 2017a) due to suspicion of the motives for harmonisation (Fonkeng, 2007), among other factors. The ongoing socio-political crisis which has affected schooling adversely in the North West and South West regions of the country for close to five years now, originated from lawyers and teachers' complaints that the Anglo-Saxon culture was being marginalised in national judicial and education affairs. Ngalim (2014) holds that harmonisation of the two education systems should be embraced as a multicultural perspective for democratic education. He argues that the lack of harmonisation is responsible for the problems of equity and quality education in Cameroon and recommends suspension of prejudices to establish a truly Cameroonian curriculum irrespective of colonial identities (Ngalim, 2017b). However, genuine harmonisation would indeed be recommended by the present authors as a solution to the problem of biculturalism, while allowing each subsystem to maintain some specificities of their colonial heritage that work to the advantage of all Cameroonians.

Another aspect of curriculum change in Cameroon meant to exploit the advantages of the relationship between language and cognition, is the introduction of national languages as academic subjects in the curriculum. This poses another challenge; selecting from the huge number of national (ethnic) languages to include in the curriculum. Division into linguistic zones has been used in Nigeria to resolve this issue of ethnic diversity, and it may be a promising alternative to solve the problem in Cameroon.

Technological advancements

Technological changes influence lifestyles and values bringing about social diversity and change. The 21st century has witnessed a great explosion of knowledge and technological advancements. The era has been aptly described by many as the information age because of the rapid growth of information and communications technologies. Many functions that took hours on end to be carried out are now effortlessly done with just a click of the computer mouse. There is social diversity resulting from technological literacy. Younger people are more versed with ICTs than older people. Many jobs now require technological literacy for better productivity, automatically classifying potential workers into different categories. Curricula reforms cannot ignore this trend.

The invention and use of the computer particularly in the digital age, has revolutionised education much more than printing did in the period of the industrial revolution. Teaching and Learning are now done with computers, through computers and from computers. This calls for the introduction and inclusion of ICTs as new school subjects, new instructional media, new methods of delivery and assessments etc. Combined with the internet, the superhighway of information, print copies of textbooks are becoming obsolete. New technologies have made distance and blended instructional delivery modes new features of modern curricula.

Part Three

The Curriculum Development Process

This part comprises six chapters that follow the sequence of the curriculum development process. Since the traditional focus of the curriculum field is curriculum development, it should not be surprising that curriculum development occupies a sizable portion of the book. Curriculum development means different things to curriculum scholars and practitioners, therefore, diverse approaches and frameworks for the process are presented and discussed beginning from curriculum planning through implementation to evaluation.

7

Curriculum Development: Approaches and Models

A curriculum may be viewed as representing a practical plan for achieving the educational goals of a nation because the aspirations and hopes of a nation for its youth are commonly enshrined in policy documents on education. These documents and related ones are exploited by specially trained personnel to come up with a general blueprint for teaching and learning. The blueprint, called a curriculum framework, is further translated into workable plans for different educational levels. Ensuing curriculum plans are implemented, evaluated, and maintained or revised periodically. All these phases of work beginning from conception to construction and maintenance of the curriculum constitute the comprehensive process of curriculum development. It is a large-scale process that seems unending. It is iterative. This chapter introduces the process, its major approaches, and models.

Conceptualising the Curriculum Development Process

According to Schubert (1986 p. 16), curriculum development is the process of deciding what is to be taught and learnt in school along with all that is needed to make such decisions. Accordingly, it is a process that consists of other processes such as planning, implementation, and evaluation of learning experiences in the schooling process including the functions of the various participants, processes and procedures that are involved in creating the curriculum (Ornstein and Hunkins, 2018 p 30). The curriculum development process may therefore be perceived as an all-embracing process of curriculum making that consists of other processes such as planning, design, implementation, monitoring, evaluation, and revision. Accordingly, curriculum development is thought to evolve through a cycle in which a situation is analysed, a program or programs designed, steps taken to implement the program and assessment made to ascertain the degree to which the program has achieved its goals (Wiles and Bondi, 2011).

From the inception of the curriculum field, writers have used different terms such as *curriculum making, curriculum construction, curriculum engineering, curriculum design, curriculum planning, curriculum development* to describe various or all aspects of curriculum work. Each of these terms does not capture in the same way all the sub-processes involved in the macro activity of curriculum development as conceptualised in the first paragraph of this chapter. For this reason, Leke Tambo prefers to call the macro activity *curriculum making,* and limits the term *curriculum development* to a micro or more specific activity that comes up after curriculum design (Tambo, 2012 p. 143).

In this book, curriculum development is conceived of as a complex and comprehensive value-laden process that comprises situation analysis, design, development of materials, implementation, and evaluation of programs and courses. Curriculum development answers the questions "What should be taught? "Why should it be taught? How should it be organised? "Who is to be taught?" "How should it be taught?" When should it be taught? Who participates in deciding what should be taught? Where should the process begin? How do we know whether it has been taught? What should we do to improve teaching and learning? Answers to these questions and many more can only be obtained after careful research, consideration of theoretical frameworks, adoption, and execution of decisions in many phases of work that have been listed above.

Characterising Approaches and Models of Curriculum Development

Curriculum development is a flexible and dynamic process that uses different approaches, models, methods, and activities.

In planning, implementation and evaluation of the curriculum, curriculum workers are generally influenced by different approaches and theories. What they choose depends, as well as their personal conceptions of the curriculum, on their philosophy, history, and culture (Print, 2020p.20 of 34). The development of curricula in literature is based on many approaches. But technical/scientific and non-technical/non-scientific approaches constitute the two most common approaches. These two approaches and some of the models for curricula development that follow their philosophies are discussed below.

Technical/Scientific Approach to Curriculum Development

The curriculum developer prioritizes the students' learning from a given subject based on the explicit goals and objectives to be achieved. Furthermore, the curriculum developer would plan the structuring of the student-friendly learning environment. In addition, the plan includes staff involvement and calls for appropriate materials and supplies. The learning experiences of the students create different forms of strategies for processing knowledge. This approach is designed by the curriculum developer using the science model, which requires the observation of components and follow-up. They include topics, goals, learning experiences and evaluations. These elements are designed to promote knowledge acquisition. The students will be helped to meet their objectives by teaching subjects, such as reading and language arts, mathematics and science, on a daily and weekly basis. The curriculum is designed within a time frame to achieve these goals and goals. Different strategies would be employed to teach the subject when implementing the curriculum. The function is to order and sequence when and which textbooks, workbooks, tapes, videos, supplies and materials students will be introduced to. The curriculum could finally be evaluated based on the knowledge of the students. In the technical science approach to curricular development the following are the key features:

- It regards curriculum development as something similar to engineering or architecture.

- The basis for the procedure is the scientific method which involves a logical step-by-step procedure of problem solving.
- The procedure is guided by well-defined objectives which are formulated based on the analysis of standard needs as defined by developmental and other psychological theories, rather than individual needs and interests
- It is a way of planning curricula to maximise students' learning and to allow them to increase their output

Non-technical/Non-scientific Approach to Curriculum Development

A non-technical approach is often used when students' needs and interests or the needs of society and culture are the principal source of the program content; intended learning outcomes are not initially indicated. Educators with a subjective interpretation of reality favour the non-technical approach as it enables them to interact with students and contents in order to develop their own reality (Ornstein & Hunkins, 2007). This approach relies heavily on teachers as the major source of curriculum knowledge because they know their students and teaching contexts. Features of the non-technical approach are outlined below:

- Subjective, personal, and aesthetic and transactional
- Focuses on learners' needs and the subject-matter
- Subject matter is critical only if students can find meaning in it
- It emphasises activity-oriented methods in teaching and learning
- Emphasises evolution of the curriculum rather than a definite plan
- Flexible and structured without predetermined objectives to guide the teaching-learning process
- Teachers should provide pupils opportunities to observe, discover and learn on their own.

Models for Curriculum Development

A model specifies or describes a procedure to be used based on theory or philosophical orientation. A model proposes a solution to a problem. There are many classifications of curriculum development models in literature. An analysis of these models reveals that some are prescriptive, others descriptive; some are linear and others non-linear; others still are deductive and others inductive. Prescriptive models state what ought to be done when developing a curriculum whereas descriptive models state what is done by curriculum developers. Deductive models begin the Curriculum development process by examining the needs of society before specifying instructional objectives. This movement from generalities to specificities is deduction. Inductive models begin with the development of curriculum materials that lead to generalisation.

Curriculum models are also described as process or product models depending on where emphasis is laid in the development process. Whereas product models emphasise plans and intentions, process models emphasise activities and effects (Neary, 2003 p.39). Also known as objectives' models, product models can be traced to Tyler's rationale and process models to the works of Lawrence Stenhouse. Curriculum development models are presented below and are categorised either as technical scientific or non-technical and non-scientific.

Technical /Scientific Models of Curriculum Development

The Tyler Model, 1949

Ralph Tyler, a notable pioneer in the field of curriculum, put forward four fundamental questions that he thought ought to be used when developing a curriculum. These questions are now referred to as Tyler's rationale. They are:

- What educational purposes should the school seek to attain?
- What educational experiences can be provided that are likely to attain these purposes?
- How can these educational experiences be effectively organised?
- How can we determine whether these purposes are being attained?

Tyler further states that in selecting educational objectives, the following sources should be considered: the contemporary life, studies of the learner and suggestions from subjects' specialists. These objectives must be filtered through psychological and philosophical screens. Tyler's model is represented in the figure 7.1.

The model is linear, prescriptive, and deductive and emphasises objectives. It is a product model. Despite its simplicity and clarity, Tyler's model has been criticised on the following grounds:

1. The linear nature makes curriculum development to appear as a chain of a one-way activity. It is not so in real life.
2. The model does not show clearly where the content and methods of instruction fit in the process.

Putting evaluation at the end of the process gives the impression that evaluation of the curriculum takes place only at the end of curriculum development.

Taba's Model (Grassroot Rationale)

Hilda Taba (1962) argued that the curriculum designers should also be those who use the curriculum. She believed that teachers knew their students better and were able to provide their students with specific teaching situations. They should adopt an inductive approach to teaching, for example, from the general approach rather than from the traditional deduction approach, from general to specific. The Grassroot model of Taba emphasises the need for a broad base of participation for the decision making of the curriculum. Taba's seven stage Grassroot model advocates a significant role for teachers. The seven stages are described below:

Diagnosis of needs: Identify the students' needs for whom curriculum is to be planned.

Formulation of Objectives: Specify the objectives which need to be attained.

Selection of Content: Select subject matter based on objectives and ensure validity of the chosen content.

Organisation of content: Arrange the content in a particular sequence keeping in mind the developmental stage of learners, academic achievement, interests and more

Selection of learning experiences: Facilitate interaction of learners with content using appropriate instructional strategies.

Organisation of learning activities: The learning activities be organised in a sequence depending both on subject matter sequence and learner characteristics.

Evaluation: To assess the achievement of learning objectives, evaluation procedures need to be identified.

However, the model has been criticised as follows: This model has employed a highly technical, complex and specialised process using the concept of participatory democracy which cannot guarantee effective curriculum. It assumes that teachers have the time and skills to engage in such extensive curricula (Hunkins and Ornstein, 1988.)

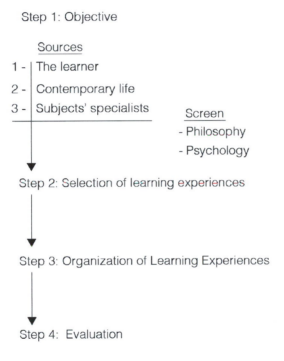

FIGURE 7.1. Tyler's Curriculum development model

Goodlad Model

An analysis of the values of existing culture is the basis of this model for formulating educational objectives. The objectives are translated into behavioural educational objectives. Learning opportunities are offered based on learning targets, such as courses or readings. John Goodlad believes that educational planners deduce from these learning possibilities specific and general educational objectives. The curriculum planners design and or select organisational centres that offer learning opportunities to students. A technical and scientific model is characterised by an interconnection between its different parts. The feedback and the adjustment of the whole model result from the students' performances and their relationship with the values of society as a whole. (Goodlad and Richter, 1966; in Ornstein and Hunkins, 1988).

Hunkin's Developmental Model

This model allows the student to adjust their decisions on curriculum actions. If the researcher finds that no content exists for a particular student during the experience selection stage for example, they can return to the beginning to change the program or go to the stage of curriculum diagnosis to recreate the desired learning experience. This model consists of seven main phases:

- Curriculum conceptualisation and legitimisation
- Diagnosis
- Content selection
- Experience selection
- Implementation
- Evaluation
- Maintenance

Wheeler Model (1967)

Building on the work of Tyler and attempting to remove its limitations, Wheeler described curriculum as a cyclical process shown in figure 7.2. This process consists of five phases which are interrelated.

Phase 1: The selection of aims, goals and objectives

He categorised goals into *ultimate, mediate, and proximate* goals: He also recognised general and specific objectives.

Phase 2: Selection of learning experiences in the attainment of aims, goals and objectives. He cited play and field trips as examples of learning experiences. He categorised learning experiences into three; that is *physical, mental, and emotional* experiences.

Phase 3: Selection of Content: This involves the selection of subject matter.

Phase 4: Organisation and integration of learning experiences and content

This phase is done depending on the design that curriculum developers choose. Curriculum organisational patterns that Wheeler identifies for selection are the subject-centred, broad-fields, activity, and core curriculum.

Phase 5: Evaluation

It is the evaluation of the effectiveness of phase 2, 3, and 4 in attaining what is set out in phase 1. In this phase, answers should be sought to question such as:

- Has the student acquired the knowledge, skills and abilities intended?
- Were the experiences chosen suitable for attaining the objectives or would other experiences have been more suitable?
- Was the integration of experience and content effective or was learning compartmentalised?
- Would a different organisation have brought about better results?

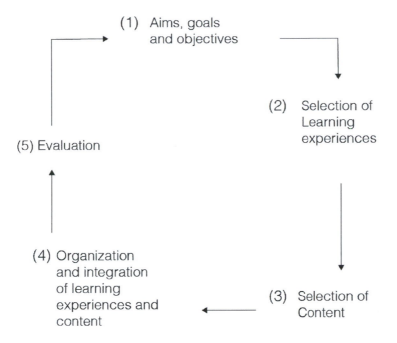

FIGURE 7.2. Wheeler's curriculum process model

Wheeler's model was an improvement upon Tyler's because it provides feedback to the process after evaluation, emphasising the cyclical nature of the curriculum development process. However, it does not specify when execution of the curriculum takes place. This model is also deductive and prescriptive but non-linear.

Tambo's Curriculum-making model (2012)

This model of the curriculum development process is presented as a more logical and comprehensive process of producing curriculum systems as guides or support systems for teaching and learning in schools. It is a general process for making a programme of studies. Tambo views it essentially as a decision-making process in five areas:

Clarifying orientations and concepts
- Situation analysis
- Curriculum design
- Curriculum development
- Curriculum implementation and evaluation

Clarifying orientations and concepts
Due to numerous and sometimes conflicting views of the curriculum and diverse approaches to

curriculum work, Tambo's curriculum-making model requires a curriculum development team to begin work by clarifying their orientations to ensure they are not heading towards different directions. He mentions various classifications of curriculum orientations and describes three major orientations to curriculum work, which curriculum developers can choose from. These are the transmission, transaction, and transformation orientations. (Miller and Seller,1990). This initial phase of curriculum making can be likened to the process defining what Murray Print terms *curriculum presage*. Curriculum presage refers to those activities and forces that influence developers in their curriculum decision-making tasks (Print, 2020 p. 1-3 of 43).

Situation analysis

This process involves analysing the different elements of the curriculum situation such as the learners and learning context. A situational analysis may be carried out using well known frameworks that include the one offered by Smith and Ragan (2005). The purpose of such analysis is to describe the current and desired situation to identify the needs of the intended curriculum. To begin work without prior analysis of the situation is like leaping in the dark (Tambo 2012 p.127). Tambo faults African governments especially shortly after independence, for calling in experts and consultants who came as 'trojan horses' bringing mainly educational practices in their home countries or those with which they were familiar. He opines that the system that needs the services of the expert or consultant should carry out the needs assessment and define the tasks to be performed instead of requesting the expert to define the tasks to be carried out (p.128).

Curriculum design

Designers can choose from subject-centred, learner-centred, and problem-centred designs. The desired pattern is chosen according to the sociological and philosophical orientations of the designers. They are guided in their choice and use of orientations by curriculum policy, goals and objectives of education and situational analysis reports. For example, in Cameroon, the 1998 law on orientation of education, the growth and employment strategy paper and policy speeches of the president of the republic are major sources that can guide designers to choose curriculum orientations and design. Design activities should take into consideration horizontal and vertical dimensions of curriculum elements, following the principles of scope, integration, continuity, and sequence.

Curriculum development

This phase begins after the layout of the curriculum has been produced and put in a generalised document by the curriculum planning group. Syllabuses, textbooks, and other curriculum support materials are then developed by curriculum writers, getting cues from the curriculum guide. If the design is subject-centred, the list of subjects or disciplines would have been made available in the curriculum guide so that developers can take off from there. Learning goals and objectives are formulated, appropriate content and subject matter, teaching and learning activities and assessment devices are selected following guiding principles.

Curriculum implementation and evaluation

The last phase of curriculum-making consists of two intertwined processes: Implementation and evaluation. This is so because during testing of materials before full adoption, there is formative evaluation. The major tasks for curriculum implementation include role definition, resource allocation, professional development, scheduling, communication, and monitoring the implementation. Evaluation processes result in formative and summative decisions. Among others, student achievement, materials and the entire program are evaluated using systematic models and techniques of curriculum evaluation.

Non-technical/Non-scientific models

There are several non-scientific models in literature. However only three of them will be discussed in this chapter. They are: Glatthorn's Naturalistic model, the Open Classroom model, and the Weinstein and Fantini model.

Glatthorn's Naturalistic Model

This is based on the following assumptions:
- Content can only be temporarily selected as students, teachers and knowledge interact
- All educational aims cannot be predefined
- Learning is based on knowledge development, particularly self-knowledge
- The development of curriculums is highly political and requires that managers and teachers cooperate.

The stages of Glatthorn's Model include the following:
1. Assess the alternatives - evaluate current approaches
2. Stake out the territory
    - define course parameters
    - define target learners
    - define learning activities
3. Develop a constituency
4. Build the knowledge base
    - identify content
    - gather data on faculty skill and support
    - gather data on student audience
5. Block the unit
    - select unit topics
    - write general objectives
6. Develop unit planning guide
7. Plan quality learning experiences
8. Select experiences which will enhance the attainment of the objectives
9. Develop course examination
    - state how learning will be documented (not test development)

10. Develop learning scenarios
11. Package the product

Open Classroom Model

The Open Classroom model is based on the program of activities. Activity curriculum proponents do not believe that children can plan any activity. Planning for them could stifle the development of the child in advance. During the teaching-learning process, learners should not be passive recipients of knowledge. William Kilpatrick supported this model. Under the model of activity, children learned and moved around in the classroom freely. Another popular supporter of the model is Herbert Kohl (1969). He believes that open classroom is a place where learners can make choices and indulge in what interests them. The teacher also recognises that the best things for him are those which arise spontaneously due to the suggestion or perception of a student. Open-class model highlights the child's freedom from teacher control and rigorous curricula. The child should select his or her own curriculum according to his or her needs, interests and skills. The model places great confidence in the ability of the child and promotes autonomy for learners.

Weinstein and Fantini Humanistic Model

This model is based on the belief that teachers are creating new content and techniques in order to keep the student central to the entire process. They can evaluate the relevance of the current curriculum, content, and the methods of learning. The curriculum is modified to meet the needs of the student based on the evaluation.

The first step in the development process is to identify the group of students. Their interest and abilities form the basis of teaching since the learners are taught in groups. The students' concerns are then identified, and the model is therefore called non-scientific or non-technical. The student's concerns determine the content organisation. They organise ideas and content based on learner needs more than on the demands of the subject matter.

The sources of content could be learners' feelings, students' identity, experiences of a growing person, and students' knowledge of the social content. The type of content will determine the skills to be developed by the students. The last stage is the identification of teaching strategies. The model aims to develop feelings of self-worth in the learners after interaction with content and teachers. It emphasises enhancement of the self-esteem of the learner and instils in them a confidence and belief in themselves (Ornstein and Hunkins, 1981).

A New Model: The Hybrid Model

In an attempt to take advantage of the strengths of both technical-scientific and non- technical approaches to development and eliminate their limitations, these authors are proposing a "hybrid model" for curriculum development. Theoretically, it would be a combination of process and product models in its approach to planning and decision making. Pending trial and validation, here is an illustrated description of the proposed model in figure 7.3.

Curriculum presage

Background forces, influences and activities at the initial stage of the curriculum development process constitute curriculum presage. Any educational system that wants to develop a new curriculum must begin to by ensuring that stakeholders make known their vision for education. At this initial stage of the process, competent authorities put in place, broad-based organisational structures. They do this by determining who participates in curriculum development projects at the macro level. They determine what curriculum conceptions and philosophies the participants are bringing with them and then try to understand the foundations that have influenced their thinking in order to harmonise and streamline towards meaningful and productive work.

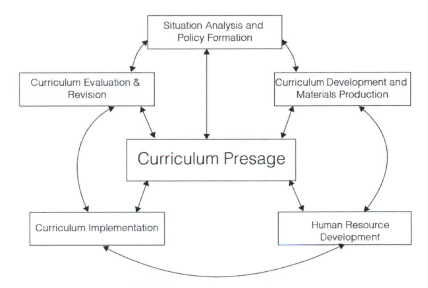

FIGURE 7.3. The Hybrid Model

Situation analysis and policy formulation

The curriculum planning council or units charged with such functions carry out a thorough needs analysis of the learners, learning task and learning context and make recommendations. Such recommendations will guide decision making that translates into curriculum policy or guidelines that regulate teaching and learning. Contemporary cross-cultural philosophies and theories of learning and development, lifelong competences and needs and aspirations of 21st century communities and societies should inform and guide the decisions that would be arrived at by the end of this stage. This is especially important for African school curricula because of the imperative to address issues of relevance, quality, and equity.

Curriculum Design and production of materials

Curriculum teams work at various levels to generate curriculum opportunities that will be laid down in flexible curriculum maps, blueprints, or matrices. Flexibility is a key consideration of design dimensions in this model. At the macro level, only curriculum frameworks are prepared. Decision making at this stage should lead to the appropriate formulation of curriculum goals, selection and organisation of varied learning experiences and determination of strategies and instruments for assessing learner achievement. This leads to the identification, production, and testing of identified instructional materials. The conclusion of activities at this stage should lead to suggestions and not prescriptions. In the spirit of the verb *currere,* each learner determines their racetrack instead of being assigned a specific pre-planned racetrack (*currus*, the noun form of *currere*), by choosing from a repertoire of activities and materials suggested. This implies that, even when the subject-centred design is used, learners are able to choose what is of interest to them. However, integrated curriculum designs are highly recommended in order to meet diverse needs of learners and the rapidly changing society. An integrated curriculum cuts across subject matter boundaries focusing on connections among concepts and experiences so that information and skills can be applied to novel and complex issues or challenges.

Human Resource Development

This stage of the curriculum development process is often taken for granted and not made clearly visible in the development process. Many curriculum innovations in Africa fail before they start because of lack of clarity and capacity to engage in change processes. Curriculum implementers must have adequate professional training before full scale curriculum implementation begins. Teacher education is of paramount importance for successful curriculum implementation. Alongside human resource development, there should be provision of infrastructure and equipment, so that practical constraints are nipped in the bud.

Curriculum Implementation

This takes place when all tentative plans and processes are translated into reality according to recommended pedagogical orientations. Trials must be carried out before full scale implementation. Classroom teachers and students are at the centre of this stage of the curriculum development process. Any interested stakeholder should be able to glean the operational curriculum from field observations and records of work done in schools. There is also monitoring of implementation and control of the taught curriculum by local education authorities. Functional curriculum management systems must be in place for effective curriculum implementation.

Curriculum Evaluation and Revision

Different types of evaluation are carried out throughout the process of curriculum development. There is diagnostic evaluation at the level of situational analysis, and the testing and refining of materials during the production stage, all of which constitute formative evaluation. During implementation in the classroom there is formative evaluation of students' achievement. At this sixth stage of the process, only summative evaluation takes place. However, it should be noted that evaluation is comprehensive involving evaluation of learner achievement, the processes, and programs, and employing different models, procedures, and instruments. After every form of evaluation, feedback is provided to the system to trigger revision where need be. There must be an inbuilt system of curriculum accountability as a channel through which reform ideas will flow.

8

Curriculum Planning: Approaches, Decision-making and Situational Analysis

Curriculum planning is the first phase of the curriculum development process. It refers to "making decisions about what to learn, why, and how to organise the teaching and learning process, taking into account existing curriculum requirements and the resources available." (UNESCO-IBE, 2019). At a general level, curriculum planning results in the elaboration of a broad curriculum framework as well as syllabuses for each school subject. At the school level, it results in course and assessment plans for different subjects while at the classroom level, the focus is on developing learning units, lessons, and sequences. In curriculum planning, curriculum developers conceptualise and organise the curriculum they want to build. Situation analysis is one of the first preoccupations of curriculum planning followed by design, and development of curriculum materials, culminating in major decisions on learning opportunities for learners before implementation can begin. This chapter begins with an overview of major curriculum planning approaches, describes the roles of resource persons in curriculum planning, and curriculum organisation structures before describing and discussing curriculum decision -making and situation analysis.

Curriculum Planning Approaches

The underlisted approaches to curriculum planning influence the dimensions and impact of decision making: 1) the intervention approach 2) the independent approach 3) the cooperative approach

The Intervention Approach

In this approach, the curriculum is designed and developed at the national level (Ministry of Education) or at the level of specialists and handed to the school through the expert or advisers. This is the top–bottom approach. It is also called the administrative or line staff model of curriculum planning. It utilises top–down line procedures in curriculum planning (Zais, 1976). Decision making in this approach is characteristic of centralised education systems. This procedure is often followed:

   i.   The highest authority in the ministry of education decides on curriculum projects to be undertaken, and thereafter forms a steering committee.

   ii.   The steering committee comprises top administrative officials and educational experts or consultants. Their duty is to formulate a general curriculum plan indicating a statement of philosophy.

iii. The steering committee appoints and selects working committees for each content area of the curriculum

iv. The steering committee receives for vetting and approval, curriculum documents that have been designed and produced by working committees.

v. The steering committee appoints administrators to introduce the curriculum plan to educators or implementers.

vi. The new curriculum is tried out and monitored for effectiveness through classroom visits and student evaluation.

Although this is the most common approach to curriculum planning and decision-making, Anja and Fonche (2001 p 99) argue that this approach is not a very effective means of causing and sustaining curriculum change because of its undemocratic principles.

The Independent Approach

It is also called the grassroots approach to curriculum planning. This is a more democratic approach based on two principles (Zais, 1976 p449)

▪ Successful curriculum implementation requires that teachers be intimately involved in the planning process.

▪ Students, parents, and lay members of the community must be included in the curriculum planning process.

In this approach, teachers in a school or within an area, form committees to carry out curriculum development activities, which may include modification of existing curriculum plans. This practice is common in educational systems that are highly decentralised. For example, in the USA, teachers in school districts form curriculum development committees and design their programs and courses. Individual schools may also plan their curricula in the bottom-top approach. Critics of this approach argue that applying the methods of participatory democracy to a highly complex and specialised process such as curriculum development, will not necessarily result in good decisions.

The Cooperative Approach

This approach brings together all relevant stakeholders (government officials, experts, lay persons, parents, and classroom teachers) to design and develop curricula. It is the participatory approach to curriculum development where stakeholders participate in identifying needs, designing and developing materials. This approach brings striking results because both top and bottom levels exchange ideas. With this approach, the development process is more dynamic, as the curriculum reflects the goals of different stakeholders, and provides guidance on the experiences needed for achievement of these goals. Secondly the final product is not far removed from the realities at the grassroots where the curriculum will be implemented.

Many successes have been recorded with the use of participatory approaches to curriculum development (PCD). In many developing countries, curriculum conferences have been used to provide a platform for training workshops involving different stakeholders in the production of curriculum materials for schools. In the Gambia, a Voluntary Service Overseas (VSO) volunteer supported a PCD approach that was applied to the development of English language teaching in primary schools. In reviewing teaching syllabuses for the first cycle of Cameroon secondary schools in 2014, the inspector-general of pedagogy stated that they used a participatory and innovative approach by bringing together experts at the various inspectorates of pedagogy, classroom teachers and trade unionists (MINESEC, 2014, p.6).

Resource Persons and their Roles in Curriculum Planning

Whatever approach is used to plan curricula, different resource persons contribute to decision-making albeit at different levels of the planning process and as the situation permits.

Government Organisations

They include the Head of State and other members of government, Ministers charged with Education, Regional and divisional delegates of Education, National and Regional, Pedagogic inspectors, and advisers. These people are responsible for formulating curriculum policy; providing infrastructure, human resources and materials required for curriculum implementation. They also follow up and supervise curriculum implementation.

National Organisations

These include examination boards, teachers' trade unions, non-governmental organisations, employers in both public and private sector and interest groups in civil society. Examination boards may develop examination syllabuses and propose changes in the design, implementation, and evaluation of school curricula. The others act as pressure groups often acting behind the scenes to influence curriculum policy and content.

Local Authorities

Non-governmental organisations like the Parent-teacher associations and municipal councils are examples of local authorities that contribute to providing and managing resources for curriculum implementation. They may be invited to participate in special curriculum planning committees at various levels of the planning process.

Curriculum Experts and Subject Specialists

Some of these experts occupy positions in government and therefore have opportunities to participate in curriculum planning. They carry out situation analysis, design and develop materials. They have professional knowledge and skills to structure the curriculum into high quality documents used for teaching and learning.

Lay Persons

Citizen participation is essential for the development of a relevant curriculum. Lay persons and parents can (i) suggest educational objectives (ii) contribute to evaluation of the curriculum. They can participate in research that aims at analysing the overall effectiveness of school programmes. Their views can be a very useful guide for future curriculum planning.

Teachers and Teacher Trainers

Classroom teachers have the responsibility of operationalising the curriculum. The teacher is the chief executive of curriculum implementation. That is, teachers translate curriculum plans into workable documents at the level of the school and classroom. Teachers' curriculum planning activities are prominent at the school level. In doing this, they participate in

- Workshops and seminars at local levels to produce schemes of work from approved syllabuses.
- They translate schemes or work into lesson plans.
- They produce learning resources (e.g., pamphlets, past questions, and answers; lecture notes) that are exploited by learners.
- The teacher is a source of feedback to school authorities and ministry officials on the effectiveness of the written curriculum.
- the classroom teacher proposes syllabus modifications to curriculum designers.

Learners

The learner is at the centre of the curriculum. In some situations, learners take part in curriculum planning. However, the major role of learners in curriculum planning is cooperation. At the school level, students cooperate in realising the goals and objectives laid down in curriculum documents by

i.   Giving feedback to their teachers to enable them to choose teaching content and methods suited to their needs and interests.
ii. Participating in decision-making in non-academic activities like student government and school sanitation.
iii. Helping to prepare teaching/ learning aids.

Curriculum Planning Organisational Structures

For development of a quality curriculum, Glatthorn (2004) proposed the creation of several organisational structures and task forces during the planning phase of the development process. Although Alan Glatthorn's proposals were primarily intended for curriculum development in school districts in the USA, these structures can be adapted to operate effectively in both centralised and decentralised educational systems. The structures comprise citizens' advisory council, curriculum planning council, curriculum task forces, curriculum writers, school curriculum council and instructional teams.

Citizens' advisory council

Such a council is made up of representatives of education stakeholders in the country or specific community. Members of this council are not directly involved in the creation of curriculum plans. Their role is to advise on curriculum policy. Curriculum policy can be defined as "the formal body of law and regulation that pertains to what should be taught in schools" (Elmore and Sykes, 1992, p. 186). Members of this council foster communication by meeting with community groups concerned about the curriculum. They discuss controversial curriculum issues affecting the community and transmit recommendations to educational authorities concerned. They may confer with the Curriculum Planning Council to convey community beliefs and opinions about curricular issues.

Curriculum planning council

This is arguably, the most significant structure in the decision-making process. It is made up of high-quality professionals. The council is charged with identifying curriculum needs, developing a curriculum calendar, appointing, and monitoring the work of curriculum task forces. Specifically, the curriculum planning council performs the following functions:

- Conduct a situation analysis or needs assessment.
- Do long term planning by producing a strategic plan, setting priorities and timelines for execution of tasks. See sample plan in 8.1 A strategic plan is influenced by priority needs, availability of resources, human resource capacity and an appropriate pace of change.
- Formulates educational goals and develops a vision for the curriculum. It is important to articulate a vision of excellence to meet the challenges of contemporary society. The vision may indicate a curriculum focus and pedagogical orientations. (See excerpts of the vision of the new Cameroon primary school curriculum in appendix A, as a sample).
- Identifies a standard design for curriculum guides.
- Develop processes and materials for effective curriculum implementation and evaluation.
- Appoint task forces and train them if necessary.
- Monitor the work of task forces.
- Arrange for leadership training and staff development.
- Make budget recommendations for curriculum work.

Table 8.1. Simplified sample of long-term planning chart

Subjects	2017/2018 academic year	2018/2019 academic year	2019/202 academic year	2020/2021 academic year
Arts and craft	plan	pilot	produce	implement
National languages		Plan and produce	pilot	implement
Mathematics	plan	Produce and pilot	implement	
Social studies	Plan and produce	pilot	implement	

Curriculum task forces

Curriculum task forces accomplish most of the work envisaged by the planning committee. Task forces are professional groups that are appointed to complete specific projects. For example, a curriculum scientific committee is a task force charged with the responsibility of reviewing the drafts of curriculum plans to ensure quality by providing scientific direction.

Curriculum writers

These are responsible for preparing curriculum materials. They write out syllabuses, textbooks, teachers guides and other support materials that may be required. Curriculum writers should have a good knowledge of the subject matter and be able to write clearly and effectively.

School curriculum council

It is a school-based group made up of administrators and other school leaders. Principals and head teachers, deans of studies and heads of academic departments meet to restructure program guidelines according to local realities. They also develop guidelines for instructional planning teams. In centralised systems, these functions may be performed at intermediate levels between the top and bottom levels of curriculum planning. In Cameroon, this council may operate at the levels of regional inspectorates of pedagogy or individual schools.

Instructional planning teams

Members work to develop yearly plans based on prescriptions in curriculum guides. They develop units of study and teaching materials to be exploited by individual classroom teachers.

Decision-Making in the Curriculum Planning Process

Curriculum decision-making entails making choices for curriculum action, requiring selection from a range of alternatives (Print, 2020p. 2 of 10). This process is not often as straightforward as it may appear. In many educational systems, selection of appropriate and relevant learning opportunities and experiences has been a controversial subject, calling for public attention. This is particularly so because curriculum decisions attempt to balance educational theories and models with political and social realities. Curriculum decisions are inundated with political and human factors. Curriculum planning involves issues of power, people, procedure, and participation. It is a political process, a social enterprise, and a collaborative activity as well.

Social Dimensions of Curriculum Decision-Making

Effective curriculum decisions must be arrived at through interactive participation of all or representatives of all education stakeholders. In this way, curriculum planning is like a social enterprise. A social enterprise is a business entity whose aim is to achieve the community mission and re-invest its profits into achieving that mission. It is in the interest of the entire education community and stakeholders in the business of schooling to participate in deciding on curriculum goals, content, instruction, and evaluation strategies.

For effectivity, it is incumbent on curriculum planners to ensure that parents, laymen, community leaders, educators, curriculum experts and community leaders or their representatives participate in curriculum decision-making. Teamwork is a characteristic feature of curriculum planning activities. Collaboration and cooperation are key elements needed to arrive at wise choices when diverse opinions present themselves.

Political Dimensions of Curriculum Decision-Making

Politics is about power. Tinder (1991) holds that a political system is a set of arrangements in which some people dominate others. The locus of curriculum control lies in the ability to influence the allocation of values. Pertinent curriculum decisions depend on who answers the question "what knowledge is worthwhile?" and who determines which persons should have access to worthwhile knowledge, instead of merely stating what knowledge is worthwhile. In addition, curriculum planners need to decide on how that worthwhile knowledge will be selected, organised, presented, and evaluated.

National and local government agencies and policies exert considerable influence on curriculum planners as they attempt to answer curriculum questions and make decisions. Amongst other tasks, these agencies

- define content areas that must be included in the curriculum according to national ideologies and philosophical orientations,
- regulate textbook adoption and supply,
- train, certify and recruit teachers and other curriculum implementers,
- monitor curriculum implementation through inspection and supervision of instruction.
- set up national examination boards and control accreditation of programs and licensure.

Curriculum leaders need to understand how political pressures are being applied and the way organisations and individuals attempt to influence what is taught in schools. Political influence is highly unequal. People with least status tend to have least influence in decision-making. The struggle for power occurs chiefly behind the scenes as interest groups attempt to persuade authorities to accept their position. Lobbying groups play important roles in the hidden power struggle especially at the macro level of decision-making. Once policy has been determined at that level, key decisions will be taken by curriculum specialists, education inspectors and superintendents, principals and teachers.

At the micro level when the classroom teacher closes the classroom door, the curriculum may become the way the individual teacher perceives what knowledge is worthwhile. Thus, at different levels of curriculum decision-making, the major sources of influence may vary considerably. Every level of the curriculum development process seems to be highly politicised.

Centralised and decentralised systems of government differ in procedures and approaches to curriculum decision making.

Arenas of Curriculum Decision-Making

Curriculum decision-making typically takes place at a broad spectrum of two levels: the top level and the grassroots or bottom level. Intermediate arenas fall between the top and bottom. Arenas for curriculum decision-making could be extrapolated from the levels of curriculum planning proposed by Van der Akker et al (2009).

Societal Level of Curriculum

This is the national level of decision-making where most school programs are conceived and created and decisions on the curriculum policy made. It is the macro level of curriculum planning.

It is the farthest from the learners since this is where the public stakeholders (politicians, groups of special interest, administrators, professional experts) participate in determining the objectives, the subjects to be studied, the time spent in education/learning and support materials.

Institutional Level of Curriculum

This is the meso level of planning which occurs in schools or institutions. The curriculum from societal level is modified by local teachers or laypeople. It is often organised based on subjects and includes subjects that must be studied. Decision-making at this level may produce curriculum standards, philosophies, courses, schemes of work and teaching guides.

Instructional Level of Curriculum

This is the micro level of curriculum and curriculum planning. Here, teachers use the curriculum that has been developed at societal level and at institutional level, at the institutional level teachers design teaching and learning in units and lessons. Teachers' instructional strategies, styles and materials give the curriculum a definite form as they choose from a myriad of alternatives.

Experiential Level of Curriculum

This is the nano level of curriculum involving individual learners. It describes the curriculum perceived and experienced by each student and therefore, varies among lessons due to individual differences. As an arena of decision-making, the scope of this level is limited.

Levels of Curriculum Decision-Making

There are two main levels of decision-making in curriculum planning. These are illustrated in the centralised and the decentralised models of the curriculum design process. Gatawa (1990) and Urevbu (1985) refer to these models as patterns of curriculum designing.

The Centralised model of Curriculum Designing

In a centralised curriculum design model, decisions about the content and the organisation of the curriculum are made by a central national office, usually the Ministry of Education. They may do so with the aid of resource persons like subject experts, curriculum specialists and experienced teachers.

Decisions about the content and organisation of the curriculum are made centrally, after which national syllabuses are produced and textbooks are adopted. Therefore, schools offer the subjects produced centrally and all students take the same examinations, though modifications may be made to respond to students with special needs. Also, the evaluation instruments are developed centrally and decisions on how to administer the instruments, remains the responsibility of the Ministry of Education and the Examination Boards. At the level of the States, districts or Regions, an Inspectorate is placed to monitor the implementation of these activities.

Advantages of the Centralised Model of Curriculum Designing
1. There is a guarantee of harmonisation in what is taught and learned making it easier to achieve national goals.
2. Assembling various resource persons to design a Curriculum guarantees a better quality.
3. Instructional materials are produced in huge quantities making them less costly for producers and more affordable for consumers.
4. It makes it easier for the Ministry of Education to communicate to schools about requirements and expectations.
5. Academic mobility is enhanced as learners can transfer from one school to another without losing much.

Disadvantages of the Centralised Model of Curriculum Designing
The design done at centralized level may not adequately address the specific needs of some groups within the country.

The limited participation of stakeholders in decision-making may result in minimal commitment during implementation.

Centralisation may retard the final production of syllabuses and other documents.

Decentralised Model of Curriculum Design
In this model, the district, local authorities, or states make decisions on the content and organisation of the curriculum. This is common in many developed countries especially countries that run a federal system of government.

With such a model, teachers work with parents to identify the content based on the local realities that meet the national goals and the learning experiences. Each school or district produces its own local curricula and texts and produces its own assessment form. There are not too many people involved in curriculum design activities. The actors may include specialists, representatives of the Parent Teachers Association, heads of schools, academics and consultants, teachers, and representatives of industry.

Advantages of the Decentralised Model
- The Curriculum design process is very realistic as it addresses local needs.
- Students can easily relate what is learned in school and its relevance to society.

- The local community is committed to the implementation of the curriculum since they are directly involved.
- There is very little delay in producing the documents as compared to a centralised system.
- The system enhances activity and initiative in the teacher with the use of local materials.

Disadvantages of a Decentralised Model
- Academic mobility is limited as learners cannot easily transfer from one school to the other.
- There is little probability that national goals will be achieved.
- Materials may be costly to develop and produce.
- The expertise at local level may not be minimal.

Situational Analysis in Curriculum Work

For wise and comprehensive decisions to be taken, any meaningful curriculum project undertaken by the curriculum planning council or any team functioning as such, must begin with analysis of the situation. Situation analysis is the process of examining factors that exist in the environment or society where the curriculum and instruction are going to be implemented. Sitwe (2010) states that it is the systematic process of analysing the situation before the curriculum is developed. Some curriculum scholars and instructional designers refer to this phase of the curriculum process as diagnosis of needs or needs analysis.

Tyler insinuated a situational analysis in the curriculum development process when he proposed the study of contemporary society, the learner, and the nature of knowledge as sources or precursors of curriculum objectives (Tyler, 1949 p.46). Factors that impact a curriculum must be studied prior to curriculum design. These factors include societal needs and needs related to school infrastructure and facilities, teachers, and learners.

Purpose and Objectives of Situation Analysis

Although situational analysis may be overlooked or resisted by local curriculum developers, with the assumption that they are already familiar with the context in which the curriculum will operate, it is an important exercise. The following reasons underscore the importance of a situational analysis. It
- Gives a clearer vision of the curriculum context,
- Provides a systematic database and up to date information about specific areas of need in order to make better policy and programme decisions (Witkin and Altschuld, 1995),
- Guides the formulation of curriculum intent, content and selection of teaching and learning activities, and
- Guides curriculum planners on what needs to be done to solve a real problem in the community for which education is the solution.

Objectives of Situation Analysis

Specifically, a situation analysis seeks to:
- Gather data using established methods and procedures.

- Set priorities and determine criteria for solutions.
- recommend action that improves programs.
- Set up criteria for allocating resources.

Approaches to Situational Analysis

It is necessary to reiterate here that, there is situational analysis before design activities in both curriculum development and instructional design processes. The distinction is found in their dimensions of needs analysis.

For Curriculum planning

In a widely acclaimed model of school-based curriculum development put forward by Skilbeck (1976), situational analysis begins with a critical appraisal of internal and external factors to the school. The factors to be reviewed to obtain needs are displayed on table 8.2.

Table 8.2. Situation analysis factors

External factors to the school	
Cultural/ social changes and expectations	Unemployment patterns, societal values, economic growth, employer expectations
Educational system requirements and challenges	Influence of external examinations; inquiry reports
Changing nature of content	Subject matter taught in schools requires to be updated
Teacher support systems	Availability and accessibility to curriculum consultants, teachers' resource centres and educational institutes
Resources	Availability and flow of financial, human, and material resources from national education authorities
Internal factors to the school	
Pupils	Similarities and differences in physical and psychological development characteristics; Aptitudes, emotional and social
Teachers	Quantity and quality of teachers; Skills, experiences, strengths, and weaknesses of teaching staff
School ethos	School climate; power distribution; social cohesiveness, operational procedures
Material resources	Buildings, equipment; books, curriculum materials
Perceived problems	Major stimulus for change: Perception of needs expressed by parents, teachers, and students

Source: adapted from Skilbeck, 1976

In another model of school-based curriculum development, Soliman et al (1981) developed an elaborate situation analysis checklist (SAC). It incorporates factors such as societal expectations, resources, educational system requirements, content, forms of knowledge, internal factors and learning processes that must be investigated to know what the new curriculum needs.

For Instructional design

The analysis phase of the instructional design process consists of sub-processes of *learning context analysis* (learning needs and description of learning environment), *task analysis* and *learner analysis*. There are various perspectives of how a needs analysis should be approached and conducted. Popular approaches to needs analysis include those outlined by Mager, 1988; Rossett, 1995; Smith and Ragan, 2005; Morrison et al ,2006; Dick, Carey, and Carey, 2009. Smith and Ragan suggest three methods of carrying out a needs assessment. They are the i) problem, ii) innovation and iii) discrepancy models. They will be described in chapter 14 (instructional design models).

Similarities and Differences Between Situation Analysis in Curriculum Planning and Instructional Design

Both situations utilise the strategy of needs analysis or assessment to get a clearer vision of the learning context. Curriculum and instructional designers are open to many perspectives and models of needs assessment. The main difference between situational analysis in the two scenarios is that situational analysis in instructional design involves *task analysis* in addition to analysis of the learner and learning context. Put differently, needs analysis before curriculum design activities consists of *learning context analysis* and *learner analysis* only. There are no tasks to be analysed.

Conducting A Situational Analysis for Curriculum Development

Print (2020) recommends a four-step procedure when conducting a situational analysis for curriculum development. It requires the curriculum developer to: i) Identify problems in the context ii) Select appropriate factors iii) do data collection and analysis iv) make recommendations.

1. **Identify problems in the context**

Specific problems in the society or community may necessitate the need for a new curriculum. For example, observations that primary school leavers cannot effectively read and write may signal the general need to improve primary school pupils' literacy abilities. For a curriculum to be relevant, the felt needs of the consumers of curriculum should be identified and investigated and considered during development.

2. **Select appropriate factors**

When the problem and general needs to be investigated have been determined, the curriculum developer can relate them to factors suggested by Malcom Skilbeck on table 8.2, to illuminate the problem. All the factors must not be used in this step. The table of factors is just a guide for the curriculum developer to select appropriate factors related to the problem identified in step 1.

3. **Data collection and analysis**

To provide useful information to the developer, a systematic approach to data collection and analysis is required. A sample of factors and techniques are found on table 8.3 which can be used for data collection.

Table 8.3. Contextual Factors and Data Collection Techniques

Factor	Techniques	Data collected
Students	Interviews	• student information and attitudes
	School records	• background and achievement data
	Systematic observation	• student behaviour patterns
	Questionnaire	• student attitudes
	External examinations	• comparative student performance
	Psychosocial environment	• student perceptions of classroom climate
	Self- reporting scales	• student attitudes
Teachers	Anecdotal records	• teacher behaviour and attitudes
	Staff profiles	• record of staff skills and abilities
	questionnaires	• teacher attitudes
School ethos	Systematic observation	• impression of school climate
	Psychosocial environment	• Aggregated classroom climate
	interviews	• Student/ teacher/parent attitudes
Resources	Inventories and Checklist	• listing of school resources
	Systematic observation	• Impression of school resources-

Collected data are analysed and synthesised. Interpretations and conclusions are drawn based on observed patterns. When curriculum developers gather this information, they use it to determine differences between the actual situation and the desired one. Data analysis brings out specific needs. A need is defined by Brindley (1989 p.65) as "the gap between what is and what should be". Armed with this information on specific needs and priorities to be considered in the new curriculum, developers can proceed to positive action towards the solution of the problem.

4. Make recommendations

A report is established containing recommendations that are helpful in devising a solution(s) to the problem. Recommendations propose direction and structure of the curriculum. For example, a recommendation relating to the hypothetical problem mentioned in step 1 could be, "Students require substantial literacy development to establish communication skills in English."

9

Curriculum Design

Being the technical part of curriculum planning, curriculum design refers to the purposeful, deliberate, and systematic organisation of curriculum and instructional blocks within a program, course, or lesson. Design activities take place at different levels of the curriculum landscape. At the macro level of curriculum planning, design involves deciding on what students should learn in a program or course in terms of knowledge, skills, and attitudes as well as how this learning should take place in terms of pedagogical orientation, assessment, and evaluation. When preparing a curriculum guide or curriculum framework document, design activities result in specifications of content in terms of the range of subjects to be offered in a program. At the level of syllabus preparation, curriculum content is specified as outlines of facts, concepts, and principles of the subject or course. At the level of lesson design, which is the micro-level of curriculum planning, content is specified according to learning sequences. Simply put, when educators design curricula, they determine and arrange what will be taught and learnt, how it will be done, and specify the schedules to be followed. This chapter presents and discusses curriculum design dimensions, patterns, attributes, and guidelines for design.

Dimensions of Curriculum Design

Curriculum design dimensions describe and define the magnitude or extent to which curriculum elements must be arranged to form a relevant, unified, and functional whole. Also called curriculum organisation, curriculum design identifies curriculum elements, their relationships, and considers organisational principles. Two dimensions or relationships have been identified and described over the years. They are relationships over time and relationships across content. These relationships between learning experiences and content are to be considered during organisation. They are illustrated in figure 9.1.

Relationship Over Time (Vertical Relationship)

This concerns relationships of curriculum elements over the entire duration of the curriculum. To produce continuous and cumulative learning, designers must ask and answer questions such as: *What learning objectives, content, and learning activities should be emphasised now and over time?* In the primary school curriculum, for example, literacy and numeracy skills and personal development may be taught in the first three years and the later years devoted to greater development of concepts and skills in mathematics, language, science, and social studies. Attitudes and values are known to develop slowly over time. To curriculum designers, this implies repetition of learning objectives that are meant to help learners acquire desired attitudes and values until they are acquired.

Relationship across content (Horizontal relationship)

Designers must determine the relationships across subject matter at given points in time in the curriculum. For example, *what is the relationship between the mathematics and physics taught to form one or students in the secondary school science curriculum? How much of mathematics and physics should be taught knowing that there are other subjects to be taught in those classes too?* Scope, integration, and balance are guiding principles of horizontal dimensions. When adding new subjects on to an existing curriculum, care must be taken to ensure a reasonable content scope that will not overload the curriculum.

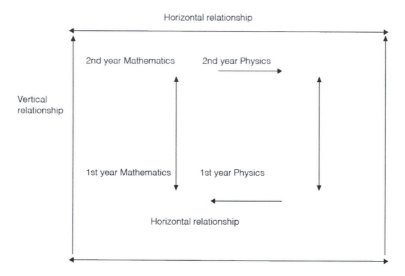

FIGURE 9.1. Relationships among Curriculum Elements

Design dimension considerations

Scope

Scope describes the number of topics and learning experiences covered at any time by a school or class. It deals with the scope and depth of the curriculum. Pertinent questions when deciding on scope are: How much should students be able to study from each domain? Do all students have to study common content? What curriculum content should be excluded from the curriculum?

The content of a year's programme or longer may be listed as topics to be studied while the content of a course (subjects), along with the cognitive, affective, and psychomotor skills to be cultivated, are listed as important ideas, concepts, principles, and skills. The content or topics are usually organised in chapters or units. It is from units that lessons are drawn. Factors that determine scope include:

- **Time available for each lesson**. Time determines the number of lesson periods that a subject can be taught. The depth of content may be compromised by breadth and vice versa due to time constraints. More subjects may be taught in less detail or fewer subjects in greater detail.
- **Core or common content**: This is the body of knowledge that all students must learn. What percentage of all learnings should be core or common content? As a rule of thumb, common content or basic knowledge should constitute at least 50% of the subject matter of a program.
- **Nature of the learner:** The scope of curriculum content should respond to learners' developmental stages and diversity. Special content may be created to meet the needs of different students.
- Content to exclude from the curriculum should be determined during design activities.

Curriculum designers may face some of the following challenges when establishing the scope of curriculum content.

- There is a problem of integrating content when subjects are taught in isolation. The scope may be extended with unnecessary repetition due to absence of adequate integration.
- Achieving balance between the breadth and depth of curriculum content is usually not easy.
- Establishing which proportion of common and special content to include or exclude in programs can be difficult.
- When a long list of topics is outlined, it is difficult to decide what should come first and justify it.
- It may be difficult to justify what should be taught at a given time or level.

Sequence

Since curriculum content is usually chunked (organised in manageable bits), the chunks must respect an appropriate sequence. Sequence refers to the order in which that which is to be taught will occur over time. There must be sequencing guidelines. Sequence falls within the vertical relationship of curriculum elements. Factors influencing sequencing include students' prior knowledge and developmental stages.

Based on the principles of sequence presented by Smith, Stanley, and Shores (1957) and Posner and Rudnisky (1994), the following guidelines to establish sequence of curriculum content and learning activities in programs, courses, and lessons are proposed.

- **Simple to complex.** The designer should present materials from easy to difficult and from concrete to abstract.
- **Whole to part**. Designers present an overview of specific content before getting into details and specificities. It could also be the reverse, that is, from part to whole.

- **Chronology**. This relates to time. The natural order of events is the basis of ordering content and experiences. One could begin from earliest to recent times.
- **Learning-related sequence**. Organisation may be based on pre-requisite learning. This means there are fundamental things to be learnt before others. Learning sequences may be informed by knowledge of how people learn. Prior learning and familiar content come before the new. Interesting content is also known to stimulate appetite for learning.
- **World related sequence**. Content is presented based on natural relationships among objects, events, and people. This could be in terms of space (top to bottom, west to East) or physical attributes like shape, size etc.
- **Concept related sequence**. Describes a situation where content and experiences are related by sharing commonalities.
- **Inquiry related**. Content follows a logical and methodological sequence based on the scientific method.

Continuity

It is a vertical reiteration where one or more of the curriculum elements are continuously stressed or repeated throughout the learning period in greater depth and breadth and with more sophistication. In such a situation a topic can be taught from a lower level to a higher level but in a more complex manner. For example, the way the topic 'Sets' is taught in primary school mathematics is different from the way it is taught is secondary school because cognitively, learners have made progress. The rationale for continuity is that there are some critical concepts and skills that learners master over time. Jerome Bruner's concept of the spiral curriculum which was discussed in chapter 5 is highly applicable here.

Integration

Integration means relating curriculum content and activities within the programme. This is to ensure that students understand how related subjects are than learning them in isolation. Problem-solving for instance requires an integration of competences from different domains. Integration can take place among different subjects that have a common thread or amongst topics in the same subject.

Articulation

Articulation refers to the vertical and horizontal relationships of curriculum experiences. Vertical articulation refers to sequencing content such that subsequent content is built on preceding content. For example, addition must be taught before multiplication can be understood. On the other hand, horizontal articulation, also called correlation refers to the process of building on the relationship among elements in one subject with those of another. For example, there are concepts in Biology that are found in Food and Nutrition and also in Chemistry. When curriculum designers consider horizontal articulation in this case, it may result in the creation of a new interdisciplinary subject known as a broad-field. The broad field may be named 'Nutrition Science'.

Balance

Balance refers to how much weighting is given to each aspect of the design. There should be equitable assignment of content and experiences vis a vis available time. How much of general courses are included as against specialised courses? How much breadth of content is included as against depth? As far as objectives are concerned, there should be a balance of the domains of educational objectives. Too much or too little of any aspects of curriculum elements jeopardises balance. Balance can be very difficult to achieve.

Two of these considerations or principles are usually represented diagrammatically in what is referred to as a scope and sequence chart as shown in table 9.1.

Table 9.1. Scope and Sequence Chart for a hypothetical Bachelor of Education program

SCOPE	SEQUENCE		
	LEVELS		
	Level 200	*Level 300*	*Level 400*
Functional French	X		
Social Studies	X		
Professional Ethics in Teaching			X
Educational Technology		X	
Research Methods		X	
Teaching Practice			X
Foundations of Education	X		
Psychology of Learning		X	

Key: **x** *means subject is offered in that level or class*

Attributes of Curriculum Design

Curriculum design is very important in creating relevant experiences and responsive teaching and learning environments for the teachers and students. It ensures that teaching is effective, efficient, and appealing. Teachers design curriculum with a specific educational purpose in mind. The main goal is to improve student learning or a response to administration requirements or quality assurance criteria. Curriculum design has certain attributes:

1. **Curriculum design is purpose driven**

It is meant primarily to improve student learning. Curriculum designers must be as clear about the purpose(s). The goals which are based on needs analysis must be clearly stated. Scholars like Robert Gagne suggest that the goals should be stated in three domains namely: the cognitive, affective, and psychomotor domains to ensure that every aspect of the human capability has been paid attention.

2.   **Curriculum design is deliberate**.

To be effective, efficient, and appealing curriculum design must be a conscious planning effort. It involves using an explicit process that identifies clearly what will be done, by whom and when. Curriculum design is creative. Curriculum design is not a neatly defined procedure that can be pursued smoothly in a rigorous series of steps. At every stage of the curriculum design process there are opportunities for innovative thinking, novel concepts, and invention as well as improvement.

3.   **Curriculum design is compatible across levels**

This is concerned with progression in knowledge and skills from one level to the next. Do the different stages align? Design decisions at one level must be compatible with those at the other levels. It must take into consideration experiences in primary school in order for those of secondary school to build on, while it must also ensure that the learning experiences in secondary school prepare the learner for post-secondary or university education.

4.   **Curriculum design requires compromises**

In developing a design that meets complex specifications, trade-offs inevitably have to be made with regard to benefits, costs, constraints, and risks. No matter how systematic the planning or how innovative the thinking, curriculum designs always end up not being everything that everyone would want.

Curriculum Design Patterns

There are three main designs or patterns of curriculum organisation. Each major pattern has variations. They are:

- Subject centred curriculum
- The learner centred curriculum
- The society centred curriculum

The Subject-centred Designs

This design is centred around different subjects or disciplines. It is geared towards helping learners build on the knowledge gained. Some subjects are subdivided into divisions or periods and subject matter is arranged according to the logic or complexity of the subject. There are usually compulsory and elective courses. The compulsory courses usually constitute the greater part of common learnings. Individual differences are met by elective courses. Variations of the subject-centred design includes the discipline design, correlated design, the broad-fields design and the core design.

Strengths of this design are:

- It is the oldest, most stable, and best-known curriculum design. Other designs like the learner-centred and problem-centred designs rely on it for content.
- It gives direction and focus on the acquisition of knowledge and constitutes a systematic and effective method of organising knowledge.
- It is organised by the disciplines on scholarly fields of specialised inquiry. Thus, it depends mainly on research findings.
- It emphasises on verbal activity; thus, the teacher plays an active role.

- It is easy to deliver because complementary materials are readily available.
- It responds to the common practices with respect to textbook treatment, how teachers are trained as subject specialists, examinations appear in subject areas and employers employ school leavers based on the subjects they studied. So, it is better accepted by the wider society.

Its weaknesses are:

- The design isolates and compartmentalises knowledge
- It overemphasises subject matter resulting in a curriculum that is too technical, inflexible, conservative, and too specialised
- It stresses content and neglects students' needs, interest, and experiences
- The use of this design encourages passivity for learning among the students.

Discipline Design

Design based on disciplines concentrates on academic disciplines. It is like the design of separate subjects. The term 'discipline' or 'subject' covers subjects or areas of study. The theoretical influence of the perennialism that deals with each subject as a specific and autonomous body of verified knowledge lies within this curriculum design. Content is divided into different topics or disciplines including language, science, mathematics, and social studies. This design is common in higher education. The students, however, "experience" the subjects which contribute to better knowledge acquisition within the discipline. Specific, current, and actual information and skills as developed by the experts on a discipline tend to be the focus of the discipline-based curriculum. It helps students master the area of content and increases independent learning. The student is involved in the design of the discipline to analyse the curriculum and draw conclusions. It helps students master the area of content and increases independent learning. The advantages and disadvantages of this design are very similar to those of the subject-centred design.

Correlated Design

Correlation is the recognition and establishment of relationships among the various subject areas or fields. *Correlation* refers to horizontal relationships, that is, relationships on the same grade level between two subjects, or among all the subjects. Correlation design is like broad-field design because it focuses on integration. The difference is that correlation design combines only two subjects while a broad-field will combine several subjects. Correlation design is a kind of simplified version of broad-fields design. The correlated design links separate subjects to reduce fragmentation. Subjects are related to one another, but each subject maintains its identity. One may correlate citizenship education and sociology.

The strengths of the correlated design are:

- It brings out the relationship between two subjects.
- The two subjects are combined in innovative ways and the students can see the connections between the two of them.

The weaknesses of the correlated design are:

- Teachers may not have enough expertise in the two subjects to successfully correlate them

in a curriculum.
- It requires teachers to collaborate with their peers which may not be evident.

Broad-fields Design

A variation of disciplinary design is Broad-fields design, also called interdisciplinary. This design combines two or more related topics into a single topic. Citizenship education, for example, combines human rights content, civics, history, and moral education and more. Broad-fields design responds to one of the major weaknesses that is the lack of integration in subject-centric design.

This design is designed to avoid the compartmentalisation of subjects and to integrate the related contents. Broad-scale designers attempt to integrate subjects with similar contents into a broader topic. Two, three or more subjects in this approach are combined into a broad study course. This organisation is a system that combines and consolidates subjects related to a major subject in the curriculum. For example, Home Science will include Needlework, Cookery, Nutrition, Home Management, Clothing and Textiles etc. It is sometimes called a holistic curriculum because it draws around themes and integration. By combining so many subjects, the subjects are studied in less depth and breadth as compared to the deeper content of a single-subject. Broad-fields design is in response to one of the major weaknesses of subject-centred design which is a lack of integration

Strengths of broad-fields curriculum design are:
- It combines separate subjects into a single course. This enables learners to see the relationship among various elements in the curriculum and the information becomes meaningful for the students
- Knowledge will no longer be fragmented or linear but multidisciplinary and multidimensional.
- It saves time on the school timetable.
- Prepares a student for self-reliance and survival skills.

Weaknesses of broad-fields curriculum design are:
- It lacks depth and cultivates shallowness.
- It provides only bits and pieces of information from a variety of subjects.
- It does not account for psychological organisation by which learning takes place.

The Core Curriculum

The core curriculum is an assumption that certain types of learnings are essential for all students. It is a common body of knowledge for everyone. It also takes the philosophy of having certain essential needs in common although learners have different needs. The core curriculum is designed to meet young people's common needs to resolve social life problems. Subject matter identity is ignored, and the content is taken from many of the traditional subject fields, as necessary.

Strengths of this design are:
- It is common. Students share a collective intellectual development experience and achieve common learning results regardless of their school or major.
- It is integrated. The core specifies learning outcomes independent of specific courses. Students can fulfil the same learning goals across the curriculum and connect their learning

across disciplines.

Its weaknesses are:
- Teachers may not be able to promote problem-solving skills and learners may end up memorizing.

Characteristics of a Subject-Centred lesson

Objectives: The objectives are often stated in behavioural terms. The objectives determine the content that the student must learn.

Contents: Subject matter is selected and organised before instruction begins. Contents may be concepts, generalisations, ideas, and processes of skills within the subject area. The experts or teachers select contents.

Material: The textbook is the most used learning material. The student does not take part in selecting the learning materials.

Activities: The traditional activities such as reading, writing, and listening are usually employed for learning the contents.

Grouping: Mostly instruction occurs in the whole class or in the large group.

Instructional Time: Time spent in the classroom is viewed as very critical. Time is divided into blocks so that each subject is taught at a specific time.

Methodology: The teacher chiefly uses lecture and discussion methods to present the contents. The teacher is an expert in the subject area.

Evaluation: An evaluation is performed to see if the student has achieved or learned the behavioural objectives. Regular assessment is frequently done. The degree of performance is indicated by marks or grades. In a subject-centred classroom, the following are characteristics of evaluation:
- Learners' interest or needs have no place.
- Memorisation is mostly encouraged.
- Learners are encouraged to learn passively.
- No place for personal experience of the learner.
- More attention is given to content than to the students.
- It is difficult to develop intellectual processes.

Learner-Centred Curriculum Design

It is an organisational pattern which shifts the focus of education from teacher to student with a view to building the student's independence by connecting the learner's path. The content, activities, materials and learning speeds are determined by the students. This model of learning puts the student (learner) at the centre. The instructor offers students the possibility to learn from each other independently and effectively, to train them in their skills. The learner-centred instruction approach includes such techniques as replacing active learning experiences for lectures, assigning open-ended problems and problems requiring critical or creative thinking. This curriculum design falls under the theoretical influence of Progressivism which stresses the need to make learning more relevant to student needs, abilities, experiences, and interests. With this design learner needs and characteristics are given priority over knowledge of facts and skill. This emphasis is due to the belief that learning is driven by learners' intrinsic motivation, whereby the intrinsically motivated will be independently driven to satisfy their natural inquiry and curiosity.

The curriculum focuses on competencies that allow for lifelong learning such as digital and technological competences, literacy, active citizenship, multilingualism and independent solution of problems. It builds on a constructivist theory of learning which emphasises the role of learners in shaping meaning through new knowledge and past experience. Students choose what they learn and how they evaluate their own learning. Students are playing a more active role here. Therefore, student-centred learning requires that the learner participates actively and responsibly in his/her own learning and in his/her own way. Here the teacher acts as a facilitator of learning for individuals rather than for the class as a whole. A similar design that incorporates the needs and interests of the learners is the experience curriculum. This design can lead to increased motivation to learn, greater retention of knowledge, deeper understanding, and more positive attitudes towards the subject being taught.

Learner-centred designs include three types of design identified as experience/activity design, child-centred design, and humanistic design.

Experience Curriculum Design

Experience, Activity or Project curriculum design is the design in which the experiences, interests and purposes of children determine the selection of and organisation of the educational programme of activities. This programme of activities is planned together by teacher and pupils and is characterised by active participation on the part of the learner, as opposed to passive learning of information from a lecture, talk or demonstration. The learning environment is open and free; no restrictions are defined. Learners choose from various activities the teacher provides and learners are empowered to shape their own learning.

Strengths of this design are:

- Learner–centred curriculum design cuts across subject boundaries and through activities students can explore the interrelatedness and applications to real life situations.
- Its approach is best suited to the natural stages of human development as learners will express needs based on their developmental stages.
- It is flexible in approach. Through teacher and pupil planning, the child is an active participant in the structure of a programme that concerns him.
- Weaknesses of this design are:
- It is too costly as the amount of human and material resources may not span the diversity in students' needs.
- The curriculum is based on children's own needs and interests certainly cannot adequately prepare those children for future life since some areas of interest cannot span the entire spectrum of desirable knowledge for any grade of learners.
- The interest of learners is sometimes difficult to identify.

- Student-centred curriculum lacks definite children's interests and contents.
- It lacks continuity of sequencing because it is based on children's interests.
- Many interests of learners are short-lived.
- Commercial teaching materials neither available nor producible.

Child-centred Design

This design is developed and implemented with an emphasis on learning by playing by children. It is based on the needs, interests, strengths, knowledge, and ability of children. It reflects a range and diversity of experiences to meet the needs, interests, and abilities of children and considers the need for them to pursue their own interests and experience. It recognises the voice of the child and captures the ideas, intentions, objectives and learning strategies of the child. The design is flexible enough to permit changes initiated by children and educators working together and reflects the interests and diversity of the children and the expertise of the teachers. It reflects the connections between children, families and communities and the importance of reciprocal relationships and partnerships for learning and values the cultural and social contexts of children and their families.

Strengths of the Child-Centred Design are:
- It helps the child develop executive skills
- It helps the child become independent, responsible, and confident
- It helps the child develop skills needed to solve his/her own problem
- It enhances the acquisition of knowledge in areas like creative representation, language and literacy, initiative, social relations, music, movements, number, space, and time.
- It gives children and adults the opportunity to invent and discover together as they explore materials, ideas, and experience events.

Weaknesses of the child-centred design are:
- Teachers are sometimes ill-prepared to adapt to changing concepts of child development
- The basic purpose of the establishment of the school is ignored
- The school values are ignored
- The selection of activities is difficult
- The focus is on activities rather than subjects

Humanistic design

The learner as a human being is central to the Humanistic Curriculum, which aims to develop and realize the student's entire human personality. The humanistic curriculum views the student as a complete entity, not as subservient to society, history, or philosophy. According to humanistic curriculum experts, if education succeeds in developing each individual's needs, interests, and aptitudes, students will willingly and intelligently cooperate with one another for the common good. This will ensure a free and universal society with shared rather than competing interests. Thus, humanists emphasize individual freedom and democratic rights in order to build a global community based on the common interests of all people.

The Humanistic Curriculum is based on the belief that education that is good for a person is also good for the nation's well-being. Individual learners are not viewed as passive or easily managed recipients of input in this context. S/he is the organism that chooses or self-selects. To create the Humanistic Curriculum, we must first consider the question, "What does the curriculum mean to the learner?" The Humanistic Curriculum's immediate concern becomes self-understanding, self-actualization, and fostering emotional and physical well-being, as well as the intellectual skills required for independent judgment. Humanists associate educational goals with the ideals of personal growth, integrity, and autonomy. They expect healthier attitudes toward themselves, their peers, and learning.

Strengths of the humanistic design are:

- Emphasises autonomy and free will. It is the only approach in psychology which places the individual's subjective experience and meanings at the centre.
- It is holistic. It places emphasis on the whole of the individual
- It adopts the Client-centred Therapy (CCT) which is supportive of individuals with problems and treats them with respect
- It views the person as an active agent
- It promotes the idea of personal responsibility
- It states that the subjective experiences are of importance and value

Weaknesses of the humanistic design are:

- Teacher is concerned with students' self-esteem and self- concept and places less emphasis on the curriculum
- Since most pedagogy trains teachers on classroom control and discipline it is not easy to find teachers for the humanistic classroom.
- The approach places emphasis on group work. This can be dominated only by extroverts.

Because the focus is on the individual's development, the idea of competition is de-emphasised and makes students less competitive

A typical Learner-centred Lesson

The learner-centred curriculum focuses on the learner. It helps to understand and improve the students.

Objectives: Objectives are not pre-determined by the teacher. Instead, the interests of the students are used for designing instruction.

Contents: Contents are selected in accordance with the needs, interests, and abilities and past experiences of the students.

Materials: Textbooks are not very important since students organise contents by themselves. A wide variety of materials are used by the students

Activities: Activities for learning are planned and selected by students. Teachers are just consulted.

Grouping: Instructional groups are formed using interests or needs of students as the main criteria. Groups are flexible, short-term, and spontaneous.

Time and space: Instructional time is not fixed but flexible. Students learn whenever time is available. The space for learning is unstructured. The classroom is only a central meeting place. Students may learn several resources in the school and community.

Teacher Methodology: The teacher is a co-learner and a facilitator in the learning process. S/he encourages the student's natural approach to learning using field trips, project methods, learning by doing are the teaching methodologies.

Evaluation: Both teacher and student jointly evaluate the learning outcome. The student does self-evaluation. Evaluation is done to determine how the student learns rather than how much s/he learns.

Society-centred Curriculum

The society-centred curriculum also called the problem-centred curriculum places emphasis on the school needs or social problems. This design is geared towards understanding and improving society. It is a curriculum design that empowers learners to conduct research, integrate theory and practice, and apply knowledge and skills to develop a viable solution to a defined problem. Learners are viewed as engaged, self-directed problem solvers, whereas teachers are viewed as facilitators. Learning is viewed as an active, integrated, and constructive process influenced by social and contextual factors in this curriculum. Learners are placed in social settings, and their learning is organized around real-life issues.

One of the hallmarks of the society/problem-centred curriculum is the use of ill-structured problems to allow for free inquiry. Students are presented with a problem that necessitates more information than is initially available. The problem is complex, open-ended, and intriguing enough to pique students' interest and encourage them to engage in inquiry and higher order thinking skills. Second, in this design, each student is assigned the responsibility of gathering relevant information and informing the group in order to develop a viable solution. By interacting, students can develop new ideas, raise questions, and consolidate each other's understanding through collaboration. This curriculum design is influenced by Progressivism whereby students learn best by carrying out real life activities in the community. Two examples of the problem-centred design are the reconstructionist design and the life situation design. These are briefly discussed below:

The Life-situations design

Three assumptions are fundamental to life-situations design: (1) dealing with persistent life situations is critical to a society's successful functioning, and organizing a curriculum around them makes educational sense; (2) students see the relevance of content if it is organized around aspects of community life; and (3) having students study social or life situations will directly involve the The strengths of the life-centred design are:

1. The emphasis on problem-solving procedures is one of the strengths of life-situations design.
2. The integration of process and content into the curricular experience is successful.
3. Another strong feature of life-situations design is that it draws on learners' previous and current experiences to help them analyse the fundamental aspects of living. In this regard, the design differs significantly from experience-centred design, in which learners' perceived

needs and interests are the sole basis for content and experience selection.

4. The design of life situations begins with students' existing concerns as well as society's pressing problems.

5. Life-situations design integrates subject matter, cutting across separate subjects and focusing on related social life categories. It encourages students to learn and use problem-solving techniques.

The weaknesses of the life-situations design are:

1. Students may not learn much about the subject.

2. It is difficult to determine the scope and sequence of essential aspects of living. Will today's major activities become essential in the future?

3. The design of life situations does not adequately expose students to their cultural heritage; additionally, it tends to indoctrinate youth to accept existing conditions, thus perpetuating the social status quo.

4. Teachers may not be adequately prepared to implement life-situations curriculum.

5. The implementation of such a curriculum is hampered by textbooks and other teaching materials.

6. Teachers may be uneasy with the design of life situations because it deviates too far from their norms.

7. The organization of life situations differs from the traditional curriculum promoted by secondary schools, colleges, and universities.

Reconstructionist Design

The primary purpose of the social reconstructionist curriculum is to engage students in critical analysis of the local, national, and international community in order to address humanity's problems. Attention is given to the political practices of business and government groups and their impact on the workforce. Advantages and disadvantages are similar to the society/problem-centred design.

The Society/Problem-centred Lesson

Objectives: The objectives are selected based on community needs. The objectives are not predetermined by the teacher.

Contents: Contents are derived from life in a society or societies. Any content related to the social problem is selected. Problem solving skills, human relation skills and social skills are emphasised rather than the subject matter.

Material: A great variety of materials and resources in the community are used. Original documents are preferred to textbooks.

Activities: Learning activities are organised by both teacher and students. Students' active participation is emphasised.

Grouping: Group work is essential in this design. Grouping of students is done on the basis of student needs and desires.

Time and Space: Instructional time depends upon the type of project undertaken by the students. Rigid allocation of time is minimised. Space for learning includes all the resources of the school and community, which are related to the problem or topic or project under study.

Methodology: The teacher is the facilitator of the learning process. Direct observation, field study and direct experience are the methods used by the teacher.

Evaluation: Evaluation is jointly done by the teacher and students. Evaluation puts emphasis on the performance or actions related to the social problems.

In many educational systems across the world, designs that are centred around subjects or academic disciplines seem to be the commonest. However, many of such designs incorporate elements of other designs to give the curriculum a holistic orientation.

Curriculum Design Tips

The following curriculum design tips can help educators direct each stage of the curriculum design process.

Identify the needs of stakeholders: A needs analysis which involves the collection and analysis of data related to the learner needs to be carried out. This data might include learners' interests, previous knowledge and what they need to know to be proficient in a particular area or skill. It may also include information about learner perceptions, strengths, and weaknesses.

Create a list of learning goals and outcomes. Based on the results of the needs analysis, goals should be stated. This helps the curriculum worker to focus on the intended purpose of the curriculum and effectively plan instruction that can achieve the knowledge, skills, and attitudes that students should achieve in the course.

Identify practical constraints: After identifying the direction to go based on the goals it is important to identify constraints that will impact the curriculum design. For example, time and resources are common constraints that must be considered. If there is not enough time to deliver all the instruction that has been planned, it will impact learning outcomes. So, priorities must be established.

Create a curriculum map (also known as a curriculum matrix). This will help you to properly evaluate the sequence and coherence of instruction. Curriculum mapping provides visual diagrams or indexes of a curriculum. Analysing a visual representation of the curriculum is a good way to identify potential gaps, redundancies, or alignment issues quickly and easily in the sequencing of instruction. Curriculum maps can be created on paper or with software programs or online services designed specifically for this purpose.

Identify the instructional methods that will be used throughout the course and think of how they will work with student learning styles. If the instructional methods are not conducive to the curriculum, the instructional design or the curriculum design can incorporate other methods to respond to diversity.

Establish evaluation methods. These will be used to assess and judge learners, instructors, and the curriculum. Evaluation helps to determine if the curriculum design is working or if it is failing. Examples of things that should be evaluated include the strengths and weaknesses of the curriculum and achievement rates related to learning outcomes. Evaluation should be both formative and summative.

Remember that curriculum design is a multi-step procedure: Curriculum design requires continuous improvement. The design of the curriculum should be assessed regularly and refined based on assessment data. This may involve adjusting in order to maximise the probability of the achievement of learning outcomes.

10

Development of Curriculum Materials

Strictly speaking, the curriculum design process focuses on creating specifications for the curriculum but development of those specifications to produce curriculum materials is intertwined with design activities. Design and development of curriculum materials constitute the central activity of curriculum planning. To ensure consistency and quality in curriculum design, curriculum materials are developed as evidence of the intended curriculum. Accordingly, conventional curriculum materials are tangible resources that guide teacher planning and implementation of lessons while curriculum support materials are those resources that direct the teacher and student how to better exploit the conventional materials.

Conventional materials include curriculum frameworks, syllabuses, and textbooks, usually designed and developed at the macro-level of curriculum planning. Schemes of work and lesson plans are designed and developed more often at the microlevel. Non-conventional materials which include teachers' guides, handbooks, student workbooks, manuals, and school timetables are developed at the appropriate levels. This chapter presents and discusses principles and procedures for developing curriculum materials that are used for curriculum implementation.

Curriculum Frameworks

The word curriculum is sometimes used interchangeably with syllabus but in strict terms, curriculum as a document is a broad description of educational goals and content with an underlying philosophy whereas a syllabus is a more detailed and operational document for teaching and learning derived from curriculum goals and focused on one subject or one theme. The general curriculum document often referred to as a curriculum framework, describes the educational environment in which syllabuses can be developed. According to Staback (2007), a curriculum framework is a technical tool which establishes parameters for the development of other curriculum documents such as subject syllabuses; it is also an agreed social document which defines and expresses national priorities for education and aspirations for the future of a nation.

A curriculum framework is most often developed at the national level, but another form of curriculum framework could be developed at the international level by a group of countries with similar goals and educational environments. For example, there are many global curriculum frameworks targeting Education for Sustainable Development.

A curriculum framework commonly contains the elements described in Table 10.1. However, elements can be added to or deleted from the framework structure to suit the needs of the education system developing it.

Table 10.1. Components of a curriculum framework

Component	Tasks for the developer
Introduction of the context	Describe the social and economic environment in which teaching, and learning occur and where the curriculum policy will operate
Policy statements	Describe the government's philosophy and vision for education, such as universal literacy and numeracy, the development of skills needed for economic prosperity in the twenty first century and the creation of a stable society.
Statements of learning goals and outcomes for each school level or cycle	Describe in broad terms what students should know and be able to do when they complete schooling. Outcomes should be expressed in a range of domains, including knowledge, skills and competencies, values, and attitudes.
Structure of the education system	Describe the school system within which the curriculum framework is to be applied. description should specify number of years of schooling, stages or cycles of schooling and their durations and number of weeks in the school year including number of hours or teaching periods per week.
Structure of curriculum content	• produce a scope and sequence chart. It shows the organisation of content within the framework and the extent to which schools and students can make choices. • state the pattern of Subjects or Learning Areas to be studied in each stage or cycle (such as compulsory and elective subjects). • give brief description of each Subject or Learning Area outlining the rationale for its inclusion in the curriculum and the contribution it makes to the achievement of the Learning outcomes • state the number of hours to be assigned to each subject or learning area in each stage or cycle
Resources required for implementation	Describe and state the quality and quantity of human, material, and financial resources needed. This should include: Teachers and qualifications, teaching load (number of classes per week); Students – number per class in each subject; Materials such as textbooks, computers, other equipment; facilities such as classrooms, furniture, and fittings.

Component	Tasks for the developer
Teaching methodology	Describe the pedagogical orientation or range of teaching approaches that might be used in implementing the framework.
Assessing learner achievement	Describe assessment strategies, techniques and instruments and frequency of evaluating learning outcomes. Certification procedures should be described as well.

Once a curriculum framework is agreed upon, syllabuses, textbooks and other documents can be developed. The curriculum framework guides syllabus and textbook writers.

Syllabuses

A syllabus is a document produced primarily for teachers' use, indicating goals and objectives, content, and strategies for teaching, learning and evaluation according to subject areas or themes (see Appendix B). Anja and Fonche (2001) describe a syllabus as an outline of work to be done over a year with a class in each subject. There are teaching syllabuses and examination syllabuses although syllabuses tend to be associated with examinations. Teaching syllabuses may be developed centrally, locally or by individual teachers depending on the system of curriculum planning practiced in the context, and they may have the status of support materials or official documents which must be used. Regardless of their contents or status, syllabuses should be consistent with statements made in the curriculum framework.

Components of a Syllabus

Syllabuses provide a range of information and can contain the following components:

The rationale for the subject

This section states the reason(s) why the course or subject is included in the curriculum and states its relationship to student outcomes stated in the curriculum framework document.

Goals and objectives of the subject

Goals provide a big picture of purpose or direction of a course while objectives describe short term learning expectations geared towards attainment of goals.

1. Learning outcomes

They represent what is achieved in a course as opposed to mere intentions. In stating learning outcomes, knowledge, skills and values to be attained must be specified possibly at each stage or year. Statements describe what a learner demonstrates to show mastery of objectives.

2. Content

This should be expressed as topics, themes, or units to be covered in each stage or year and requirements for teaching the content.

3. Teaching strategies

There should be a description of general ways to approach instruction. These could be stated in terms of direct teaching, indirect teaching, learner-centred strategies, experiential learning, problem and project-based strategies etc.

4. **Strategies for evaluating student achievement:**

The frequency and purpose of assessment as well as the assessment instruments should be stated. Evaluation and certification (where applicable) criteria should be stated.

Relationship Between a Curriculum and a Syllabus

As noted earlier, the term curriculum is sometimes used interchangeably with other related terms like syllabus and course, but clarification needs to be made by showing their relationships and differences. Curriculum can refer to any level of an educational experience, ranging from that of a particular area within a course, to the course itself, to a broader programme of study that comprises several different courses around a particular content area. It is therefore appropriate in this sense to talk about a primary school curriculum, a science curriculum, or a biology curriculum. Curriculum is therefore, broadly used to refer to a focus of study, consisting of various programs and courses all designed to reach a particular proficiency or qualification while syllabus refers to the content or subject matter, instructional strategies and evaluation means of an individual course (Musingafi, Mhute, Zebron, Kaseke, 2015). In effect, a syllabus is contained in the curriculum. Both a curriculum framework and syllabuses may appear in a single document, or they may be prepared as two separate documents. The differences between a curriculum and a syllabus are summarised in table 10.2.

Table 10.2. Differences between curriculum and syllabus

BASIS FOR COMPARISON	SYLLABUS	CURRICULUM
Meaning	Syllabus is the document that contains all the portions of the concepts covered in a subject or course.	Curriculum is the overall content, taught in an educational system or a program.
Origin	From a Greek term.	From a Latin term.
Coverage	A subject or course	A program or school level
Nature	Descriptive	Prescriptive
Scope	Narrow	Wide
Duration	For a fixed period, normally a year.	Till the program lasts.

Textbooks

A textbook is an organised body of written material for the formal study of a subject area (Coolidge, 2014). Written material may be presented in print or electronic form. Textbooks are schoolbooks. They are developed by subject matter experts or experienced teachers in collaboration with editors and publishers. Textbooks grow out of syllabuses and in some cases, they are the main curriculum reference materials for students. Students use textbooks for self-directed learning, preparation, and revision of formal lessons. Teachers use them as resources for lesson planning.

Characteristics of a Good Textbook

1. Content (subject matter). A high-quality textbook contains current, relevant, and accurate subject matter that aligns with the goals and objectives of the syllabus or curriculum document from which it derives. Sources of information are usually indicated either in-text or as references or bibliography at the end of the book. Concepts presented in textbooks should be precise and relevant to students' prior experiences. There should be a balance between breadth and depth in the treatment of concepts. The level of subject matter difficulty should be consistent with curriculum requirements and cognitive level of students. To avoid bias, it is important for textbook writers to have multiple perspectives and balanced viewpoints of issues raised, when presenting subject matter.

2. Pedagogical features. Well written textbooks contain features that facilitate teaching and learning. A textbook should be capable of instructing a learner with or without support from a live teacher. This requires the textbook writer not to be limited to subject content knowledge but also have pedagogical content knowledge (PCK). By pedagogical content knowledge, it is meant the way knowledge about teaching relates to the subject matter under consideration; to produce a blend of pedagogy and content. Three components of PCK are: knowledge of tasks, knowledge of students' prior knowledge and knowledge of instructional methods (Krauss et al, 2008). Pedagogical features of a textbook should therefore include:

- Examples and illustrations to help the student grasp ideas and concepts better. Visuals in the form of tables, pictures and highlighted keywords capture attention and motivate learners.
- An internally consistent style that arouses the reader's interest and stimulates active engagement in the learning process.
- Opportunities for learners to practice newly acquired knowledge through interesting learning activities.
- Coherent presentation of subject matter in suitable learning chunks.
- A balance of learning experiences for factual knowledge acquisition, building of intellectual skills and the development of positive attitudes and values.
- Utility for future reference for example glossary, index of words and bibliography.
- For e-textbooks, special features like multimedia, interactive learning activities and hypertexts enhance learning effectiveness.

3. Textbook structure. The main body of a textbook consists of parts, chapters, sections, and subsections. To facilitate exploitation, there is a table of contents, chapter titles, headings, and outlines. Chapter beginnings often have learning objectives, an introduction and focus questions; Chapter endings include summaries, learning activities and revision questions.

4. Language. The language used in textbooks should be concise and tailored to the level of the target audience. Rules of grammar and sentence construction should be respected. New vocabulary should be introduced progressively, and students provided with the meanings of words in a special section called the glossary.

5. Design. The overall layout of a textbook should make it appealing and easy for teachers and students to use. Physical features such as font type and size, line spacing, margins and paper quality are as important as the content relevance and accuracy of the book.

Procedures of Textbook Development

Student needs and expected learning outcomes are the starting point for textbook writing. In addition, textbook writers must seek to understand national textbook policies before engaging in textbook writing projects. Information should be sought concerning the subjects that require textbooks, the language of instruction, evaluation and authorisation of textbooks, printing, and publishing.

Textbook Writing, Manufacture, and Distribution

From experience in curriculum practice, these steps can be gleaned and recommended as guidelines for textbook writers to follow.

- Write the first draft
- Give to editor for review and comments
- Do a second draft based on editors' comments
- Obtain further comments from editor and make revisions
- Try out the material
- Do further revision
- Submit manuscript to publisher.
- Publisher produces and distributes textbooks according to the model of textbook development practiced in the country.

Models of Textbook Development

1. Ministry of Education publications. In some countries, there are publishing units in ministries of education charged with the production of all textbooks.

2. Market-driven textbook development. In other countries, there is decentralisation and market liberalisation. Government authorities issue syllabuses and guidelines to the public and invite writers to make submissions. After evaluation, one or more texts are selected for each subject and recommended to schools for adoption. Schools may be empowered to choose the textbooks which they believe will best support their teachers and students in achieving the learning outcomes prescribed in the syllabuses.

3. Supplementary resources. Teachers are trained in developing teaching and learning resources which supplement the textbook, and which support specific learning activities in their classroom. These resources can be sourced from the media, the internet or other print, video or digital material. The result is the development of a bank of resources which make learning interesting and cater for the individual differences of students in particular locations and circumstances. teachers should have teaching-learning resources available in addition to textbooks. Access to the internet opens enormous opportunities for the provision of materials to supplement textbooks and enrich the learning environment.

Textbook Evaluation

Before they are allowed for use in schools, textbooks are evaluated on selected criteria that include social relevance and interest. Only approved textbooks are authorised for use. Each of the models cited has advantages and disadvantages. In some countries where there are multiple choices of textbooks, publishers have complained on several occasions of inconsistencies in appraisals by evaluation commissions, insinuating favouritism and conflict of interest (Hunt, 2006)).

Schemes of Work/ Course outlines

When syllabuses are prepared centrally, they are sent to schools by the authorities concerned. There is a need to divide the yearly content of the syllabus into a definite amount of work that may be covered per term or semester. If, for instance, there were thirty topics to be covered for first year mathematics, this content may be divided into ten topics per term. When the mathematics teacher splits the year's work into portions to be studied per term, indicating weekly attributions, we have what is called, schemes of work (See Appendix B). Accordingly, a scheme of work describes the content and learning experiences that should be treated every term of the academic year (Okai, 2010).

Schemes of work are also called course outlines notably at the university level (see Appendix C). The scheme of work or course outline is very important to the teacher in that it guides the planning of instructional units and consequently the daily lessons in line with the time available for each topic in the term or semester. The scheme of work also guides supervisors of schools in determining the efforts of the schools and teachers towards meeting the societal demands on them. In some educational systems, schemes of work are handed to classroom teachers by local education authorities and classroom teachers only engage in unit and lesson planning.

In educational systems where course syllabuses are prepared by individual classroom teachers, syllabuses take the form of schemes of work and course outlines.

Elements of a Course Outline

The essential components of a course outline are the same as those of a syllabus in addition to a time frame for execution of the teaching plan. However, other elements like a teacher's name, room and telephone number, subject code, subject title, and description of class where applicable, may be added. All the elements described here may not feature on all course outlines. Teachers may leave out what they consider non-essentials depending on the learners they are dealing with.

Basic information: The course title and number, meeting times and location, credit value, and semester.

Instructor information: Office location and hours, appointment scheduling, phone numbers, contact information for teaching or lab assistants.

Prerequisites: Courses, knowledge, or skills students should already have.

Required texts and materials: List of all required textbooks, technology, and other materials (packets, programs, Internet access, and so on) with information about editions, volumes, and other details; for difficult-to-find materials and hints on locating copies.

Course description: Summary of what the course covers, with more details than the short catalogue descriptions, to give the students a more complete picture of what you will (and will not) include.

Course purpose: Explanation of why students should take this course, how it is relevant to them, how it will help them now and in the future.

Course learning outcomes: List of three to five learning outcomes of the course which is what you want the students to really "get" from their experience, the ideas/experiences they will remember many years from now. These should be related to students' lives, should be challenging yet attainable, and inspiring.

Student learning goals: A space for students to record their own goals and hopes for the course. Ask students to fill in these goals and refer to them regularly.

Classroom procedure: Summary of the basic routines and learning activities for the course, how you will assess students' knowledge and skills, what they can expect from you and what you expect from them.

Participation: Explanation of how you expect students to participate in your class, how they should prepare, and how you will assess their participation.

Recommended: Helpful tips and hints for students about how to get the most out of your course, how to study for the assignments and exams, and other suggestions that will help them excel in your class.

Tips on using the plan: Explanation of how students can use the course plan to best advantage.

Grading procedures: A breakdown of each assignment and examination, what it is worth, how you weight scores, and percentages for each grade level.

Assignment descriptions: Descriptions and directions for each type of assignment, quiz, exam, and so on, or directions to more detailed directions; this is the information students need to understand the course assessments. Again, assignments should be linked to students' lives, challenging yet attainable, and inspiring.

Course schedule: A calendar of class days, dates, topic titles, learning outcomes, assignments, exams, and so on, with an explanation of how the teacher will handle scheduling changes if necessary.

Course policies: Policy statements and standards you expect the students to meet. These may include standard statements from the University, college, or department. Be sure to add the University's required policy statement.

Lesson Plans

A lesson plan is a document that guides teachers on what to do to a certain group of students in a certain time. For every lesson, it is a sort of roadmap. There are a variety of lesson plan models and templates that teachers can choose from depending on context. These are available in Pedagogy textbooks and some educational websites. Lesson plans ensure a logical, systematic process for teachers that maximises the learning of students. At least four essential parts of an ideal lesson plan should be included: educational objectives, warm-up activity, techniques, and procedures for achieving teaching goals and assessment.

The importance of Planning Lessons

- Helps teachers to think through what learners will achieve in the lesson.
- Provides a framework for organising ideas, methodology, materials etc.
- Helps teachers to know where they are going and how they are going to get there.
- Helps make the lesson coherent.
- Avoids over-reliance on coursebooks.
- Demonstrates to learners that the teacher knows what s/he's doing.
- Being prepared boosts teacher confidence.
- Helps to identify any problems or difficulties which may arise during the lesson.
- Helps teachers to adapt to different classes.
- Helps to identify the kinds of activities and materials to include to achieve aims. (British Council, 2008 p.4).

Essentials of a Good Lesson Plan

It should be written. A lesson plan should preferably be written and not remain at the oral or mental stage. A plan is a written note of a teachers' preparation efforts. Writing helps in clarifying thoughts and concentration.

It should have clear objectives. The lesson plan should clearly state the specific instructional objectives to be attained.

It should be linked with the previous knowledge. The plan should make provision for relating the lesson to students' prior knowledge.

It should show methods of teaching. It should clearly state the various steps that the teacher is going to take, and various questions that he will ask.

Instructional materials. The illustrative aids to be used should be indicated in the lesson plan.

Suitable subject matter: The content of instruction or subject matter should be carefully selected or organised.

It should be divided into stages: The plan must indicate the various stages of the lesson, the activities of the teacher and the learner and the duration per stage.

It should provide for activity: The children must be given enough opportunity to actively participate in the lesson.

It should provide for individual differences: The plan should be prepared in such a way as it does full justice to all the students of varied abilities.

It should suggest reading resources: The plan indicates other reading material. This will motivate the bright students to do extra reading. Care should be taken to suggest only that material which is available.

It should include assignments for students: A good lesson plan cannot be thought of without appropriate assignments for the students to help students apply knowledge learnt. Assignments can take different forms.

General Principles for Development of Curriculum Materials

In chapter one, the main components of a curriculum were described. The principles presented here are guidelines on how these components should be decided on and presented inside curriculum documents and materials.

Guidelines lines relating to setting goals and objectives

Goals and objectives should be derived from various sources such as:

- The nature of the subject matter,
- Philosophical sources,
- The cultural and economic needs of the society,
- Student growth and development needs,
- The nature of the learning process and
- Situational analysis reports and
- Educational forces (Print, 2020)

Goals and objectives should be comprehensive. This means that they should cover all areas of development of the learner in a consistent manner. Goals should aim at the intellectual, physical, social, and emotional development of the learner.

Goals should be realistic. They should be statements of purpose that are attainable given the resources and facilities present in the community. They should be stated clearly in the curriculum document in such a way that the classroom teacher can exploit them to develop instructional objectives (objectives at the level of lesson plans).

Selecting appropriate content

The content of a curriculum is determined to a large extent by the nature of knowledge, the sources of knowledge and the knowledge that society considers as worth passing on to younger generations. It is known that knowledge can be obtained by revelation of authority; discovery or experimentation, logic or reflection and collective perception (common sense). Selection is crucial because everything that qualifies as worthwhile knowledge cannot possibly be fitted into a curriculum. Knowledge must be filtered somehow to obtain that which is necessary. There should be established criteria for selecting content. There is no doubt that subject content selection is a highly political activity because syllabus committees argue, negotiate, and debate to control the content (Print, 2020).

After different subjects or themes of knowledge have been selected and stated in general curriculum plans, these knowledge domains are broken down and stated in subject (course) syllabuses in the form of content outlines. In a syllabus, the content of a subject consists of the facts, concepts, laws, principles, and themes of that subject. One of the challenges of selecting content to include in syllabuses is to determine what to include or leave out. How broad or how deep should the content be? The following guidelines may guide curriculum developers to overcome some of these challenges.

1. A curriculum document should not be loaded with subject matter that cannot be covered by the school, given the time and resources available.

2. Select content according to importance, validity, and suitability, social relevance, learnability, and utility (Tyler, 1949; Wheeler, 1967; Ornstein and Hunkins, 2018; Print 2020). By validity it is meant that the content should be related to the objectives, and it should not be outdated.

3. Sources of content should be indicated where possible for example, recommended textbooks, oral tradition etc.

4. An outline of subject matter for each topic or theme chosen should be provided in order to facilitate instructional planning. This process should follow the scope and sequence determined at the design stage.

Selecting teaching/ learning strategies

Only broad indications of teaching/learning strategies should be stated in syllabuses so that teachers can adapt their work to the specific groups of learners they have to deal with. There are learner-centred teaching strategies and teacher-centred teaching strategies can be found in many texts on teaching methods. It is important to include in a syllabus, different types of teaching/ learning strategies. The principle of variety has been articulated extensively in many curriculum development texts. It is also important to select the strategies in relation to the ages of the learners, the environment, time available and competence of the teachers. These broad statements should be made in a suggestive rather than a prescriptive manner.

Selecting teaching/learning materials

A syllabus should contain a suggestion of materials like textbooks. Textbooks could be basal, co-basal or supplementary. Selecting textbooks to include in syllabuses is very crucial because there are myriads of books in the world but not all of them are suitable for teaching and learning. Textbooks for inclusion in syllabuses should be selected with care. Some factors to be considered when selecting textbooks are:

- The content and scope of the book. Is the author competent in the field? Are the required topics treated in sufficient depth and breadth? Is the writing style suitable for the age of the learners? Mechanical features of the book such as typing, printing, legibility and quality of paper should not be neglected.
- Other materials suggested should be of different types. In addition to print materials, audio, visual, electronic, and integrated media could be suggested.

Selecting teaching/learning activities

Learning experiences are embedded in materials and methods as well as in activities. For example, if a learning goal in primary mathematics is that "pupils should know how to calculate the volume of objects" they should not only listen to lectures on the required formulae, but they should be given written exercises requiring the calculation of volumes of objects.

Instructional activities for inclusion in a curriculum document must be carefully selected in a way that each one reflects the kind of learning experience desired for the learner. Syllabuses and other curriculum documents should therefore indicate suggestions of learning activities that provide learner with experiences that can result in the attainment of stated goals and objectives.

It is important to note that learning experiences that may result in the development of attitudes and values are not necessarily the same as those that stimulate thinking or enhance motor activity. Different goals may call for different instructional activities. One activity may also produce multiple outcomes. For example, singing the national anthem would teach pupils patriotism, pronunciation of some new words and music. Stated activities should be varied. Activities could take the form of laboratory work, field trips, drama etc. Variety is very important and necessary to meet the needs of different individuals. Learners have different learning styles. There are visual, auditory, and kinaesthetic learners. So, it would be profitable to all learners if activities that emphasise the stimulation of different senses are included in the curriculum document.

Selecting evaluation instruments

It is characteristic of school programmes to end with examinations, for the purpose of certification. Syllabuses are therefore often associated with examinations. Evaluation of learner achievement is usually made through examinations. Assessment refers to the collection and analysis of data regarding the extent to which learning objectives have been achieved. After assessments, value judgments are made to qualify them thus completing the process of evaluation. Put differently we can say evaluation equals assessment plus value judgments.

- A well written syllabus should indicate the purpose of assessment. (i.e., the assessment goals and objectives)
- There should be an indication of various assessment instruments and strategies to be used in the process for example, written test, oral t tests, performance tests; criterion- referenced or norm referenced testing.
- The frequency of evaluation should be indicated. Continuous evaluation versus terminal evaluation should be decided upon.

Development of Curriculum Support Materials

Support materials like teachers' guides and student manuals are developed following the same procedures as the development of textbooks and conventional curriculum materials. The school timetable is a special kind of support material for curriculum and instruction. It needs to be carefully constructed.

The School Timetable

A timetable is a schedule of events that guides school activities throughout the day, week, term, or year. It is a four-dimensional table that considers the teacher, the student (class), classroom and time slot (period). A timetable specifies a starting time and an ending time for each activity. In some cases, it indicates who is involved and how the activity will be conducted. A well-prepared timetable will impact significantly on the teaching and learning process in the classroom. The shortest duration on the timetable is called a period or module. The length of a teaching period or module varies from school and from level to level although the range is normally between 30 minutes and

40 minutes. However, there are schools that use blocks instead of periods. A block is generally an hour or more. Blocks of periods can be used to teach science, language, and practical subjects when more than one period is needed. Timetables can be prepared manually or using specialised software.

Types of Timetables

Master Timetable: It is a general timetable prepared by the Head teacher or school principal. This timetable shows when the school day begins and ends and also shows the activities for each day. It further shows which teacher will teach which subject to which class, on what day and at what times.

Department timetable: From the master timetable or general timetable, each department prepares the timetable that should be followed by all the members of the department. Each teacher notes their class and subject from the department timetable and create a class timetable or individual timetable. Class and individual timetables can be extracted from the master timetable.

Class timetable: A class timetable is drawn either from the general timetable or department timetable. A class timetable shows the starting and ending time for each subject or activity of each class or level in the school and teachers or personnel in charge of each activity.

Individual timetable: Teachers and students can extract their timetables from the general timetable to obtain individual timetables. Individual timetables for teachers show when, where and at what time they are expected to teach during the school week.

The role of a school timetable

Communication. All stakeholders of the school are informed about what is done, when, where, by whom and at what times.

Resources Allocation: Time is distributed according to specifications in the syllabus. Teachers are assigned according to school needs and their levels of experience. Facilities are scheduled in a way that benefits all users. Equipment needed for each class is identified and allocated.

Control: Starting and ending times are specified for each activity. Staff responsibilities are indicated for each person to know and act accordingly.

Accountability: Timetables can be used to check on what has been done, when and by whom. This is the responsibility of designated curriculum managers like Vice principals, dean of studies and heads of department.

Monitoring tool: Teachers can easily plan and monitor their own work and the children's progress with a timetable. Heads of Ministry of Education authorities can monitor what is happening in the schools.

Factors That Influence Timetabling

Available time: It determines the number of activities that can be accommodated in a school day as well as how often each subject is taught, also considering the number of contact hours prescribed by education authorities.

Number of teachers: It determines how many subjects or classes a teacher will teach in a school and determines class size.

Facilities available: They determine distribution of learning resources and the number of sessions that facilities can be in use.

Number of subjects: Determines size of periods and what time can be allocated for co-curricular activities.

Principles for effective timetable construction

Official regulations: The duration of an academic year determines the time available for studies and co-curricular activities. Workload for each course or subject should match the time available according to official regulations. Curriculum policy usually defines the duration of a school day and weekly schedules for individual subjects. The length of teaching time should not fall below the minimum required by the Ministries of Education.

Incidence of fatigue: Some subjects are more fatiguing than others so they should not be put on the timetable consecutively. Mental freshness is more in the morning and after recreation. Subjects that are mentally demanding should come in the morning or after break. Length of periods for young learners should be shorter and depend on the nature of the activity.

Principle of justice: For fairness and equity, the teaching load for every teacher should be almost the same. The timetable should be planned by the entire staff to avoid unnecessary conflicts among them. Some teachers and school subjects should not consistently appear in the morning periods and others in the afternoon.

Principle of variety: The same teacher should not be programmed to teach consecutively for many periods. Where possible the same room should not be used for all the subjects. Theory should alternate with practical lessons.

Play and recreation: Lesson periods should be punctuated with break periods. This enables learners to satisfy their physiological needs and relax their brains. The number and length of the break periods should depend on the length of the school day and the age of learners.

Free periods for teachers: Teachers are entitled to free periods within the working week. This increases teachers' efficiency and provides time for correction of work. Such free periods should be spent in the staff room.

Maximum utilisation of resources: Learners should benefit from more experienced staff. Therefore, qualification of teachers, room size, should be kept in mind when constructing a timetable. More experienced staff to be assigned to beginners.

Flexibility. Timetables should not be rigid. They should be revised from time to time as need arises.

11

Curriculum Implementation and Change

Curriculum implementation and curriculum change are two highly interwoven processes, to a point where one cannot be discussed without the other. It is commonplace for educators to think of curriculum implementation narrowly in terms of instruction only. Mkpa (2007) defines curriculum implementation as the task of translating the curriculum document into the operating curriculum by the combined efforts of the students, teachers and others concerned. This definition points to the process of instruction only. Other definitions imply that other important tasks and change processes are involved in implementation, without which the instructional process cannot effectively take place. Curriculum implementation therefore entails all that it takes to put into practice the officially prescribed courses of study, syllabuses, and subjects (Chikumbi and Makamure (2005). This includes curriculum management and instructional supervision. Perspectives, tasks and models of curriculum implementation and change will be presented and discussed in this chapter.

Perspectives

To support the broader view of curriculum implementation that incorporates change processes, Hawes in his book *Curriculum and reality in African classrooms*, states that curriculum implementation involves:

- Workshops for the training of pilot teachers
- Training and re-training of educational administrators, inspectors, head teachers, principals, tutors and teachers or lecturers
- Introduction of new plans and materials into schools
- Changes in organisation at school or class level, e.g., staff deployment
- Provision of material resources and facilities for teachers and other curriculum workers
- Changes in patterns of assessment and examinations
- Explanation of changes to parents and other stakeholders (Hawes, 1979).

Ornstein and Hunkins (1988) recognise implementation as a different component in the process of curriculum development seeing it as the logical step once a programme has been developed and piloted. They also point out that implementation involves change. It includes changing individuals' knowledge, actions, and attitudes. Obviously, this takes time. They also suggest that implementation is an interaction process between those who have created the programme and those who are to deliver it and the end users.

Curriculum change means introducing a new instrument in the curriculum, to give it a new direction. This may include modifications to its philosophy, aims and objectives, content, methods, and assessment modes. Curriculum change is a process that includes curriculum innovation and improvement. When a new element is introduced in the curriculum that increases its quality, some improvement has taken place. Curriculum reforms and change are inevitable. Society is dynamic and values change over time. Globalisation has also brought unintended and unpredictable educational and curriculum implications. Education must reflect changes in society because education reflects social needs. Thus nations, states, local communities, and schools are renovating their curricula, as their current curricula are no longer relevant. The curricular change is an important educational process which can transform the capacity and quality of the institutions. The curriculum change process includes defining what needs to be changed and identifying possible solutions to problems as well as achieving the necessary changes.

Some educational goals of many African countries have not been achieved because of setbacks in curriculum implementation. Among other factors impeding curriculum implementation in Nigeria, Ahmadi (2015) identified challenges relating to adaptations to change resulting from new programs, as a significant factor.

Tasks Relating to Curriculum Implementation and Change

Professional training of key implementers

Faced with school-based curriculum work, teachers and other key implementers need to understand the underlying philosophies and expectations laid out in a curriculum framework document. Exposure to such knowledge means preparing needed human resources for curriculum implementation through pre-service and in-service training. Pre-service training takes place in teacher training colleges. Duration of training varies with entry qualifications and level of certification. In service training usually takes the form of refresher courses, seminars, and workshops for personnel already in the field of practice. Such training is necessary to help teachers effect curriculum change that comes with introduction of new curricula.

Resource Allocation

Resource is a collective name given to means, money, materials, or skills available to individuals or an institution for the purpose of achieving specified objectives. Allocation in this context alludes to decisions on the quantity of resources to be made available or set aside for achieving an objective. Resource allocation therefore refers to how government, local authorities and schools make resources available for the achievement of educational goals and objectives as specified in the curriculum. When resources made available for schools to achieve curricular goals and objectives are scarce and limited, there is need for them to be carefully allocated.

Educational resources can be grouped into three categories: financial, human, and material resources.

1. **Financial Resources**

Financial resources allocated for curriculum implementation are used for:
- Paying teachers and administrators salaries,
- Purchase of teaching and learning materials such as books and chalk,
- Training and professional development of teachers,
- Providing school infrastructure,
- Maintenance and repair of school equipment and infrastructure,
- Taking care of running costs of schools and
- Learner's welfare.

2. **Human Resources**

Human resources are needed for implementation and invariably, the attainment of curriculum objectives. These are teachers, inspectors, counsellors, and school administrators. The quantity and quality of human resources determine the quality of teaching and learning which in turn determines the extent to which curriculum objectives are attained. For effective implementation of new programs, staff recruitment, deployment and redeployment needs to take place.

3. **Material Resources**

Material resources for smooth functioning of activities in an educational establishment include buildings, playgrounds, laboratories, libraries, vehicles, and equipment. These are needed for effective curriculum implementation and change. Inadequate supply or absence of these materials hinders effective school administration, teaching and the learning process. There must be changes in building and equipment policies to accommodate curriculum innovations during implementation.

Curriculum resources come from different sources. Sources of curriculum resources include the government, Ministries of Education, local authorities, the school, parents, and teachers.

i) Government: The government allocates financial resources to the Ministry of Education yearly in the form of budget. The government also trains, recruits, and pays teachers and other school personnel.

ii) The Ministry of Education: The Ministry of Education shares the financial resources allocated by the government in cash or in terms of materials to education establishments in the regions, divisions, and sub-divisions.

iii) Local Authority: Local authorities such as urban and rural councils generate financial resources and allocate a fraction for education. Local authorities also allocate resources to schools for the construction of buildings and playgrounds. They also hire teachers when they are in short supply.

iv) Schools: The following resources are available in schools:
- Money generated from school fees/tuition, sport fees, levies, and government grants.
- Infrastructure or physical facilities (classrooms, laboratories, libraries, playgrounds).
- Equipment (radio, television, and computers).
- Teachers and
- Books.

v) Parents: Parents provide financial resources to schools through school fees. Parents also make donations to schools and buy the school needs of their children. Financial and other contributions also come in through parent teacher associations.

vi) Teachers: Their resourcefulness consists of knowledge, skills, and time. Teachers use their expertise to translate curriculum objectives into learning experiences for their students.

At the school level, resource allocation is the responsibility of the school head. The head teacher or principal deploys teachers to subject areas and/or classes based on the teachers' competence, experience, and specialisation. Material resources are allocated to teachers and classes based on the amount available and the number of students to benefit from these resources. The teachers in turn ensure equitable allocation of resources amongst their students. The timetable is used to allocate time for instruction.

Procedures in Curriculum Implementation

After the technical process of curriculum design and production of curriculum materials in the form of syllabuses, teachers and learners' guides, textbooks and support materials, the next phase of the curriculum process is implementation in schools. Curriculum work expands from a central focus on a national framework to efforts by classroom teachers, learners, educational administrators (curriculum managers), parents, and other community members at the school level. Major tasks and steps include piloting, diffusion and dissemination, adoption, adaptation, integration, and monitoring.

Piloting

This is the trial phase of implementation. Curriculum materials are usually tried out with a smaller population before full implementation. Trials could be done in a few schools called pilot schools or in all the schools. In the latter case, it is called a field trial. The present Cameroon secondary school teaching syllabuses underwent field trial in the 2012/2013 academic year before full implementation in 2014. This phase can pass for both curriculum implementation and curriculum evaluation. Both pilot and field trials aim at identifying areas for improvement. thus performing the function of formative evaluation.

Adoption

It is the official launching of the curriculum. Together with piloting, adoption constitutes the initiation phase of the newly minted product, the curriculum. Adoption usually takes the form of an official ceremony presided over by educational authorities and attended by a cross section of stakeholders. For example, the present nursery and primary school curricula in Cameroon were adopted on 19 July 2018 in Yaoundé. The ceremony was presided over by the Minister of Basic Education.

Diffusion and Dissemination

Information about the curriculum must spread to its end users and stakeholders. Effective communication is needed for the survival of a curriculum system. Information must flow among key participants in the implementation process. In addition to government officials and few representatives of teachers usually present in curriculum adoption ceremonies, parents, learners, textbook writers, and producers ought to have adequate information on the nature of new curricula.

Adaptation and Integration

Classroom teachers have the duty of operationalising the curriculum. In this process they make adaptations to the contents by integrating local realities in their pedagogic practice. New curricula tend to prescribe new pedagogical orientations. The process of instruction ensures that officially prescribed content and methodologies are followed as much as possible, to reduce discrepancies between the written and the taught curriculum. Instructional planning and design are pertinent during curriculum implementation.

Monitoring

This is a crucial task in the curriculum implementation process. It involves gathering information on how the implementation process is progressing. Such information facilitates the process. It is a type of formative evaluation. Monitoring is done by Heads of Departments, principals, and pedagogic inspectors. Monitoring may lead to modification in scheduling and communication.

Key Players in Curriculum Implementation

Curriculum implementation involves different agents, each with their roles. Their roles must be clearly defined by curriculum developers to ensure the success of a curriculum. Below are the roles of various agents in the curriculum implementation process:

The Role of Learners in Curriculum Implementation

Learners are central to curriculum planning. The curriculum is planned for their consumption. The learner makes the curriculum alive through cooperation. The learners are an important element in the entire process of curriculum implementation since learners hold the key to what is translated and adopted from the official designed curriculum that is meant for them.

Learners constitute the basis in the selection of learning experiences because the school consists of many levels and class grades calling upon the teacher to prepare for the disparities among the learners like individual differences between the slow learners and the quick learners. Therefore, a teacher selects the appropriate learning methods and teaching aids to suit each category of learners.

The learner exhibits desirable discipline both in and outside the classroom through maximum obedience to the school rules and regulation and attending to the classwork and the entire school program, like doing all assignments, tests and examinations. This results in some level of desirable learning. For the implementation of curriculum to be effectively done, the learner should be physically, mentally, and emotionally responsive to instruction so that the planned program is implemented.

The Role of the Principal in Curriculum Implementation

The principal should ensure that he/she is versed with the regulations, policy documents and circulars. He/she should study these documents and master the details of the curriculum changes. He/she should be able to diagnose the problem, plan for change, implement change, monitor implementation, assess developments, and engage the staff in decision-making from the level of planning while allowing people to express their concerns. To transform and improve the school, the principal should ensure that educators understand what they are going to do. The principal should also focus on changing the mind-set of all stakeholders, improving the internal functioning of the school, and improving the key function of the school, namely teaching and learning. The principal should improve the competence of teachers by organising a staff development programme related to the proposed change. He should encourage teamwork and motivate staff to implement changes.

The Role of Teachers in Curriculum Implementation

The teacher's role in curriculum implementation is very important because the teacher with his or her knowledge, experiences and competencies, interprets the curriculum structures into learning experiences. The interpretation of the curriculum policy into practice depends mainly on the teacher. The teacher selects the actual learning experiences to be provided and so he/she must be involved in the planning and development process. A teacher enriches and alters the program according to the characteristics of the learners. The teacher transforms the curriculum into small units and looks for the teaching and learning material that students can understand. In order to enhance student learning, the teacher employs the appropriate methodology and motivates learners to create interest and a desire for learning. He/she will evaluate the students to see whether the students have achieved the curriculum goals and objectives and to see if there are gaps requiring corrective action. In order to keep track of the correct direction throughout the course of the study, the teacher provides counselling and guidance. The teacher is not just a receiver of the curriculum but a modifier and transmitter; and for her/him not to derail from the objectives, goals and aims of the planned curriculum, s/he must be part of the planning and development processes.

Role of Government

Government activities include providing facilities and materials for learning, human and material resources, salaries, facilities for all personnel involved in both teaching and non-teaching, and support for teachers' professional advancement. Government also certifies and issues licenses for teachers to qualify for teaching.

Role of School Management Board (SMB) in Curriculum Implementation

SMB consists of the principal, Heads of Department, senior teachers in a school and parents' representatives. SMB is entrusted with day-to-day responsibility for the management of the school under the leadership of the principal. It should provide support to teachers and make available resources that teachers need for teaching. SMB is expected to understand the curriculum change and manage it effectively. It has the task of measuring teaching outcomes in schools to meet national goals and to plan ahead to ensure that there are enough teachers to be assigned for classes. They should have a hold of school timetables, procure teaching materials and organise for retraining of teachers for the task ahead.

Role of Community Resources

Participation in the community is a collaboration that could include information sharing and is the home–school intervention for family members working with the school. Family members are paraprofessionals, instructors, volunteers, board members, tutors and curriculum planners, and other resource persons.

Models of Curriculum Implementation

There are many different models for implementing curriculum. Three of them will be discussed in this section. One common model is the Overcoming-Resistance-to-Change Model (ORC model), the Leadership Obstacle Course Model (LOC) and the Linkage Model. These three models bear similarities as discussed below:

Overcoming-Resistance-to-Change (ORC) Model

This model focuses on the acquisition and sharing of power between administrators and teachers, which also allows teachers' personal needs to be addressed by preserving a high level of flexibility in the implementation. It concentrates on change from the teacher's perspective. As described below, this model has four phases:

Stage 1: Unrelated Concerns

The first stage is that of indifference. A teacher knows about change but does not see how it relates to their own life. As such the teacher is not worried about whatever innovation is coming. For example, a shift to the problem-based learning approach. The teacher knows this innovation is out there, but it has not influenced his or her actions yet.

Stage 2: Personal Concerns

The teacher is now interested on how the innovation or curriculum will impact their life personally. For example, a teacher how the use of the problem-based learning approach will affect what they are trying to do in the classroom.

Stage 3: Task-Related Concerns

In stage 3, the teacher is thinking about how to use the new curriculum or innovation. Questions begin to go through their minds on how to apply them. The teacher may wonder about issues like how much time will it take to learn the new activity, what the best ways are to use this innovation, what kind of support they will get.

Stage 4: Impact-Related Concerns

The teacher has started implementing but is now worried about how this will affect students. At this stage, teachers are focusing on their students, peers, and school. The shift here is from self to others.

Leadership-Obstacle Course Model (LOC) model

LOC is the acronym for Leadership-Obstacle Course model. This model treats staff resistance to change as a concern and proposes that we should collect data to determine the extent and nature of the resistance. We can do this by making sure that the following five conditions exist:

- The organisational members must have a clear understanding of the proposed innovation.
- Individuals within the organisation must be given requisite skills so that they possess the capabilities requisite for carrying out the innovation
- The necessary materials and equipment for the innovation must be furnished.
- If need be, the organisational structure must be modified to align with the innovation being suggested.
- The participants in the innovation must be spurred to spend the required time and effort to make the innovation a success.
- This model, which is like the OCR model, has a feedback and monitoring mechanism to determine if problems once solved keep reappearing.

Linkage Model

The "linkage model" recognises that innovators exist in research and development centres, universities, and so on. However, educators in the field do not find some of their innovative attempts to solve the problems. Therefore, it is important to align problems with innovations, such that any innovation is a problem solved. This model foresees two systems: user system and resource system. There must be a link between these two systems. The resource system should have a clear picture of the curriculum user's problems if it is to retrieve or create appropriate educational packages. An effective resource system must proceed through a cycle of diagnosis, search, retrieval, fabrication of solution, dissemination, and evaluation in order to test out its product. Thus, in the linkage model, the basic process is the transfer of knowledge.

Change Management

The concept of change management dates to the early to mid-1900s. Kurt Lewin's 3-step model for change was developed in the 1940s; Everett Rogers' book *Diffusion of Innovations* was published in 1962, and Bridges' *Transition Model* was developed in 1979. However, it was not until the 1990s that change management became well known in the business environment, and formal organisational processes became available in the 2000s.

Change management has been defined as "the process of continually renewing an organization's direction, structure, and capabilities to serve the ever-changing needs of external and internal customers" (Moran & Brightman 2001). Many new programs are failing. This shows a basic lack of a valid framework for how organisational change is implemented and managed. For management of these challenges to change in education, motivation is very important. People need incentives to engage in new practices because it is sometimes difficult to get people out of their comfort areas. In order to develop a new system, it requires good leadership.

There are at least three major factors which constitute the change design when a planned change is attempted. These include full understanding of technological innovation, having comprehensive information on pressure in and around school, and a change strategy. To manage change, some scholars have come up with change models.

Procedure for an Effective Change Management Process

Education must keep up with societal changes and so change is constant and necessary for growth and profitability. A consistent change management process will aid in minimising the impact it has on an organisation and its staff. The following steps are essential to ensure that change is successful:

1. **Determine areas for improvement**

Since most change occurs to improve a process, a product, or an outcome, it is critical to identify the need and to clarify goals. This also involves identifying the resources and individuals that will facilitate the process and lead the endeavour. Most change systems acknowledge that knowing what to improve creates a solid foundation for clarity, ease, and successful implementation.

2. **Present a Solid plan to Stakeholders**

There are many categories of stakeholders like parents, teachers, school management who both direct and finance and implement the new programme. All have different expectations and experiences and there must be a high level of interest from these different stakeholders. It is important to provide plans that enhance time, patience, and communication.

3. **Plan for the Change**

This is the blueprint that identifies the beginning, the route to be followed, and the destination, the resources needed, the scope and costs entailed. A critical element of planning is providing a systematic process rather than sudden, unplanned general changes. This involves outlining the project with clear steps and measurable targets, incentives, measurements, and analysis.

4. **Provide Resources and Use Data for Evaluation**

The identification of resources and funding are critical elements as part of the planning process. These include software systems, infrastructure and equipment. Consider the necessary tools to re-educate, retrain and refine priorities and practices. Various models identify data collection and analysis as an element which is not being used. The clarity of clear progress reports enables better communication, correct and timely allocation of incentives, and measurement of successes and milestones.

5. **Communication**

This is a very important tool for managing change. It is a matter of good communication to identify, plan, integrate and execute a good change management plan. Clear and open communications lines are an important part of all processes of change. They promote transparency and two-way communication structures that offer a way to overcome frustrations, applaud what works and change what doesn't work seamlessly.

6. **Monitor and Manage Resistance, Dependencies, and Budgeting Risks**

Resistance is typical in change management, but it can threaten the success of a change process. Most resistance occurs because of fear of the unknown. It also occurs because there is a fair amount of risk associated with change – the risk of impacting dependencies, return on investment risks, and risks associated with allocating budget to something new. Previewing and preparing for resistance by arming leadership with tools to manage it will help in a smooth change lifecycle.

7. Celebrate Success

Recognising milestone achievements is a critical part of any project. When managing a change through its lifecycle, it's important to recognise the success of teams and individuals involved. This will help in the adoption of both the change management process as well as adoption of the change itself.

8. Review, Revise and Continuously Improve

This is a key tool to manage change. The identification, planning, integration and implementation of a good Change Management Plan is a matter of good communication. Clear and open lines of communication are an important element of all transformation processes. They support transparency and bidirectional communication structures, which can overcome frustrations, applaud what works and change the things that do not work properly.

Change Management Models

Change Management Models have been developed based on research and experience on how to best to manage change within an organisation or in one's personal life. Most Change Management Models provide a supporting process that can apply to your organisation or personal growth. Four of such models are described below:

Lewin's Change Management Model

Lewin's Change Management Model is one of the most popular and effective models that gives a concrete understanding of organisational and structured change. This model was designed and created by Kurt Lewin in the 1950s, and it is still relevant today. His model consists of three main stages namely: unfreeze, change, and refreeze.

1. Unfreeze

This first stage of the process of change involves the preparation for the change. Here, the organisation must get ready for the change and for the fact that change is important and needed. This phase is important because most people around the world try to resist change, and it is important to break this barrier. It is important to explain to people why the present situation needs to be changed and how change can bring about profit.

2. Change

This is the stage where the real change takes place. The process may take time to happen as people usually take time to embrace changes. At this stage, good leadership and reassurance is important because these aspects not only lead to advancing towards the right direction but also make the process easier for staff or individuals who are involved in the process. Communication and time are critical at this stage.

3. Refreeze

At this point the change has been accepted, embraced, and implemented by people, the company or organisation begins to become stable again. Therefore, the stage is referred to as refreeze. This is the time when the staff and processes begin to refreeze, and things start going back to their normal pace and routine. This step requires the help of the people to make sure changes are used all the time and implemented even after the objective has been achieved. Now with a sense of stability, employees get comfortable and confident of the acquired changes.

Kotter's change management theory

This theory was propounded in 1995 by John P. Kotter, who is a Harvard Business School Professor and author of several books based on change management. His change management theory is divided into eight stages where each one of them focuses on a key principle that is associated with the response of people to change. The eight stages are as follows:

1. **Increase urgency**

This step involves creating a sense of urgency among the people so as to spur them to move forward towards objectives.

2. **Build the team**

Getting the right people on the team by selecting a combination of skills, knowledge, and commitment.

3. **Get the vision correct**

This stage is related to creating the right vision by considering, not only the strategy but also creativity and the objectives.

4. **Communicate**

Communication with people regarding change and the rationale for this change is were important. It may take the form of short presentations during a staff meeting or workshops.

5. **Get things moving**

To get into action, one needs to get support, remove the barriers, and implement feedback in a constructive way.

6. **Focus on short term goals**

Focusing on short term goals and dividing the goal into small and achievable parts is a better way to achieve success without too much pressure.

7. **Do not give up**

Persistence is the key to success, and it is important not to give up while the process of change management is ongoing, no matter what the constraints may be.

8. **Incorporate change**

Besides managing change effectively, it is also critical to reinforce it and make it a part of the workplace culture.

Bridges' Transition Model

Bridges' transition model was developed by William Bridges who is a change consultant, and this theory became popular after it was published in the book *Managing transitions*. The peculiarity of this model or theory is that it concentrates and focuses upon transition and not change as such. The difference between transition and change may be subtle, but it is important to understand it.

Where transition on one hand is internal, change on the other is something that happens to people, even when they do not realise it. Transition is something that happens to people when they are going through the change. Change can be immediate, but transition may take time.

The model focuses on three main stages that are given as follows:

1.   **Ending, Losing, and Letting Go**

When people are first introduced to change, they may enter this first stage that is characterised by resistance and emotional discomfort. Some of the emotions experienced at this stage include fear, resentment, anger, denial, sadness, frustration, and most of all-disorientation. One must realise that he/she is getting to accept new beginnings.

2.   **The Neutral Zone**

This is the stage of uncertainty, impatience, and confusion. This stage can be considered as the bridge between the old and the new when people are still attached to the old but trying to adapt to the new. This stage is associated with low morale and reduced productivity, and one may experience anxiety and scepticism as well when going through this stage. But despite this, the neutral zone may also include innovation, renewal, and a burst of creativity.

3.   **The New Beginning**

When the neutral phase is passed with the help of support and guidance, the stage of acceptance comes in. At this level, people begin to accept the change and understand its importance. They are beginning to build the competences needed to reach the new goals and may start to experience benefits of the change already. It is associated with high levels of energy, new commitment, and a zest to learn.

Reasons for Change Management Failure

In most cases, failure to achieve organisational change is caused by one of the following factors:

- limited understanding of the change and its effect
- negative employee attitudes
- failure to involve employees in the change process
- poor communication
- inadequate resources or budget
- resistance to a change in organisational culture
- lack of management support for the change
- lack of commitment to change
- past experience of failed change initiatives
- lack of skills
- lack of staff
- inadequate organisational infrastructure
- Mobility of key employees who influence change

Consequences of poor change management

The costs and outcomes of poorly managed change can be significant. They include:

- financial losses
- productivity and performance drops
- decline in quality of work
- wasted time and resources
- inability to retain staff
- increase in employee sickness levels
- poor staff morale

Curriculum Management

Curriculum management is a set of activities aimed at making the most efficient and effective use of resources in order to achieve one or more curriculum goals. It is the art of creating an environment in which people can perform and individuals can work together to achieve curriculum goals (Chesterton & Chesterton, 2019). Curriculum management entails managing change, training principals and teachers in the new curriculum, and monitoring and supporting principals and teachers. Second, it covers curriculum coordination, policy implementation, staff development, and resource management, as well as curriculum evaluation, all at the school level. Finally, it covers curriculum development in the classroom. Curriculum management is essentially concerned with curriculum improvement and effective implementation. Curriculum management is sometimes used synonymously with curriculum leadership. The quality of management contributes significantly to the quality of life and the standard of work of both teachers and learners.

Who is responsible for Curriculum Management?

The answer requires a description of the roles of the people involved in curriculum management. In decentralised education systems like the USA, Canada, Australia which emphasise school-based curriculum development, school district officials, the Curriculum Committee, the principal/ Head Teachers, Vice principals/Deputy Head Teachers and the classroom teacher are responsible for curriculum management in K-12 (kindergarten to twelfth grade). In a college or university, the most senior professionals are in charge of curriculum management and leadership. In centralised education systems like what obtains in Cameroon, curriculum leadership is entrusted to the national inspectorate of pedagogy with limited devolution of powers to regional inspectors of pedagogy and divisional pedagogic advisers. Although such people in both centralised and decentralised systems have many specific responsibilities, the main interest of a school which is effective learning, is the principal responsibility of these actors.

The Curriculum Management Process

The Curriculum Management Process (CMP) is primarily concerned with the effectiveness of teaching and learning. The procedure entails managing what students are expected to learn, assessing whether or not it was learned, and looking for ways to improve student learning. Graduates who are well prepared to succeed after college in any organisation or in advanced education are evidence of an effective curriculum management process. A requirement is that the curriculum be current, responsive, and innovative. It should be delivered in a suitable format and through an effective channel. Above all, students need to gain appropriate knowledge and skills as they progress through and complete the program.

The CMP is made up of two major areas: curriculum development/review and Assurance of Learning (AOL), which refers to demonstrating that students are meeting learning expectations through assessment processes, as well as the process of continuous program improvement. It provides a mechanism for improving student learning by examining areas of weakness. Schools use AOL to demonstrate accountability and assure educational stakeholders such as potential students, parents, government, public officials, supporters, and accrediting organisations that the school meets its students' learning goals. Curriculum development analyses what students should be taught. This process includes developing curriculum content that meets the needs of internal and external stakeholders, responds to new developments in business practices and issues, and aligns with the college and university's mission and strategy. Curriculum development may include the creation of new courses or programs, the use of new tools, and the application of novel approaches. However, the process also includes ongoing improvement mostly through revision and redesign of existing content, pedagogy, tools, and approaches.

Key Characteristics of Curriculum Managers

Beare, Caldwell, and Millikan (1989) identify the following three curriculum management requirements:

- Curriculum managers collaborate with others to create a shared curriculum.
- Commitment to a shared vision of teaching excellence
- The curriculum manager has a vision for teaching excellence as well as a vision to guide the school into the future and the ability to articulate this vision to the staff and students.
- Curriculum managers and their teaching colleagues have the knowledge and skills to make the vision a reality.

The Role of various Actors in the Curriculum Management Process

Local education authorities

The role of district officials who function as local education authorities in curriculum management is fourfold. First, they must manage the mental shifts that principals and teachers experience when a new curriculum is implemented. Second, they ensure that principals are trained in the new curriculum. One of the most important activities in the curriculum management process is the training of principals and teachers. It is a prerequisite for meaningful and successful curriculum implementation in the classroom, as well as an important strategy when implementing a new curriculum. Thirdly, they monitor and support principals and fourthly they carry out curriculum evaluation.

The following four guidelines developed by Pratt (1980) provide district officials with strategies for monitoring and supporting teachers:

- Contact with teachers on a regular basis to provide advice and assistance, to encourage mutual contact among teachers, and to maintain contact with students and parents.
- Clear communication to illustrate roles, explain terminology, illustrate possible methods of evaluation, and provide answers to frequently asked questions.
- Provision of a support service, such as explaining timetables, supplying materials, setting an example, creating a climate in which trust and security are prominent, and also encouraging teachers.
- Compensation such as praise and acknowledgement, but also intrinsic aspects of compensation where successful implementation is considered sufficient compensation. This provides an opportunity for professional development through expanded perspectives and increased responsibilities.

The Curriculum Committee

Education requires participation from various community members in order to play its roles in the overall development of society, because the involvement of these school staffs in the teaching – learning process is important in making the curriculum relevant. To achieve a better outcome in curriculum implementation and improvement, principals, teachers, learners, counsellors, and supervisors must work as part of a team, with each individual accepting an appropriate share of the responsibility. This group is known as the school curriculum committee. Incidentally, the organisational structure of education systems in some countries does not provide for curriculum committees at primary and secondary school levels.

The Curriculum Committee or its equivalent where it exists, is responsible for researching the identified problems, recommending solutions, and assisting or coordinating the implementation of the solution. This committee is specifically tasked with developing, reviewing, renewing, and recommending curriculum to the Board of Trustees or its equivalent structure. Curriculum renewal and development are typically the result of a collaborative decision to meet student needs for course work that includes basic skills, general education, transfer, and major programs of study. This school curriculum committee also advises teachers and administrators on how to improve student achievement and teacher practice in curricular issues.

Effective curriculum renewal and development necessitate the use of standards of practice by each school's curriculum committee to ensure the highest possible quality for curriculum offerings that can be made available within allocated resources. This demonstrates how the school curriculum committee is a highly responsible body in the implementation and improvement of the school curriculum in order to increase learners' learning outcomes by involving various stakeholders in curricular matters.

The Principal

The following characteristics are expected of the principal as curriculum leader or manager, according to Smith and Andrews (1989):

- Have policy knowledge and management skills in curriculum matters, which leads to improved teaching practices.
- Be an effective communicator in one-on-one, small-group, and large-group settings.
- Be visionary in terms of creating a visible presence for the school's staff, students, and parents on both the physical and philosophical levels.

The functions of principals in curriculum management include the following:

- Principals plan the curriculum by ensuring that students receive appropriate instruction in areas identified by the school district through policy.
- They ensure that the school's academic goals are met by providing the necessary resources.
- While implementing the curriculum, principals should assist teachers in interpreting curriculum policy.
- The principal should ensure that teachers are developed in accordance with their abilities and skills.
- Principals must develop both themselves and their staff.
- Principals ensure that curriculum content is consistent with both learning outcomes and assessments used to assess achievement of those outcomes.
- Principals work hard to ensure that the learning and teaching materials used in their schools are consistent and effective.
- They establish curriculum evaluation procedures and ensure that these evaluations take place on a regular basis.
- Principals plan staff meetings for curriculum co-ordination which address curriculum outcomes and activities, monitoring curriculum activities and modifying practices in the light of curriculum demands.

The Teacher

Aside from the main function of the teacher, which is to implement the curriculum at the classroom level, or what is more commonly known as the teaching process, the teacher also has a management function to perform that comes before curriculum implementation. This management function is primarily responsible for developing the curriculum that will be implemented. The teacher plays a critical role in curriculum decision-making. The teacher decides which aspects of the curriculum, new or ongoing, to implement in a specific class.

The teacher also decides whether and how much time is spent on developing basic skills versus critical thinking skills, decides where to place emphasis as far as the content is concerned. Teachers participate in curriculum committees in addition to being curriculum implementers in the class-room. Teachers are unquestionably the most effective curriculum implementers.

Supervision of Instruction

Instructional supervision is a set of activities carried out with the goal of improving the learner's teaching and learning. Instructional supervision is a necessary activity for a good school system to function properly. It is a method of supervision that involves advising, guiding, refreshing, encouraging, stimulating, improving, and supervising specific groups in the hopes of gaining their cooperation in order for the supervisors to be successful in their supervision tasks. Pre-training programs should include instructional supervision courses to prepare school administrators, particularly principals, for an instructional supervisory role.

Importance of Supervision of instruction

One approach to improving teacher effectiveness has been identified as supervision. One of the most important reasons for instructional supervision is to ensure that each individual teacher in the school system is carrying out the duties that have been assigned to her/him. Another reason is to improve teachers' effectiveness so that they can contribute as much as possible to the system's goals. In addition, as the educational system evolves, supervision becomes more important in order to improve the quality of instruction in schools. Furthermore, modern instructional materials are being introduced and used as teaching aids in the classroom. In order to cope with these demands, supervision has an important role to play.

Who is an Instructional Supervisor?

An Instructional Supervisor is any certified individual who is in charge of directing and guiding the work of teaching staff members. This implies that the supervisor's role is to assist teachers in doing their jobs better through collaborative efforts. Instructional supervisors could be either internal or external to the institution. External supervision is conducted by the government and delegated agents such as regional Inspectors of Education, whereas internal instructional supervision is conducted by school-based supervisors who occupy supervisory positions in the school and provide leadership to teachers. They are known as instructional supervisors because they are primarily responsible for collaborating with teachers to improve the quality of student learning through improved instruction and may include principals (head teachers), assistant principals, specialist consultants, curriculum directors, instructional lead teachers, departmental heads, and master teachers. Specifically, the roles of an instructional supervisor include the following:

- Provides direction for the development of schools in accordance with the Ministry of Education's strategic plan; and
- Ensures quality standards by supervising, inspecting, and evaluating school operations.
- Through program proposals, training seminars, and workshops, s/he leads in professional development for principals and teachers.
- Ensures the growth of school-based management. For teachers and school administrators, it provides a rich resource of exemplary coaching, training, and apprenticeship.
- Mentoring or arranging for mentoring of new teachers in order to facilitate a smooth transition into the profession.

- Bringing individual teachers up to minimum effective teaching standards (quality assurance and maintenance functions of supervision).
- Improving individual teachers' competencies, regardless of how skilled they are deemed to be.
- Collaborating with groups of teachers in an effort to improve student learning.
- Collaboration with teacher groups to adapt the local curriculum to the needs and abilities of diverse student groups while also aligning the local curriculum with state and national standards.
- Connecting teachers' efforts to improve their teaching to larger goals of schoolwide improvement in support of quality learning for all students.

Characteristics of Good Instructional Leadership

A component of instructional leadership is instructional supervision. Effective instructional leadership ensures that educational programs have the desired effect. An effective leader motivates others to take action and has a positive outlook on the future. A positive attitude is essential for a successful supervisor. Teachers are more likely to be satisfied and interested in their work when their supervisor has a positive attitude toward work and their school. He or she also sets a good example by being truthful, honest, and fair to others.

A good school-based supervisor should be approachable, empathetic, patient, and a strong leader. Furthermore, supervisors must be able to motivate employees as well as instil trust in others. He/she encourages and supports subordinates while confidently inspiring the team to achieve instructional goals. Furthermore, two-way communication allows leaders to solicit ideas for improvement, make informed decisions, and keep an educational organisation on track. An instructional leader is unlikely to succeed unless he or she possesses these characteristics.

Supervision Models

There are many instructional supervision models in literature. Four of them have been summarised below:

Clinical Supervision

Clinical supervision is focused on improving instruction through systematic cycles of planning, observation, and intensive intellectual analysis of actual teaching performance in the interest of rational modification. It necessitates face-to-face contact with teachers with the goal of improving instruction and fostering professional development (Sergiovanni & Starratt, 2002). Clinical supervision is used by supervisors who collaborate with teachers and provide expert assistance to teachers in order to improve instruction.

The goal of clinical supervision is to assist teachers in modifying existing patterns of teaching in ways that make sense to them and support agreed-upon content or teaching standards. The supervisor's role here is to assist the teacher in selecting goals to be implemented and teaching issues to be illuminated, as well as to better understand his or her practice. Clinical supervision of instruction consists of five steps. A pre-conference, observation and data collection, data analysis, a post-conference, and reflection are all part of the process.

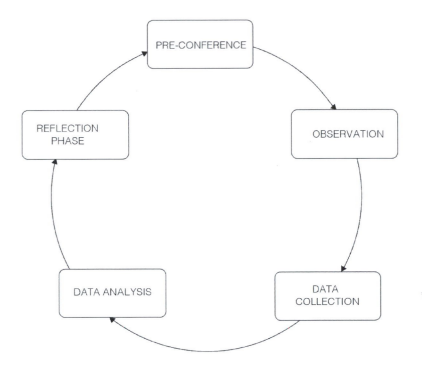

FIGURE 11.1. The Clinical Supervision Process

The pre/planning conference is intended to inform the instructional leader of the lesson objectives. The teacher creates a detailed lesson plan that the instructional leader can critique and use as a foundation for suggestions. The instructional leader observes the teacher teaching the lesson outlined in the lesson plan during the classroom observation/data collection step. The instructional leader should collect data on the lesson being taught using an observation instrument. This procedure provides the teacher with written information to analyse (highlighting strengths and weaknesses) during the post-observation conference.

The post-observation conference allows the instructional leader to discuss the observed lesson with the teacher and allows the teacher to provide feedback on the lesson. The teacher reflects on the feedback as the instructional leader and teacher collaborate to set goals to be met at the next observation date. The purpose of the post-conference analysis is primarily for the instructional leader, who must determine whether the best supervisory practices were used with the teacher. This analysis includes a reflection exercise that will assist the instructional leader in improving the next supervisory conference.

The Conceptual Model

The conceptual model includes the following elements: teacher commitment to teaching, school commitment, trust in administration, trust in teachers, and a desire for collaboration. The model is supported by organisational theory, which states that individuals are united by a common set of values and collaborate within a structured system to achieve specific goals and objectives. A conceptual model identifies organisational factors such as role ambiguity, work overload, decision making, supervisor support via supervision, classroom climate, role conflict, and colleague support and personal factors such as life stage, teaching assignment, experience in education, and knowledge of subject as having a direct influence on teacher performance. Based on organisational and personal factors that influence the teacher's performance, the supervisor and teacher establish certain benchmarks. Changes in organisational and personal factors should be made if possible, and the teacher's progress toward the benchmarks will be evaluated during each supervisory visit. For example, if the teacher is concerned about his or her classroom management skills, the supervisor can work with him or her on that aspect and assist him or her in overcoming it. This type of supervision is relationship-based and is initially used to build trust between the supervisor and the teacher.

Developmental Supervision

Glickman et al. (2001) define developmental supervision as "the match of initial supervisory approach with the teacher or group's developmental levels, expertise, and commitment" (p. 197). The instructional leader operating in developmental supervision gives three types of assistance: 1) directive, 2) collaborative, and 3) nondirective.

The instructional leader is designated as the expert in charge of writing goals for the teacher under directive supervision. Teachers with moderate levels of abstract thinking, expertise, and commitment benefit most from collaborative assistance. With this type of assistance, the instructional leader and teacher establish goals, determine how they will be met, and note when the achievement should be recognised as a team. Teachers who think abstractly and have a high level of expertise and commitment to teaching are best matched with nondirective support (Glickman et al., 2001). Nondirective assistance gives the teacher control over how and when the goals are met. The instructional leader remains involved, but in a more passive role in the supervision process. Glickman et al. (2001) define the instructional leader's behaviours in this role as listening, reflecting, clarifying, encouraging, and problem solving.

Collaborative Supervision

The supervisor's role in a collaborative model is to collaborate with teachers rather than to direct them. The supervisor actively participates in any decisions made with the teacher and attempts to establish a sharing relationship. The teacher and supervisor collaborate to solve a problem in the teacher's classroom teaching. They propose a hypothesis, test it, and implement strategies that appear to offer a reasonable solution to the problem at hand. Rather than telling the teacher what he should have done, the supervisor could have asked, "How did you like the lesson?" How did it turn out? Did you achieve your goal"? This would be said in a positive, enthusiastic tone.

Challenges of School-Based Supervision

Several factors tend to work against effective supervision of instruction in schools. Some teachers have a negative attitude toward their bosses. They may perceive supervision as fault-finding at times. The supervisory exercise will not have the desired effect unless teachers perceive it as a process of promoting professional growth and student learning. In addition, a lack of supervisory training, a strained relationship between teachers and supervisors, and a lack of support for supervisors from higher levels of administration all have an impact on supervisory practice in the school. Secondary school principals are so weighed down by routine administrative burden that they hardly find time to visit classrooms and observe how the teachers are teaching. Lack of financial and material resources also constrain supervision.

12

Curriculum Evaluation

Despite agreement on the necessity of evaluation in the curriculum development process, there is discord among curriculum scholars as to the meaning, purposes, approaches, and uses of curriculum evaluation. Because evaluation is the process of collecting and analysing data to determine the extent to which objectives have been achieved to make effective decisions (Gay,1985), it involves making assessments and value judgments. Curriculum evaluation implies these two concepts, with assessment preceding value judgement. However, some writers restrict the meaning of curriculum evaluation to making of value judgement only, and others describe the term to include assessment. To a few others like Ornstein and Hunkins (2018 p. 286), assessment and evaluation are synonyms. In curriculum theory and practice, there are several types, approaches and models of curriculum evaluation. They will be presented and discussed in this chapter alongside assessment and evaluation instruments and techniques.

Definitions, Purpose and Nature of Curriculum Evaluation

Some widely used and accepted definitions of curriculum evaluation are:

- the process of measuring and judging the extent to which planned courses, programmes, learning activities and opportunities as expressed in the formal curriculum produce the expected results (UNESCO IBE, 1995-2021).
- "The formal determination of the quality, effectiveness, or value of a program, product, project, process, objective, or curriculum" (Worthen and Sanders, 1987)
- "The process of judging, based on gathered data, the success level of an individual's learning, or a product's effectiveness" (Brown and Green, 2006)
- "Assessment of the merit and worth of a programme of studies, a field of study or a course of study" (Ornstein and Hunkins, 2018).
- "The process of delineating, obtaining, providing, and applying descriptive and judgmental information about the merit and worth of some object's goals, design, implementation, and outcomes to guide improvement decisions, provide accountability reports, inform institutionalization/ dissemination decisions, and improvement decisions, and understanding of the involved phenomena" (Stufflebeam, 2003, p.34).

There is a prolific use of the words *worth* and *merit* in many definitions of curriculum evaluation.

While merit describes the intrinsic value of the curriculum, worth refers to its value relative to a particular context. Both the worth and merit of a curriculum deserve attention in curriculum evaluation practice, and they are ascertained from assessment data. Assessment is therefore the starting point of curriculum evaluation.

Purposes of Curriculum Evaluation

Curriculum developers are always eager to know the quality of their products; the implementer too wants to know whether classroom instruction is effective, and the larger society wants to know whether their educational investments are yielding the desired profit. Education stakeholders have different interests and reasons for curriculum evaluation. McNeil (2005) shed light as to the purpose of curriculum evaluation by stating that it answers these two questions: "Do planned learning opportunities, programs, courses, and activities as developed and organised produce desired results?" "How can a curriculum be improved?" Therefore, the main purpose of curriculum evaluation is to:

- Identify the strengths and weaknesses of an existing curriculum and its implementation, to provide a basis for maintaining, revising, or replacing the curriculum.
- Provide critical information for curriculum policy decisions and instructional changes after assessing students and teachers in matters of teaching and learning.
- Find out whether curriculum contents and practices are consistent with global, national, and local realities and educational expectations. This is a form of quality assurance and control.

Nature and Scope of Curriculum Evaluation

Curriculum evaluation is a human-made enterprise and a political exercise since it involves groups of people assigning values to activities. Put differently, curriculum evaluation has a human element influence. Supporting Parlet and Hamilton's argument that the principal purpose of programme evaluation is to inform decision makers, Urevbu (1985) went further to assert that an evaluator must recognise the value stance of the decision makers who exploit evaluation reports. He argues that placing value on specific acts or objects implies choice among a range of value systems. This act is not neutral because evaluation results are influenced by external group criteria.

Contrary to the connotation of some curriculum development models that evaluation is a tail-end phase of the process, evaluation begins at the initial stages of curriculum conceptualisation and spans through the delivery stage as well. The overall process is also subject to evaluation. Curriculum evaluation is an iterative process that occupies a central position in the entire development process. It takes place in the stages of analysis, design, production of materials and implementation of courses and programs. The evaluation process itself can be subjected to evaluation.

Curriculum evaluation is comprehensive and complex. Although many curriculum texts see evaluation in terms of student achievement (product evaluation) only, there are other issues surrounding the learning environment that need attention. The instructors, instructional methods, curriculum materials, programs and support services need to be evaluated too. (Borg and Gall, 1989; Hezel,1995). In this process, evaluators collect and analyse information about a program's activities, characteristics, and outcomes for the purpose of making judgments to improve the program's effectiveness and inform programming decisions (Patton, 1987).

Affirming the broad scope and multi-level nature of evaluation activities, Romiszowski (1988) identifies four levels of curriculum evaluation namely:

- Level 1: project level; Level 2: curriculum level; Level 3: unit level; Level 4: learning step
- Curriculum evaluators include classroom teachers, students, peers, and professional evaluators.

Differences Between Measurement, Assessment, and Evaluation

Although many educators use these terms interchangeably, it is necessary to make a clear distinction between measurement, assessment, and evaluation. Measurement is the assignment of numerals to objects and events according to rules (Kerlinger, 1973). Educators record observations of students' degree of competence by making measurements. Educational measurements use a variety of instruments with different scales, some of which do not yield as precise measurements as those used in the physical sciences. Unaided human senses also make measurements aptly referred to as estimates. Counting the number of ticks on a student's test script and stating a score of 90 is measurement. That is a measure of learner achievement.

Table 12.1. Differences between Assessment and Evaluation

BASIS FOR COMPARISON	ASSESSMENT	EVALUATION
Meaning	Assessment is a process of collecting, reviewing, and using data, for the purpose of improvement in the current performance.	Evaluation is described as an act of passing judgement based on set of standards.
Nature	Diagnostic	Judgemental
What it does?	Provides feedback on performance and areas of improvement.	Determines the extent to which objectives are achieved.
Purpose	Formative	Summative
Orientation	Process Oriented	Product Oriented
Feedback	Based on observation and positive & negative points.	Based on the level of quality as per set standard.
Relationship between parties	Reflective	Prescriptive
Criteria	Set by both the parties jointly.	Set by the evaluator.
Measurement Standards	Absolute	Comparative

Source: Surbhi, S. (2016). keydifferences.com

Assessment takes place when the teacher states that the score is 90 out of 100, after counting the ticks. Assessment interprets the score obtained by measurement against set objectives. Because assessment and measurement instruments are most often the same, in this example a test, these two processes often mean the same. Tests and examinations are the most common assessment instruments used in teaching and learning. As a result, measurement, assessment, and testing are often used synonymously in education.

However, educational assessments are not limited to tests. Portfolios, projects, classroom discussions and journal entries can also be used to assess learner achievement. Assessment of learning deals with how well a student or group of students have learned a particular set of skills or kind of knowledge. And it uses various forms of measuring techniques, tests, or examinations. Interview, questionnaires, and observations are other tools widely used in assessing other aspects of the curriculum different from learner achievement.

Evaluation takes place when the teacher, in our example, goes further to judge the score of 90 out of 100 and state that it is excellent, based on predetermined criteria. Evaluation yields information about the worthiness, goodness, the appropriateness, or validity of something for which a reliable measurement or assessment has been made. Measurement, assessment, and evaluation are closely linked concepts although assessment and evaluation differ in some respects as shown in table 12.1.

Types of Evaluation

Evaluation can be classified based on functions or tasks to be performed.

Types of evaluation based on functions

Diagnostic Evaluation

It is the type of evaluation carried out for the identification of students whose learning or classroom behaviour is adversely being affected by factors not directly related to instructional practices (Madaus and Airasian,1972). Here, assessments and judgements are made at the beginning of a lesson or a program to identify the status of the learner or prerequisites of the program.

Placement Evaluation

It is the type of evaluation used to place students according to prior achievement or personal characteristics at the most appropriate point in an instructional sequence. (Madaus and Airasian,1972).

Formative Evaluation

It is the kind of evaluation that is made to improve or modify a programme, a course or a lesson, a textbook, or any curriculum system. Taking place before and during project implementation, it guides and aids the development of instructional sequences and curriculum projects. Also called rapid prototyping by instructional designers, formative evaluation is essential at the initial stages of the development process. Formative decisions lead to modifications of curriculum and instruction (Bloom, Hastings and Madaus, 1971).

Urevbu (1985) opines that the essence of formative evaluation is to ensure the results of summative evaluation are positive.

Formative evaluators construct test items, validate the test instrument, administer, analyse the results, and state the implications and modifications to be made. They collect and analyse data whose interpretations determine the nature and magnitude of modifications.

A variety of strategies can be used to conduct formative evaluation during instruction. Brent Ducor (2014) holds that through questioning, a classroom teacher can engage students in deep reflection, allowing them time to ponder and generate in-depth and rich responses. The questions are distributed to members of the class and records of responses kept for later analysis and interpretation. In addition to questioning, teachers could collect data for formative decisions by simply walking round the class and listening to students (Taylor and Nolen, 2008).

Summative Evaluation

Commonly associated with macro level evaluation, summative evaluation is the kind of evaluation that comes at the end of a curriculum project or a segment of instruction. Evaluation here is a terminal process. It is the process of determining the worth of or value of a curriculum system to maintain or reject it. It also determines student learning over a period and reports to stakeholders on whether a program should be maintained or discontinued. When summative evaluation is carried out at the school level, it takes the form of semester and end of year examinations often leading to award of grades and certificates. It is done at the end of an instructional program to check quality and quantity of learning and to compare the processes with the products to understand if the objectives have been achieved or not (Gronlund, 1990).

Types of Evaluation (Based on Evaluation Tasks)

Some classifications of curriculum evaluation produce dichotomies such as student evaluation and program evaluation, evaluation of learning outcomes and evaluation of learning systems. Gagne, Wager, Golas and Keller (2005) identify five categories or types of evaluation in the instruction design process that can be applied to curriculum development:

- Materials evaluation
- Process evaluation
- Evaluation of instructional consequences
- Evaluation of learner achievement
- Learner reactions

Materials Evaluation

This is the process of evaluating curriculum materials that a team has produced or is producing. Different forms of materials evaluation are:

i) Pilot trial: testing of material is carried with a small group. The group is preselected and given the materials to use. Evaluators observe teaching and learning processes and activities. Learners are given achievement tests and results obtained. From the naturalistic observations, learners test results and other documented evidence of how the materials are perceived, evaluation experts make judgements and recommend modifications.

ii) Field trial: A larger real-life group is tested with materials that have been produced. This final try-out aims at finding out the conditions that sustain the new materials. The Cameroon secondary school syllabuses that went operational in 2014 underwent a field trial in some parts or the country in 2012/2013 academic year (Republic of Cameroon, MINESEC Teaching syllabuses p.4).

iii) Development try-out: This is one-on-one evaluation carried out with individual learners. Experts recommend that students of varying abilities should be included in such try-outs to reflect a balanced view of learners' perception of the new materials being developed.

iv) Expert or stakeholder review: It is done by specialists to find out if material is accurate and up to date. Educational experts are often grouped and called a scientific committee for the purpose of reviewing and giving their opinions on the suitability of the materials.

In all the forms of materials evaluation, formative decisions are taken; modifications are made until the final draft is of a textbook, a syllabus or timetable is adopted.

Process Evaluation

It focuses on reviewing the whole process of curriculum making. Evaluators try to find out how well each of the stages or phases of the curriculum process was carried out. It leads to formative decisions.

Instructional Consequences

This involves examining the relevance of the objectives and content of a program vis a vis the outcomes. How successful are the graduates of a programme? Can they find jobs? Can they improve their lives or that of the community after undertaking the programme? Can learners transfer skills they have acquired to a job or other life situations? These and many more make up evaluative questions at this level. This kind of evaluation usually leads to summative decisions.

Evaluation of Learner Achievement

It deals with gathering empirical evidence on how learners are performing or achieving the objectives of a course, unit, or lesson. It comprises teacher-made tests, examinations, quizzes, (written and oral). This is otherwise called instructional evaluation. It leads to both formative and summative decisions.

Learner Reactions

A curriculum can be evaluated by requesting learners to give their opinions about a course or programme. Opinions are sought concerning curriculum objectives, content, learning activities, materials, teaching and assessment strategies. Such value judgments may lead to formative or summative decisions.

Approaches to Curriculum Evaluation

Two major approaches to curriculum evaluation falling along a continuum have been identified in the literature (Cronbach, 1982;). These are the scientific modernist approach and the humanist, post-modernist approach. The former is also called the utilitarian and the latter is the intuitionist approach. (Ornstein and Hunkins, 2018).

Scientific, Modernist Approach

Evaluators in this category are behaviouristic and prescriptive in their approach. They utilise methods of physical scientists. They would begin work by stating objectives of the curriculum and instruction then proceed to use standardised tests and other instruments to measure their level of attainment. Cause and effect relationships are established from the data gathered and program decisions are made. For a modernist evaluator, a student's score of 90 per cent in a test denotes high understanding of subject matter and indicates teacher effectiveness. This approach dates as far back as the 19th and 20th century with emphasis on the scientific method. Ralph Tyler, Robert Stakes and Stufflebeam's CIPP evaluation models use this approach.

Humanistic, Postmodernist Approach

Humanists and post-modernists may not pay as much attention to students' achievement as they do to how planned curricula have enabled students to improve their self-concept. An evaluator using this approach would focus on the reason why a student obtained a 90 percent score in a test. To obtain evaluation data they utilise qualitative methods such as ethnography, autobiographies, and phenomenology. Evaluators using this approach engage in the art of interpretation. Hunkins and Ornstein (2018) identify and discuss five major humanistic approaches to qualitative evaluation: interpretive, artistic, systematic, theory driven, and critical-emancipatory.

1. In the *interpretive approach,* the evaluator considers the educational setting and interprets to get the meaning and significance of teachers and students' actions. Attention to social context is very important.
2. In the *artistic approach,* the evaluator engages in aesthetic inquiry, observing classes and co-curricular activities and then publishing what is good and bad about the curriculum. The evaluator pays attention to the quality of the relationships between teacher and students.
3. In the *systematic approach,* evaluators try to be as objective as possible in their descriptions. They employ logical analysis and base their judgments on facts. However, they do not rely mainly on statistical techniques, the hallmark of the scientific approach.
4. In the *theory-driven* approach, the evaluators apply philosophical, political, or social theories when judging the quality of curricula.
5. *Critical-emancipatory* evaluators tend to be the most radical. They judge a curriculum's effectiveness according to how well the curriculum works against social forces that slow down individual development and fulfilment.

Models of Curriculum Evaluation

The Tyler Model, 1949

Also called the objectives model because of its approach to educational evaluation, Tyler advocates that curriculum development begins with formulation of objectives. He cites the learner, contemporary society, and subject matter as sources of objectives. Objectives are filtered through the screens of psychology and philosophy. There is coherence between learning experiences and content. Both are selected and organised with objectives in the background. The purpose and process of evaluation is to determine the extent to which objectives are being realised by curriculum and instruction.

The Tylerian evaluation process according to Glatthorn et al. (2019), follows these steps:
Predetermine intended learning outcomes. State them as behavioural objectives.

1. Identify the context that gives opportunity to develop and achieve objectives
2. Select, modify, or construct evaluation tools. Check them for reliability, validity, and objectivity.
3. Utilise the tools to obtain results
4. Compare the results obtained before and after instruction
5. Analyse the results to obtain strengths and weaknesses
6. Use results to make necessary modifications.

Instructional evaluation is the prime focus of this model. Evaluators begin by specifying objectives, collect performance data and make comparisons of student performance and expected standards. They use the results to make the necessary modifications in the curriculum. Although pre-assessments and post-assessments are made, the model supports summative evaluation. Over time, more attention has been given to formative evaluation, which includes evaluation during planning and implementation (Billings and Halstead, 2009).

Although the Tyler model is easy to understand and apply, and it laid a foundation for subsequent evaluation models, it has been criticised for not being useful in identifying reasons for curriculum failure because it ignores the process of education, focusing on the product. In addition, it does not suggest how objectives are evaluated.

The CIPP Model, 2003

The author of this model, Daniel Stufflebeam describes it as "a comprehensive framework for guiding evaluations of programs, projects, personnel, products and evaluation systems" (Stufflebeam, 2003, p.31). The CIPP model as it is popularly called outlines four different dimensions of evaluation: Context, Input, Process and Product.

Context evaluation deals with assessing needs and problems of the operating context. When evaluating the educational quality of a school, the history, goals, and background of the school are studied. The aim is to identify and address the problems resulting from school needs. The actual and intended needs are compared. Methods for collecting evaluation data at this level include surveys, document analysis and interviews with stakeholders. Some of the questions posed at this level are:

are the aims of the school suitable or not? Do the objectives generate from aims? Are the courses taught relevant to the aims? Is the school fulfilling social needs? (Aziz, Mahmood, and Rehman, 2018)

Input evaluation identifies resources used to develop programs: people, funds, space, and equipment. The goal is to evaluate competing strategies, the work plans, and the budgets for the strategies chosen to implement programs or projects.

Process evaluation is used to monitor and assess activities carried out during programs or projects' implementation.

Product evaluation helps to identify and evaluate short term, long term, intended or unintended outcomes of programs or projects.

During each of these four stages, specific steps are taken:
- The kinds of decisions are identified.
- The kinds of data needed to make those decisions are identified.
- Those data are collected.
- The criteria for determining quality are established. The data are analysed based on those criteria.
- The needed information is provided to decision makers (as cited in Glatthorn, 1987, pp. 273–274).

The CIPP model has some strengths. It emphasises decision-making which is appropriate for administrators concerned with improving curricula. Its concern for the formative aspects of evaluation makes up for a serious deficiency in the Tyler model. The detailed guidelines and forms created by the evaluation committee provide step by step guidance for users.

Critics have, however, identified some of its weaknesses. The main one seems to be its failure to recognise the complexity of the decision-making process in organisations. It assumes more rationality than exists in such situations and ignores the political factors that play a large part in these decisions. Also, as Guba and Lincoln (1981) noted, it seems difficult and expensive to implement.

Eisner's Model, 1979

This model breaks away from the traditional scientific models by involving narratives more than numerical summaries. It emphasises qualitative appreciation based on two constructs: i) connoisseurship and ii) criticism. Being an art educator by profession, Eisner believed that evaluators should use perceptual memory to appreciate curriculum practice. A curriculum evaluator should have expert knowledge in education and also know how to appreciate and value what is happening in school. Such an individual is a connoisseur.

Connoisseurship is the art of appreciation. Appreciation requires creativity, exploration and helping others to see hidden aspects of a phenomenon. An educational evaluator perceives essentials of educational life and relates it to classroom structure. Five dimensions of connoisseurship are i) intentional, ii) structural, iii) curricular) iv) pedagogical and v) evaluative.

The intentional refers to what schools are intended to achieve. What is truly important in schools? Defining intentions refers to both the overall goals of education and the specific goals of the subjects being taught. The structural aspects of education refer to how subjects, time, and roles are organized. Some schools have a section devoted solely to the sciences, another to the fine arts, and yet another to business and computer studies. Separation is emphasized and reinforced through a departmentalized structure.

The curricular dimension looks at the intended curriculum which includes what is to be taught - the materials, outlines, projected activities, and goals - as well as the manner in which the curriculum will be organized. The operational curriculum is the curriculum that takes place in the context of the classroom. Pedagogy is essential in this process. Pedagogy is an essential component of school reform. Changes on paper, whether policy or curriculum, are unlikely to have much impact on students unless classroom practices change.

The evaluative dimension requires attention in school reform. As a result, redesigning assessment instruments so that they provide information about what teachers and others care about most from an educational standpoint, is a critical component of school reform. Schools cannot move in one direction while being evaluated by procedures that represent values in another. The processes of teaching and the quality of what is taught, as well as their outcomes, are the proper subject matters of an adequate approach to educational evaluation.

Criticism has four aspects.

- Descriptive: The evaluator describes relevant qualities of educational life giving details of classroom life.
- Interpretive: Ideas from theories are used to explore meanings and develop explanations for the rules and regularities of classroom life.
- Evaluative: Value judgments are made to present the evaluator's understanding of the curriculum.
- Thematic: Various themes that are meaningful within the curriculum are identified.

In this model, curriculum evaluators might observe lessons and other school activities or use videos of students and teachers in action to perform their functions. Although Eisner's model broadens the view of evaluation to include aesthetics, it has been criticised for lacking methodological rigour (Glatthorn et al, 2008). Connoisseurship requires a lot of expertise.

Robert Stake's Model, 1967

Assessment of training programmes. "Description and judgment are important" for educational assessment according to Stake (1967). The conceptual evaluation framework conceived by Stake required a variety of methods to collect data from various sources. Stake's model includes information about the educational background, transactions, and outcomes. Robert Stake (1967) presented an evaluation framework which called for two basic acts in the Stake's definitions of these attributes of evaluation were as follows:

Antecedents: An antecedent is any condition existing before teaching and learning which may relate to outcomes. The status of a student before his lesson and the investments in community resources are examples of educational antecedents.

Transactions: Transactions are the many interactions between students with teacher, student with student, author with reader, parent with counsellor — the various engagements which comprise the process of education.

Outcomes: Outcomes are the abilities, achievements, attitudes, and aspirations of students resulting from an educational experience. Outcomes are the consequence of educating.

Stake stated that history, transactions, and outcomes are components of assessment statements and are a part of the description and judgment. Stake has been synonymous with educational goals or outcomes. According to this model, educational efforts included more than just the desired results of a learning tool. In Stake's view, intents include the planned-for environmental conditions, the planned-for demonstrations, the planned-for coverage of certain subject matter, etc., as well as the planned-for student behaviour.

Providing the rationale for processing descriptive evaluation data depends on (1) finding the relationship among intended antecedents, transactions, and outcomes; and (2) finding the congruence between intents and observations. When their intended backgrounds, transactions and results occur, a school program is said to be consistent. Thus, it proposed that an evaluator collect information on the intended and observed backgrounds, transactions and results of a program and describe the discrepancies and consistency that results from these.

Stake (1967) noted, however, that relationships or contingencies between variables deserve additional attention in that evaluation is a search for links that allow for better education, and that the assessor's task is to identify results that depend on preliminary conditions and instructional transactions. Suggestions for both the formative and summative evaluators were contained in the accompanying education assessment framework. Stake suggested that formative evaluators should look for covariations across studies, as a basis for guiding development of present and future programs.

Stake further suggested that summative evaluation of educational entities should follow a different model. In that model, summative evaluators would judge the goodness-of-fit of an available curriculum to an existing school program by learning whether the intended antecedents, transactions, and outcomes for the curriculum are consistent with the resources, standards, and goals of the school.

Michael Scriven's Goal-Free Evaluation Model, 1972

The Goal Free Evaluation (GFE) is any assessment that is conducted without knowledge of or reference to established or predetermined objectives and objectives. The evaluation does not involve the evaluator. The goal-free evaluator attempts to monitor and measure all real results, effects or impacts, intended or unintended. Objective-free evaluation is also used naturally when program objectives have not been identified previously or goals have not been identified. Goal-free evaluation is not a comprehensive stand-alone evaluation model, but rather a perspective of an evaluator's goal orientation throughout an evaluation. It can be used or adapted for use with several other evaluation approaches, models, and methods if the other approaches do not mandate goal orientation.

There are two methodological requirements of GFE. The first is that the goal-free evaluator comes from outside the organisation and is independent of the program and its main stakeholders (program funders, designers, administrators, managers, staff, volunteers, vendors, etc.); the second is that someone be appointed as the goal screener. A screener is an impartial party (i.e., someone who is not assigned to GFE design or data collection, such as an administrative assistant, a third party, or even the screener intervenes between the evaluator and the program people to eliminate goal-oriented communications and documents before they reach the goal-free evaluator. While the objective evaluator normally receives the objectives with a description of the program and then develops outcomes actions, the goal-free evaluator often begins with the collection of data. The goal-free evaluator cannot know what the program (goals and objectives) is supposed to do, so the first task of the goal-free assessor is to try to define and describe the program. This is accomplished by measuring, observing, and reviewing literature and documents regarding the program's actions and activities. Once the goal-free evaluator begins to understand what the program does and whom it serves, relevant outcome measures often reveal themselves.

Evaluation Methods and Instruments

A variety of methods or tools and instruments are utilised in gathering data for determining the worth or merit of a curriculum. Prominent among them are surveys, questionnaires, interviews, observations, checklists, rating scales, and tests. These are described here.

Surveys

Surveys are used to gather data from representatives or samples of a defined population at a particular time. There are cross sectional and longitudinal surveys. Evaluators use them to gather opinions from stakeholders on a wide range of curriculum issues. For example, surveys could be used to collect data on manpower resources, socioeconomic background of learners or features of various learning environments. The questionnaire, interview and focus group discussions are common instruments for this purpose.

Questionnaire

It is a self-reporting instrument consisting of a set of questions to which the subject responds in writing. It is carefully designed to collect needed data in a simple format that covers a great deal of information. It is relatively inexpensive and may cover a wide geographical area. However, questionnaire construction requires methodological competence and extensive experience. Another limitation of this instrument is that respondents must be literate to fill it out. In curriculum evaluation, the questionnaire is particularly useful in process and program evaluation and not suitable for instructional evaluation. Curriculum developers may be interested in finding out the perceptions of learners about a new course in mathematics and use this instrument.

Interview

The interview gathers data through verbal interaction with participants, usually in a face-to-face situation. In-depth information is collected because interviews allow flexibility in framing and reframing questions. Useful information from parents and laypersons in communities can be collected readily through interviews.

Observations

An observation is a method in which one or more persons examine what is happening in naturalistic settings. Evaluators use the senses to view, classify and record pertinent happenings according to planned schemes. To avoid confusion, observation is systematic, implying that it requires the observer to define aims, select, and define objects or events to be observed and define characteristics of each item or behaviour to be observed (Amin, 2005p. 17).

When properly executed, observations provide unique insight that is not achievable through other methods. They also have the advantage of providing first-hand evidence of certain behaviours because the results approach reality in the natural structure. Despite its advantages, observations are prone to bias, selective perception, and memory. They may also not be readily used to evaluate large groups. Instruments used to record observations include rating scales, checklists, anecdotal records, and inventories. Modern multimedia tools may also be used.

Checklists

A checklist is a set of specific criteria that the observer examines its presence or absence in the product. Used in the diagnosis of learning strengths and weaknesses.

Rating scale

Rating scales require the user to assign a value, sometimes numeric or qualitative to an object as a measure of the attribute being observed. For example, the Likert scale is typically used to measure teachers and learners' attitudes toward curriculum and instruction interventions.

Inventories

An inventory is a complete set of items or behaviour listed by the observer. Self-assessment inventories can be used to help learners identify and assess their learning strategies and approaches to learning.

Anecdotal records

These are detailed written narrative accounts of specific events under observation and occurring in classrooms, playgrounds, or other learning environments. Such records are subjective and provide qualitative data. A classroom teacher may keep a record of the behaviour of uncooperative students, then analyse and evaluate behaviour to determine an appropriate classroom management strategy. Figure 12.1 is a sample template of an anecdotal record that can be adapted for use in different classes at all school levels.

Tests

In education, a test is a tool, a method or an instrument intended to measure the level of student knowledge or skill. Tests fall in two categories depending on their intended uses: achievement and aptitude tests.

```
Name: —————————— Date:—————— Time:————
Observer: ————————————— setting: —————

Description of Event: ———————————————————
————————————————————————————
————————————————————————————
————————————————————————————
————————————————————————————




Signature: —————————————————
```

FIGURE 12.1. Template for anecdotal records

Aptitude tests

Amin (2005) defines aptitude tests as cognitive measures that are commonly used to predict how well an individual is likely to perform in the future. An aptitude test is a systematic means of finding out a candidate's ability to perform specific tasks and react to a range of situations. It is designed to test the innate ability of the test taker towards a competency. Many aptitude tests focus on verbal and numerical reasoning. Examples of internationally known aptitude tests are SAT (Scholastic Aptitude Test), IELTS (international English language testing system), GMAT (graduate management admission test) and GRE (graduate record exam). They are often mandatory for selection of candidates suitable for studies in higher education.

At national and local levels, many competitive entrance examinations into professional schools are aptitude tests. Often used by school counsellors, psychometric tests are also aptitude tests. Psychometric tests are designed to test an individual's personality and cognitive abilities in relation to learning and learning difficulties. Aptitude tests are commonly used for diagnostic and placement evaluation.

Achievement tests

An achievement test is one that determines the extent to which a student has acquired knowledge or skill in a content area after instruction. Such tests can be subdivided into teacher- made-tests and standardised tests according to the design process.

Standardised tests. These are large scale assessments administered to substantial groups of students. Experts in testing construct, administer and score them. All test takers take the same questions. They are built on the principle of consistency.

Teacher-made-tests. As the name indicates, these are tests constructed, administered, and scored by classroom teachers. They take the form of written, oral and performance tests. These are widely used in instructional evaluation.

Another dimension of testing is the interpretation of test scores. In that direction, there is norm referenced and criterion referenced testing.

Norm referenced tests

A test is said to be a norm referenced test when a student's performance score is compared with that of peers. This kind of test addresses a wide range of content and identifies students who are successful and those that need remediation. As a group the students establish a norm. This may be represented statistically in a normal curve. Related to but different from norm referenced assessment are ipsative assessments or self-referenced assessments. Here, assessments are made to measure the progress of individuals by comparing their present performance scores with previous ones. This is to determine intra-individual differences in performance as opposed to inter-individual differences in norm referenced assessments.

Criterion referenced tests

This kind of test is designed to show how well a student performs a task or skill or how well the student understands a concept in relation to a predetermined criterion or standard. Criterion referenced testing is the process of evaluating and grading the learning of students against a set of pre-specified qualities or criteria, without reference to the achievement of others (Brown, 1998; Harvey, 2004). The pedagogical orientation of the competence-based approach to teaching (CBA) favours criterion referenced testing over norm referenced testing.

Key Considerations for Successful Programme Evaluation

Program evaluation is carefully collecting information about a program or some aspect of a program to make necessary decisions about the program. Curriculum evaluation is like programme evaluation. Whatever type of programme evaluation needs to be undertaken, certain considerations are important. The following key questions should guide the design of programme evaluation:

- For what purposes is the evaluation being carried out? i.e., what do you want to be able to decide because of the evaluation?
- Who needs the information from the evaluation, e.g., education stakeholders, customers, bankers, funders, board, management, staff, customers, clients, etc.?
- What kinds of information are needed to make the decision you need to make and/or enlighten your intended audiences, e.g., information to understand the process of the product or program (its inputs, activities, and outputs), the stakeholders or clients who experience the product or program, strengths and weaknesses of the product or program, benefits to customers or clients (outcomes), how the product or program failed and why, etc.?
- From what sources should the information be collected, e.g., employees, customers, clients, groups of customers or clients and employees together, program documentation, etc.?
- How can that information be collected in a reasonable fashion, e.g., questionnaires,

interviews, examining documentation, observing customers or employees, conducting focus groups among customers or employees, etc.?

- When is the information needed (so, by when must it be collected)?
- What resources are available to collect the information?

Part Four

Instructional Design

This part of the book is devoted to instructional design. Curriculum and instruction can be studied as separate entities but cannot be successfully practised in mutual exclusion. Accordingly, instructional design is an integral part of curriculum development, but we have decided to give instructional design prominence by treating it in a separate part. Consisting of two chapters only, terms related to instructional design are first clarified and the theoretical basis of instructional design discussed in chapter 13. Various instructional design models and their applications are described subsequently in chapter 14.

13

Theoretical Basis of Instructional Design

Curriculum development and instructional design are intricately related in the same way that curriculum and instruction are. This relationship has been discussed elsewhere in this book. Curriculum planners cannot develop effective curricula without considering how instructional systems would be designed. To fully grasp the theoretical underpinnings of instructional design and instructional systems design, some commonly used terms need to be clearly explained first. Learning theory, instructional theory, systems theory and communication theory will then be presented and discussed.

Definition of terms and concepts

Instruction

It is a process that deliberately assists someone to learn with or without the help of a human being. This means that a textbook or a website for example, can instruct someone the way a live teacher does. Instruction is the intentional facilitation of learning towards identified goals (Smith and Ragan, 1999, 2005). From this definition, the instructional process is one that offers a solution to the problem of learning. Solutions to problems do not come easily. They often result from collection, analysis and synthesis of data, reflection, insight, and much effort. Instruction is therefore a painstaking process that needs to be carefully planned.

Design

It is the deliberate and systematic arrangement of ideas to form a pattern or plan. When a plan has specifications for its realisation, it becomes design. Smith and Ragan (1999 p. 4) describe design as an intensive planning and ideation process prior to the development of something. Design may be influenced by knowledge, for example, architectural design is informed by facts, concepts, and principles in engineering sciences among others.

Instructional system

Since a system is a set of interrelated parts working toward a common goal and instruction is the intentional facilitation of learning, an instructional system can be defined as a set of interacting parts functioning together to facilitate learning for a particular purpose. Examples of instructional systems include the curriculum, syllabus, a course, module, a lesson, a form 4 physics class, a training workshop, an educational website and web blog.

An instructional system defined by Inyang-Abia (1988) is "a deliberately organized combination of people, materials, facilities and procedures which interact cooperatively for the purpose of achieving predetermined learning objectives" (see figure 13.1). The aspect of "deliberately organising" constitutes design. Instructional systems are not just created. They are designed. Large systems are called macro-instructional systems and smaller ones, micro-instructional systems. Examples of macro-instructional systems are the education system of Cameroon and Secondary education in Cameroon; an example of a micro-instructional system is form 3 physics class.

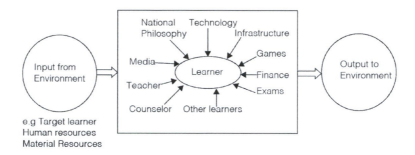

FIGURE 13.1. Flow chart of an instructional system

Instructional design

The term instructional design can be defined from different perspectives. This includes a process, a discipline, a science, and a system.

Instructional Design as a Process

It is the systematic planning of instruction. The process leads to creation of specifications for plans, products and materials that are used for face to face or distance delivery of instruction. For instruction to accomplish its essence of facilitating learning, it must not be haphazardly carried out. It must be designed. Instructional design is a creative, goal-oriented process with practical utility. The careful and well-thought-out input into the process of instructional planning influences the quality of the output. This is what qualifies it as instructional design. Instructional design is distinguished from other forms of instructional planning by the level of precision, care, and expertise (Smith and Ragan, 2005) The overall purpose of instructional design is to create effective, efficient, and appealing instruction.

Instructional Design as a Discipline

It is a branch of knowledge dealing with research and theory about instructional strategies, and the procedure for developing, implementing, and evaluating these strategies.

Instructional Design as a Science

The process of instructional design is objective, observable, and systematic. It is based on a needs assessment and not the designer's interest. The outcomes are observable and measurable, and it follows a step-by-step procedure.

Instructional systems design (ISD)

Instructional systems design is the systematic planning of instructional systems. Instructional design (ID) and instructional systems design (ISD) have basically the same operations and these terms can be used interchangeably. The difference between them lies in the magnitude and sphere of operations. This explains why writers use the term *instructional design* when describing work carried out for micro-instructional systems and use the term *instructional systems design* for work carried out for macro instructional systems. There are many theories and models of instructional design. Some are suitable for designing macro-systems and others more suitable for the design of micro-systems.

Basic Assumptions About Instructional Design

There are important assumptions or principles that constitute the basis for instructional design. They are:

- Instructional Design is a systematic process
- Instructional Design is geared towards problem-solving
- Students learn from many different media: the live teacher is not the sole source of instruction.
- The best instruction is that which is *effective* (facilitates learner acquisition of desired knowledge and skills); *efficient* (requires the least possible amount of time for learners to achieve the goals and *appealing* (motivates learners).
- Instructional Design insists on alignment among objectives, instruction, and evaluation.
- To design instruction the designer must have a clear idea of what the learner should acquire from instruction.
- There are principles of instruction that cut across all age groups and content areas – for example active participation.
- Evaluation should include evaluation of instruction as well as evaluation of learner performance.

Learning Theory (LT)

Learning theories are an organised set of ideas that explain how people acquire, preserve, and retrieve knowledge. A foundation for ISD lies in learning theories. The theoretical approach of an instructional designer to learning affects the design, implementation, and evaluation of education. Theories can be used as guidelines for selecting instructional tools, techniques and learning strategies. There are three main theories on how human beings learn namely Behaviourism, Cognitivism and Constructivism will be summarised here. (These theories have been discussed in detail in chapter

5 of this book).

Behaviourism

Behaviourists are of the opinion that learning takes place when new behaviours or changes in behaviours are acquired through associations between stimuli and responses. Therefore, association leads to a change in behaviour. They also believe that learning entails the formation of associations between stimuli and responses. Behaviourists explain learning in terms of observable phenomena, and reinforcing consequences making the responses more likely to occur whereas punishing consequences make it less likely to recur. The role of the environment specifically how stimuli are arranged and presented and how responses are reinforced are critical.

Implications of Behaviourism on instructional design includes the fact that the instructional designer/teacher should prepare the environment that will help learners to learn, by selecting activities that will bring about the intended learning outcomes. Teachers also need to help learners practice what they have learned. This is important as learning is subject to the rate of occurrence of behaviour. Also, teachers should reward any desired behaviour in learning and punish undesired behaviour.

Cognitivism

To the cognitivists, learning is an internal mental phenomenon measured by what people say and do. The theory is based on the idea that humans process the information they receive, rather than merely responding to stimuli (for example, they think about what is happening). The changes in behaviour indicate what is going on in the learner's head. Learning involves the reorganisation of experiences, either by attaining new insights and changing old ones. Thus, learning is a change in knowledge which is stored in memory, and not just a change in behaviour. Examples and applications of cognitive learning theory include classifying or chunking information, linking concepts (associate new content with something known), providing structure (organising your lecture in efficient and meaningful ways), real world examples, discussions, problem solving, analogies, mnemonics. Such knowledge is important to the instructional designer/teacher in organising content and activities. Teachers need to use different teaching techniques. This helps them lead students to explore the concepts from different perspectives.

Constructivism

Constructivist theorists believe that learning is a process where individuals make meaning or construct new ideas or concepts based on prior knowledge and/or experience. Constructivism perceives each learner as a unique individual with unique needs and complex backgrounds. The instructional designer/teacher therefore should assess students' prior knowledge before they launch new concepts. The constructivist approach insists that instructors/ facilitators must help the learner to get to his or her own understanding of the content. They encourage critical thinking and inquiry by asking students thoughtful, open-ended questions, encouraging them to ask questions to each other so that students can construct their own meaning when learning.

Some major branches of constructivism are:

Individual constructivism:

Knowledge is constructed from experience. Learning results from a personal interpretation of knowledge. Learning is an active process in which meaning is developed based on an individual's experience.

Social constructivism:

Learning is collaborative with meaning negotiated from multiple perspectives. Many instructional designers would recommend that collaborative learning groups are part of a powerful instructional strategy.

Principles of Learning

There are different perspectives of learning principles. However, the following guidelines constitute common elements in principles of learning:

1. Learning is a process of actively constructing knowledge

Learners should engage in experiences that encourage individual construction of knowledge such as hands-on activities and field trips.

2. Learning is enhanced when it takes place in a social and collaborative environment.

In small groups, students can share ideas and learn from each other. They also develop their interpersonal skills and learn to deal with conflict. When cooperative groups are guided by clear objectives, students engage in numerous activities that improve their understanding of subjects explored.

3. Learners have different ways of knowing and representing knowledge.

Learners generally have different interests and learning styles. Effective teaching should be able to respond to differences in the classroom.

4. Repetition

Repetition is essential for all students, regardless of their ability or age. Generally, the more a learner encounters material, the better the likelihood of retaining the information in the long-term. New learning has to be repeated and reinforced for it to be truly remembered and understood. Repetition (practice) is important in teaching skills.

5. Reinforcement

Reinforcement (reward) plays a key role in the condition of operant behaviour and acquisition of learning. It encourages desired behaviour. The use of positive reinforcement is an effective, high-impact strategy for improving students' behaviours. A student who receives a prize for academic excellence for example, is likely to continue working hard.

6. Readiness

Learner readiness is that individual state of a learner where he or she is physically, mentally and emotionally ready to learn. Learning readiness is important for a successful academic performance.

Generally, readiness in children include physical well-being and motor development; social and emotional development; approaches to learning; language development emergent literacy, cognition, and general knowledge.

Instructional Theory (IT)

Instructional theory offers explicit guidance on how to better help people learn and develop (Reigeluth,1999a). It differs from learning theory in that it is prescriptive whereas learning theory is descriptive. Learning theory describes how people learn while instructional theory prescribes how to influence learning. There is however a close relationship between the two. Learning theory informs instructional theory. Accordingly, instructional theory is highly influenced by behaviourism, cognitivism, and constructivism.

Two of the most influential instructional theorists and their contributions to knowledge and implications for instructional design will be summarised and presented here.

Gagne's Conditions of Learning

Robert Gagne's theory of instruction has provided a great number of valuable ideas to instructional designers, trainers, and teachers. His theory of instruction is commonly broken down into three areas: Gagne's taxonomy of learning outcomes, conditions of learning and Events of Instruction. These sub-theories have significantly influenced instructional design.

Conditions of Learning

Critical to Gagne's ideas of instruction are what he refers to as conditions of learning. This theory states that there are several different types or levels of learning. The significance of these classifications is that each different type requires different types of instruction. Gagne identifies five major categories of learning: **verbal information, intellectual skills, cognitive strategies, motor skills** and **attitudes**. Different internal and external conditions are necessary for each type of learning. Instruction must consider internal and external factors to the learner that affect learning.

Internal Conditions of Learning

Internal conditions of learning encompass different conditions within the learner, ranging from processes within the learner that must be present for learning to occur, for example how information is registered, stored in memory and retrieved. It also includes what the learner knows prior to the instruction as well as other psychological factors peculiar to the learner. These factors are explained below:

State of mind of the learner: Learning is efficient when the learner is fully engrossed in the learning process. Learning is maximised when the mind is stable. Too much happiness, sadness, anxiety and fear can impede the learners' ability to concentrate on a lesson and this negatively affects learning.

Previous knowledge: The knowledge students possess may either promote or hinder their learning. It is the basis on which a person may relate or associate to new information and construct new and improved knowledge.

Personal goals: Students who are goal-oriented are highly motivated especially if instruction is aligned with their aspirations. Such students are likely to perform better than students who do not have any specific goals.

Level of interest/Motivation: Highly motivated students are very committed and likely to perform better than students who are not motivated. Motivation is a critical factor in learning, be it intrinsic or extrinsic motivation.

Personal Abilities and Traits: Being open to experience or being intellectually curious or imaginative, is fertile for learning. People with high score on this trait are likely to be more adventurous, creative and can think outside the box. People with low score on this trait are likely to be more conventional and may struggle with abstract thinking. Personal factors such as age and gender, influence learning. People of a young age have a good grasping memory necessary for learning but may have low concentration levels that affect their learning. Studies also indicate that the brains of girls usually mature faster than that of their male age mates and this can be attributed to the high level of concentration by girls in class as compared to boys. Learners with a well-developed language find it easy to learn as compared to those that have no developed language. Also, a learner with high intelligent quotient (IQ) is likely to learn faster and deeper than a person with a low IQ

Social Factors: Social factors like peer pressure affect learning in many ways. The type of friends that a learner keeps influences their behaviour which may affect their attitudes towards learning. If the learner is influenced to get involved in other activities and skip classes, it may affect their concentration and consequently their performance.

External Conditions of Learning

These are circumstances that exist outside of the learner's control. These conditions include the learning situation, the learning environment, and any external aids used by an instructional designer or teacher to facilitate the learning process, such as books, videos, or audio. External conditions differ at each stage of the learning cycle for the same learner. This is due to the fact that learning can begin at a different point each time, and the external environment is usually different at that time.

Nine Events of Instruction

Gagne's 'Nine events of instruction' is based on the information processing model of the mental events that occur when adults are presented with various stimuli and focuses on the learning outcomes and how to arrange specific instructional events to achieve those outcomes. Events of instruction help trainers, educators and instructional designers structure their training or teaching sessions and so provide a framework for effective teaching. Learners are more likely to be engaged in the teaching-learning process and retain the information or skills taught.

The following illustration of the nine events of instruction has been adapted from Gagne, Briggs, and Wager (1992).

1. **Gain attention of the students**

Ensure the learners are ready to learn and participate in activities by presenting a stimulus to capture their attention.

These are a few strategies for capturing learners' attention:

- Stimulate students with something new, unexpected or surprising
- Pose thought-provoking questions to students
- Have students ask their own questions
- Lead an ice breaker activity e.g., greeting

2. Inform students of the objectives

Inform students of the objectives for the lessons to help them understand what they are expected to learn and do.

Here are some methods for stating the outcomes:

- Describe required performance
- Describe criteria for standard performance
- Have learners establish criteria for standard performance
- Include course objectives on assessment prompts.

3. Stimulate recall of prior learning

Help students make sense of new information by relating it to something they already know or something they have already experienced.

There are numerous methods for stimulating recall:

- Ask questions about previous experiences
- Ask students about their understanding of previous concepts
- Relate previous content to the current topic
- Have students incorporate prior learning into current activities.

4. Present the content

Use teaching strategies to present content to provide more effective instruction. Organise and sequence content in meaningful ways and provide explanations after demonstrations.

The following are ways to present content:

- Present multiple versions of the same content (for example video, demonstration, lecture, podcast, group work, etc.)
- Use a variety of media to engage students in learning
- Incorporate active learning strategies to keep students involved
- Provide access to content such that students can access it even outside of class.

5. Provide learning guidance

Encourage students to use strategies to aid them in learning content and of resources available. In other words, help students learn how to learn. Learning guidance can be done in the following ways:

- Provide instructional support as needed. Scaffold and remove slowly as the student learn and masters the task or content
- Model different learning strategies – for example mnemonics, concept mapping, role playing, visualising
- Use examples and non-examples
- Provide case studies, visual images, analogies, and metaphors – Case studies provide

real world application, visual images assist in making visual associations, and analogies and metaphors use familiar content to help students connect with new concepts.

6. Elicit performance (practice)

Get students to apply what they have learned to reinforce new skills and knowledge and to confirm correct understanding of course concepts.

Here are a few ways to activate learner processing:

- Facilitate student activities – for example ask deep-learning questions, have students collaborate with their peers, facilitate practical laboratory exercises
- Provide formative assessment opportunities – for example written assignments, individual or group projects, presentations
- Design effective quizzes and tests – for example test students in ways that allow them to demonstrate their comprehension and application of course concepts (as opposed to simply memorisation and recall).

7. Provide feedback

Provide timely feedback of students' performance to facilitate learning and to allow students to identify gaps in understanding.

The following are some types of feedback you may provide to students:

- **Confirmatory feedback** informs the student that they did what they were supposed to do. This type of feedback does not tell the student what she needs to improve, but it encourages the learner.
- **Evaluative feedback** informs the student of the accuracy of their performance or response but does not provide guidance on how to progress.
- **Remedial feedback** guides students to arrive at the correct answer but does not provide the correct answer.
- **Descriptive or analytic feedback** provides the student with suggestions, directives, and information to help them improve their performance.
- **Peer-evaluation and self-evaluation** help learners identify learning gaps and performance shortcomings in their own and peers' work.

8. Assess performance

Test whether the expected learning outcomes have been achieved on previously stated course objectives. Some methods for testing learning include the following:

- Administer pre- and post-tests to check for progression of competency in content or skills
- Provide formative assessment opportunities throughout instruction using oral questioning, short active learning activities, or quizzes
- Implement a variety of assessment methods to provide students with multiple opportunities to demonstrate proficiency
- Craft objective, effective rubrics to assess written assignments, projects, or presentations

9. Enhance retention and transfer

Aid learners retain more information by providing them opportunities to connect course concepts to real-world applications.

The following are methods to help learners internalise new knowledge:

- Avoid isolating course content. Associate course concepts with prior (and future) concepts and build upon prior (and preview future) learning to reinforce connections.
- Continually incorporate questions from previous tests in subsequent examinations to reinforce course information.
- Have students convert information learned in one format into another format (e.g., verbal or audio-visual).
- To promote deep learning, clearly articulate your lesson objectives, and align learning activities to lesson goals.

Gagne's Learning Outcomes and Their Conditions of Learning

Gagne (1985) classified learning outcomes into five categories. The five learning outcomes include: intellectual skills, cognitive strategy, verbal information, motor skills, and attitude. The intellectual skills, cognitive strategy, and verbal information are in the cognitive domain while motor skills are in the psychomotor domain and attitude is the affective domain as seen below:

1. Intellectual Skills

Intellectual skills incorporate procedural knowledge (how to do things). Intellectual skills are broken down into different levels of learning: discrimination, concrete concept, defined concept, rule, and problem-solving (Gagne et al., 1992).

Discrimination is the ability to make a difference between objects based on their physical characteristics. For example: differentiate between an orange and a lemon. To facilitate learning the teacher should use reinforcement and repetition to assist and enhance learning of this skill.

Concrete concept is the ability to identify an object as a member of a group based on common physical characteristics. For example, organisms that have four legs are considered animals. As such dogs, cows and horses will be considered animals. Learning a concrete concept is more complex than learning discrimination. Discrimination only requires identifying a difference while concrete concept requires the ability to identify an object correctly based on its main features. Students must be able to discriminate before they learn concrete concepts. They must be able to understand concrete concepts before they can understand abstract concepts. To enhance learning of this skill, the teacher should present different examples of an object (concept) as well as non-examples and ask students to identify a correct answer.

Defined concept is the ability to understand the meaning of an object, event, or relation. It requires more than stating a definition or defining a concept. For example, to understand the meaning of love, justice, kindness, intelligence etc. Although defined concepts may overlap with concrete concept, the former represents more abstract learning. To enhance learning of this skill, the teacher should first ask students to recall all aspects in the definition of a concept, including the relations among those components. The teacher can facilitate this skill by having students watch a demonstration, video, or film on how the concept works.

Rule is the ability to understand the relationships among concepts (objects and events). For example: know how to multiply numbers, to construct a house or to play a game. To learn the skill, teachers should help students recall the components that make up the rule and their relationships. They should clearly communicate the rule to students and provide guidance (e.g., prompts, cues, strategies) during learning.

Problem-solving is the ability to combine rules to solve a problem. Teachers should teach or have students recall relevant rules and information essential to solving the problem. They should offer cues or prompts to help students solve the problem or engage them in discovery learning (guided and unguided) to reach a solution.

2. Cognitive strategy

Cognitive strategy is another type of intellectual skills for learning and thinking. Learning strategies include rehearsal (verbally repeating, underlining, or copying materials), elaboration (associate new information with the existing one through paraphrasing, summarising, note-taking, and questions and answers), and organising (arranging material in an organised and meaningful order through outlining, concept mapping, advance organiser, etc.). The metacognitive strategies (thinking) involve students setting learning goals, tracking learning progress, and modifying strategies to achieve the goals. The affective strategies are used to focus and maintain attention, to control stress and anxiety, to manage time effectively, and so on.

3. Verbal information

Verbal information or declarative knowledge includes facts, information, names, places, etc. To assist learning of verbal information, the instructor may teach students different mnemonic techniques (e.g., keyword, loci, imagery, etc.) and help students relate new information to what already exists in memory to make learning meaningful and memorable. The teacher should enhance learning strategies like rehearsal, elaboration, and organise to enhance memory.

4. Motor skills

Motor skills also known as psychomotor skills are sequences of motor responses or movements, which are combined into complex performances. For example: dancing, jumping, writing, playing, etc. The motor skills can be further divided into sub skills (part skills), which are performed simultaneously or in sequential order to produce performances. These skills are best learned through rehearsals. To teach the part skills, the teacher should provide clear instruction to learn the skills. Pictures or diagrams will also be useful. The teacher should encourage students to practice the skills repeatedly, accompanied by timely and appropriate feedback from the instructor.

5. Attitude

Attitude is an internal state that affects personal choices and actions over an object, person or event. Although it is a complex human state, it can be measured by observing the person's choice or action. The measurement of attitude is often seen in a form of a self-reported questionnaire, which may use Likert-scale and/or open-ended questions. Attitudes can be taught using a role-model. Other methods involve using reinforcement to encourage a desired behaviour and using a conditioned response method to promote certain attitudes. To change attitude, teachers should help students recall a situation to which the attitude applies, present an appealing and credible role model, use the model to communicate or demonstrate the desired choices or actions for the given situation, and demonstrate satisfaction the model obtains because of the selected choices or actions.

Bloom's Taxonomy of Educational Objectives

This was created in 1956 by Benjamin Bloom and his associates to promote higher forms of thinking in education, such as analysing and evaluating knowledge and processes rather than just memorising facts. It is most often used when designing educational, training, and learning processes.

The taxonomy of educational objectives identified three domains namely:

- **The Cognitive domain**: This domain is made up of mental skills (**knowledge**)
- **The Affective domain**: This includes growth in feelings or emotional areas (**attitude or self**)
- **The Psychomotor domain**: It involves manual or physical skills (**skills**)

Each of These three domains is broken down into subdivisions, made up of a hierarchy starting from the simplest cognitive process or behaviour to the most complex.

The Cognitive Domain (original version, 1956)

This domain is made up of six hierarchical levels that are presented below.

Knowledge: This level requires a learner to acquire information by memorising or identifying facts and it provides the basis for greater understanding. Questions that ask students to define, label, locate, recite, select, memorise, recognise, name, state, identify or repeat information are designed to achieve objectives at this level. Knowledge is the lowest level of Bloom's taxonomy.

Comprehension: It requires understanding information focusing on the meaning and intent of the material. Whenever students are asked to restate, paraphrase, rewrite, convert, give examples, illustrate, summarise, explain, locate, express they are employing comprehension level skills, the level of comprehension is targeted.

Application: It has to do with making use of information; gives student practice in the transfer of their learning to other situations. Some action verbs associated with the application level are apply, modify, dramatize, translate, demonstrate, and construct.

Analysis: It requires examining specific parts of information to "see" the underlying ideas; utilised before decisions are reached and problems are attacked. Analyse, classify, distinguish, subdivide, separate, differentiate, examine, calculate, compare/contrast are verbs that could be used to express the analysis level of Bloom's taxonomy.

Synthesis: It involves doing something new and different with information; involves the ability to put parts and elements together in a new form. Students who combine, compose, design, organise, invent, develop, plan, or create are using synthesis level skills.

Evaluation: It has to do with judging information using some criteria or standard. Asking students to evaluate, recommend, summarise, debate, criticise, or judge, challenges them to incorporate the evaluation level in their thinking process.

The Cognitive Domain (new version, 2001)

Benjamin Bloom's former student named Lorin Anderson led a new assembly in the 1990s to review and update Blooms taxonomy. Published in 2001, the revision includes a few significant changes (see Tables 13.1 and 13.2). The revised version of the taxonomy has more relevance for 21st century teachers and students. Both versions provide educators with a way to organise thinking skills into six hierarchical levels, from the most basic to the most complex levels.

Remembering: It means recalling information, recognising, listing, describing, retrieving, naming and finding information

Understanding: It means explaining, describing, interpreting, differentiating, paraphrasing, classifying, explaining ideas or concepts.

Applying: This implies using information in another familiar situation. Verbs used at this level include implementing, carrying out, using, demonstrating, executing etc.

Analysing: It means breaking down information into its constituent parts to explore understandings and relationships. It is a higher level of understanding. Verbs used at this level include comparing, organising, deconstructing, interrogating, finding

Evaluating: This implies justifying a decision or course of action. Checking, hypothesising, critiquing, experimenting, and judging are some of the verbs used at this level.

Creating: This means generating new ideas, products, or ways of viewing things. Verbs commonly used here are designing, constructing, planning, producing, inventing.

Table 13.1. Minor Differences between Original and New Versions of Blooms Taxonomy

Basis of comparison	Original version	New version
Description of each level	Use of nouns	Use of verbs to emphasise the learning process
Highest mental skill	evaluation	creating
Position of last two levels	They are swapped	

Major differences between original and new versions
- Knowledge is a dimension common to all six levels, consisting of facts, concepts, procedures, and metacognition
- Taxonomy can be presented diagrammatically in a matrix as shown in table 13.2

Table 13.2. New Bloom's Taxonomy matrix

Knowledge dimension	Cognitive dimension					
Factual knowledge	Remembering	Understanding	Applying	Analysing	Evaluating	Creating
Conceptual knowledge						
Procedural knowledge						

Knowledge dimension	Cognitive dimension					
Metacognitive knowledge						

Source: Anderson and Krathworl (2001)

The Affective Domain

The affective domain describes learning objectives that emphasise a feeling tone, an emotion, or a degree of acceptance or rejection. Affective objectives vary from simple attention to selected phenomena to complex but internally consistent qualities of character and conscience.

Beginning from simple to complex, the affective domain has five levels as follows:

1. **Receiving** is being aware of or sensitive to a stimulus or the existence of certain ideas, material, or phenomena and being willing to tolerate them. Examples include: to differentiate, to accept, to listen (for), to respond to.

2. **Responding** is reacting to the ideas, materials, or phenomena involved by actively responding to them. Examples are, to comply with, to follow, to commend, to volunteer, to spend leisure time in, to acclaim.

3. **Valuing** is willing to be perceived by others as attaching some worth or valuing certain ideas, materials, or phenomena. Examples include: to increase measured proficiency in, to relinquish, to subsidise, to support, to debate.

4. **Organisation** is to relate the value to those already held and bring it into a harmonious and internally consistent philosophy. Examples are, to discuss, to theorise, to formulate, to balance, to examine.

5. **Characterisation** by value or value set is to act consistently in accordance with the values he or she has internalised. Examples include: to revise, to require, to be rated high in the value, to avoid, to resist, to manage, to resolve.

The Psychomotor Domain

There are three versions of the psychomotor domain in literature. In this section Elizabeth Simpson's version will be discussed. The psychomotor domain by Simpson, (1972) includes physical movement, coordination, and use of the motor-skill areas. Development of these skills requires practice and is measured in terms of speed, precision, distance, procedures, or techniques in execution. Thus, psychomotor skills rage from manual tasks, such as digging a ditch or washing a car, to more complex tasks, such as operating a complex piece of machinery or dancing. There are different versions of the psychomotor domain. That of Simpson (1972) is presented below.

Perception (Awareness): The ability to use sensory cues to guide motor activity. This ranges from sensory stimulation through cue selection to translation. Verbs at this level include chooses, describes, detects, differentiates, distinguishes, identifies, isolates, relates, select etc.

Set: Readiness to act. It includes physical and emotional sets. These three sets describe dispositions that pre-determine a person's response to different situations or mindsets. Verbs here include begins, displays, explains, moves, proceeds, reacts, shows, states, volunteers etc

Guided Response: The early stages in learning a complex skill that includes imitation and trial and error. Adequacy of performance is achieved by practicing. Verbs include copies, traces, follows, reacts, reproduce, responds etc.

Mechanism (basic proficiency): This is the intermediate stage of learning a complex skill. Learned responses have become habitual and the movements can be performed with some confidence and proficiency. Verbs include assembles, calibrates, constructs, dismantles, displays, fastens, fixes, grinds, heats, manipulates, measures, mends, mixes, organises, sketches etc.

Complex Overt Response (Expert): The skilful performance of movements that involve complex movement patterns. Proficiency is indicated by a quick, accurate and highly coordinated performance requiring a minimum of energy. This category includes performing without hesitation and automatic performance. For example, players often utter sounds of satisfaction as soon as they kick towards the goal post because they can tell by the feel of the act what the results will produce. Verbs include assembles, builds, calibrates, constructs, dismantles, displays, fastens, fixes, manipulates, organises, sketches etc.

Adaptation: Skills are well developed, and the individual can modify movement patterns to fit special requirements. Verbs include adapts, alerts, changes, rearranges, reorganises, revises etc.

Organisation: Creating new movement patterns to fit a particular situation or specific problem. Learning outcomes emphasise creativity based on highly developed skills. Verbs include arranges, combines, composes, constructs, creates, initiates etc.

Systems Theory

Systems thinking is a process of understanding how things influence one another as a whole. It is an approach to solving problems by focusing on the whole (that often tends to be bigger than the sum of its parts). Systems thinking looks at the bigger picture of things. As far back as the 17th century, Isaac Newton accomplished the system theory through a mathematical analysis of the solar system. He analysed the components of the solar system and their relationship with the force of gravity. Today, Bertalanffy, a biologist who propounded the general systems theory in the mid-twentieth century, is considered the father of modern systems theory.

Within the field of education, systems' thinking has been found to be useful in educational technology, administration, evaluation and pedagogy. Systems' thinking is very beneficial in education for the following reasons:

- It helps educationists to see problems in wholes and not piecemeal.
- Holistic approach to problem solving enables exploration of all related alternatives of the solution to a problem.
- It is a scientific and technological way of thinking.

Characteristics of a system

A system is a set of interrelated parts that work toward a common goal (Smith & Ragan, 2005). There are natural systems like the human body, ecosystems, climatic system, the biosphere. And human-made systems like an automobile, a wristwatch, a sewing machine, a school, and a nation. A system is a holistic organisation of elements that function interpedently towards achieving specific functions. Malfunctioning of any part of the system would render the system partially or entirely non-functional. Specifically:

- It is composed of parts or elements often known as components. These components are related to one another. A change in one component causes a change in the whole system.
- A system has a boundary and anything outside the system is in the environment.
- Some systems are open, and others are closed. Open systems are those that interact with the environment. They receive inputs from the environment and send outputs into the environment.
- A system can be nested inside another system. In that case the larger system is the supra system and the nested one, the subsystem.
- A system consists of processes that can transform inputs into outputs.
- Systems are often self-regulating. That is, they are self-correcting through feedback.

Applicability of System Characteristics to Education and Instruction

Systems approach to instruction is not a method of teaching; it is a way of thinking that involves carrying out certain practices.

1. Systems components organisation

In education there are systems such as the school, the class, the regional delegation of education, the inspectorate of education. Each of these systems has components referred to as a subsystem, for example, the school. Some of the subsystems are classes, timetables, schemes of work, administrative staff, teaching staff, learners etc. The system components are systematically arranged and organised to produce a definite structure.

2. Goals and objectives

All human-made systems have clearly defined goals. A system goal is a general description of the purpose of the system, for example, the Cameroon Education system has goals. Long-term goals, medium and short-term goals. The goals of education in Cameroon as outlined in law no. 98/4 are:

3. Open and closed systems

Most systems in education are open systems. The school interacts with other systems in its environment, like the home. The social, economic, political, and cultural systems found in a school's environment affect the educational system. Complete openness is however not very healthy for the survival of a system.

4. Supra systems and subsystems

Secondary education is nested in the education system of Cameroon. Secondary education is therefore a subsystem of education in Cameroon.

5. Inputs, throughputs and outputs

The inputs of an instructional system are the learners, the instructional objectives, materials, methodology, personnel, and environmental instruments. Throughputs are the interactions with one another; the style and methods of mixing them together. The throughput is an active processor. The throughput of an instructional system consists of instructional processes. The output refers to the school graduates. They have acquired new abilities, good morals and marketable skills.

Communication Theory

There are many communication models. However, three prominent ones and their underlying approaches will be discussed here. There are many perspectives in the definition of communication as presented by West and Tuner (2000).

Shannon and Weaver (1949) described communication as a linear process. They were inspired by the radio and telephone technology and wanted to develop a model that could explain how information passed through various channels. This led to the conceptualisation of the linear model of communication. This approach to human communication comprises several key elements: a source, or transmitter of a message, sends a message to a receiver, the recipient of the message. The receiver is the person who makes sense out of the message. This communication takes place through a channel. Channels frequently refer to the visual, tactile, olfactory, and auditory senses.

This communication process was highly appreciated many years ago. However, there are some limitations of this approach. First, the model assumes that there is only one message in the communication process. Yet there are several circumstances in which we send several messages at once. Also, communication may not have a definable beginning and ending and may not involve only two persons.

Based on these limitations of the Linear model, Schramm (1954), conceptualised the interactional model of communication, with a two-way communication process between communicators: from sender to receiver and from receiver to sender. This cyclical process suggests that communication is dynamic. The interactional view shows that a person can perform the role of either sender or receiver during an interaction, but not both roles simultaneously. One element which is key to the interactional model of communication is feedback, or the response to a message.

14

The Instructional Design Process and Models

Classroom teachers, programme and course designers, textbook writers and curriculum developers at all levels want to create high quality learning environments and experiences for learners. To do this effectively, they must engage in the instructional design process. There are three basic questions that the instructional design process provides answers to. *Where are we going? How do we get there? How do we know when we get there*? These questions must be asked and answered by instructional designers themselves. The answer to the first question lies in the formulation of instructional goals and objectives. It is essentially what learners should know and demonstrate because of learning. To know in advance where one is heading to, reduces waste of time in trial and error. The second question requires designers to make decisions on instructional methods, activities and materials and media. The last question leads to the design of assessment strategies and instruments. Generally, instructional design (ID) involves the following steps:

- Step 1: Analyse Requirements. Analysis is perhaps the most important step of the Instructional Design process.
- Step 2: Identify Learning Objectives.
- Step 3: Develop Design.
- Step 4: Develop Prototype.
- Step 5: Develop Training.
- Step 6: Deliver Training.
- Step 7: Evaluate Impact.

In this chapter, we begin with a general description of the ID process and move on to present in detail, various instructional design models.

General Description of the Process

The Instructional Design process as conceived by different scholars and illustrated by their models has more commonalities than differences. The differences are found more in the structure than in the content. Generally, the content and what is required in the equivalent stages of different models, are the same. Below is a broad discussion of what is expected at different stages with explanations from different models where necessary to better illustrate a point. Generally, five stages can be identified in the instructional design process.

Analysis

According to a generalised model popularly known as ADDIE model (pronounced adee), the first step in drawing up a new educational programme is referred to as needs analysis or needs assessment. The rationale of needs assessment is to determine whether instruction should be designed in the first place. At the end of this exercise the reasons for developing instruction will be very clear. The outcomes one would expect to see when the problem is solved will be very apparent.

Smith and Ragan (2013) identify three factors that call for a needs assessment:

- When there is a problem or crisis (Problem Model)
- When there is something new that learners need to learn e.g., change in policies or change in tools (Innovation Model)
- When it is a result of summative evaluation – the difference between the goals and the outcomes. The discrepancies form the foundation (discrepancy model)
- The above analysis could be carried out through document analysis, interviews, observation, focus groups, questionnaire, surveys. Once you have completed these analyses, you will have a much better idea of the who, what, where, and why of your envisaged programme. The following elements are analysed:
- The Learning Environment
- The Learner
- The Learning Task

Analysing the Learning Environment

There is a need to assess the location in which the instruction will be implemented. The following questions will guide the assessment of the context: what are the characteristics and attitudes of teachers who will be using the material? What is their experience with the content? Are there existing curricula that the instruction can fit in? What instructional materials exist in that context? Are specific resources available? What is the class size like? What are the organisational values? Is the proposed instruction in consonance with the organisational values?

Analysis of the Learner

Once you confirm that training is needed, it's time to analyse your learners. Knowing key demographics and background information about your learners will help you identify the information they need to know and the best way to present it to them. Learners are similar and different in various aspects. Individuals are similar in sensory capabilities (information processing), physical, psychosocial and language developmental processes. They are however different in their aptitudes, styles, developmental stages and prior learning. Designers can assess learner characteristics using the instruments listed above.

Task Analysis

The first step to task analysis is the interpretation of the goals. This interpretation results in the statement of objectives. There are two kinds of task analysis: The procedural task analysis or

Information processing task analysis and the Learning task analysis.

The Procedural Task Analysis. Procedural task analysis describes the steps for performing a task. It involves breaking down tasks to steps the learner must perform to complete the task. These are physical and mental steps a learner will go through in order to complete the learning task. This provides a clear description of the **target objectives** or the competences. In order to know these steps, the designer can read about it and confirm with subject experts.

The Learning Task Analysis. Once the target objectives have been identified, an analysis to identify prerequisite competencies (enabling skills) can be done. Prerequisite skills can be classified into:

- Essential prerequisites
- Supportive prerequisites

Essential prerequisite skills are those a student should learn to be able to demonstrate content knowledge e.g., the ability to explain and analyse concepts. Supportive prerequisites on the other hand are skills that are helpful but not essential in the acquisition of intellectual skills. Language skills and attitudes for instance are supportive skills. It must be noted that different learning outcomes constitute prerequisite skills for others. This results in a learning hierarchy. For instance, intellectual skills constitute a prerequisite skill for cognitive strategies or knowledge is a prerequisite for comprehension (based on Bloom's taxonomy). A diagrammatic representation of the breakdown from the target objectives to the prerequisite skills is known as an *Instructional Curriculum Map*.

Design

The design phase includes the identification of objectives, content, instructional strategies, practice activities, instructional materials, and duration. The designers determine how objectives will be assessed and what forms of assessment will be used. The objectives and assessments should also align. Specifically, objectives are stated in three domains:

- Cognitive-Knowledge
- Affective -Attitudes
- Psychomotor -Skills

Concrete decisions are made at this point about selecting the content to be taught, the sequence to follow in teaching the content, the teaching strategies/activities that will be used, the media and delivery mode (online, face to face or blended), the duration per unit, the assessment items. It is here that the skills to be taught and strategy for teaching are determined. Smith and Ragan propose the following specifications for the design phase: Organisation, i.e., the structure and sequence of content; Delivery, i.e., the media involved in the delivery and specific tools designed for that. Also, the grouping strategies (i.e., either large or small groups) and management, i.e., the scheduling and the acquisition of resources. Smith and Ragan (2013) propose that the organisational strategy should be guided by information processing. The designer should select organisational strategies which facilitate mental processes like rehearsal, elaboration, organisation, and meta-cognition. Some general procedures for organisational strategies in delivering content are: introduction, body and conclusion or Gagne's events of instruction.

Different outcomes call for different teaching strategies which could be direct (supplantive) and indirect (generative). For example, declarative knowledge calls for elaboration, rehearsal, organisation (chunking). At the end of the instructional design phase, the designer creates an instructional design document (a blueprint) that provides a high-level overview of the entire instructional plan.

The product of design is a blue-print; a set of specifications or plans for developers to follow. This includes:

Translating course goals into course objectives while identifying the type of learning outcomes involved:

- Determining the major units or topics of instruction, the major outcomes per unit and how much time will be spent on it.
- Fleshing out the unit objectives by specifying the learning outcomes for each unit; Breaking units down into lessons and learning objectives.
- Developing specifications for lessons and learning activities.
- Determining media and delivery modes
- Designing specifications for the assessment of students' learning (usually criterion referenced).

Development

The development phase entails the process of authoring, reviewing, producing and validating the learning materials. At this stage samples of the materials are created. This phase focuses on developing the instructional material and the delivery system. In some cases, materials may be available from another course which can be incorporated, adapted, or even adopted. In other cases, material relating to that instruction may be unavailable and these must be produced. However, looking around for what is available minimises cost. Development could also mean changing a course from one delivery system to another, for example from the classroom to web-based. Depending on the design specifications, designers may work in project teams with authors, subject matter experts, editors, language practitioners, graphic designers, artists, film/video or other media producers, book designers and desktop publishers in order to ensure accuracy.

Implementation

This phase involves implementing instructional materials to the real world environment, providing support to users, and using evaluation instruments to find out the worth of the instructional material and programs. The validation involves a process of formative evaluation, which entails collecting and interpreting people's opinions on the learning programme and instructional materials because the material developed is usually a new element to be used by people other than the designer and this makes implementation complex. Smith and Ragan (2013) suggest that even though the content has been sequenced it should still be tested with representative members of the target audience. Formative evaluation should go through many phases. It must go through design reviews where all data gathered at the analysis stage can be submitted for formative evaluation. Also, expert review should be carried out before developing material. Content experts, design experts and teachers need to check the content to find out if it is authentic, realistic, or accurate. The feedback from this will lead to further improvement of the material. After this the material is tried out with representations of the target audience at different levels. There is one-to-one evaluation consisting of 2-5 members of the target audience. Feedback from this small group leads to revision of the material. The next level is small group evaluation consisting of a larger group and then field trials consisting of a much larger group. This is referred to as material evaluation.

Formative evaluation is important when the designer is a novice, when the content area is new to the designer, when the technology is new, when the instructional strategy is new to the designer and when opportunities for later revision are slim.

Evaluation

Once the final product has been produced and learners use the learning materials, the evaluation at this stage is referred to as summative. Usually, independent evaluators are called upon to conduct the summative evaluation to ensure objectivity, and not the designer who was closely involved in all the design and development stages of the final product. Evaluators are concerned with questions such as: what is the impact of the new learning materials on the institution/organisation? How are grades and graduation rates or job performances affected? Are the learning objectives relevant? Are the materials being used correctly? Is the course content relevant? What aspects need to be changed or updated?

Gagne et al (2005) identify five types of evaluation namely:

Materials Evaluation: This review is done by subject experts. They look at the objectives and materials and trial testing take place. This type of evaluation takes place at the implementation stage as seen above.

Process Evaluation: This evaluation focuses on instructional design processes. It looks at how well each stage of the design process was conducted. This leads to continuous improvement.

Learner Reaction: This evaluation focuses on learner perception of the programme relating to the quality of the instructor, instructional strategies etc. A self-report questionnaire may help.

Learner Performance: It is the extent to which learners are achieving the objectives, generally and in specific areas. This feedback is important in improving the programme.

Instructional consequences: It is the transfer or application of training on the job, the benefits of training to the community etc.

While the evaluation is both formative and summative, formative evaluation leads to improvement of the programme while summative evaluation leads to decisions about the worth and value of a programme.

Often, the instructional systems design process may be portrayed as linear. In practice, however, it is frequently iterative, moving backwards and forwards between the activities as the project develops and that is why Smith and Ragan (2013) describe this process as a "ball of worms".

Instructional Systems Design Models

Instructional design models are conceptual tools to visualise the process of instructional design. It guides the practitioner in completing the process in a step-by-step manner. There are many instructional design models in literature, five of which are discussed below.

The ADDIE Model (Gagne, et al. 2005)

Analysis

- First, establish the needs for which instruction is the solution
- Conduct an instructional analysis to determine the target cognitive, affective, and motor skill goals for the course
- Determine the entry qualifications/skills students have and which will impact learning in the course
- Analyse the time available and how much might be accomplished in that period (context analysis).

Design

- Translate course goals, performance outcomes and major course objectives
- Determine the instructional topics or units to be covered and how much time will be spent on each
- Sequence the units regarding the course objectives
- Flesh out the units of instruction, identifying the major objectives to be achieved during each unit
- Define lessons and learning activities for each unit
- Develop specifications for assessments of what students have learned.

Development

- Make decisions regarding the types of learning activities and materials
- Prepare draft materials and/or activities
- Try out materials and activities with target audience members
- Revise, refine and produce materials and activities
- Produce teacher training or adjunct materials.

Implementation

- Market materials for adoption by teachers and students
- Provide help or support/training as needed

Evaluation

- Implement plans for student evaluation
- Implement plans for program evaluation

- Implement plans for course maintenance and revision
- These stages are shown in the diagram below:

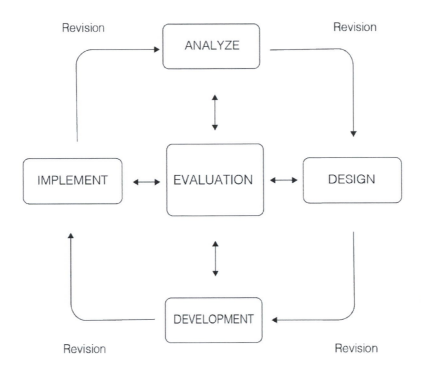

FIGURE 14.1. The ADDIE model

The Dick and Carey Model

This model has ten stages similar to the models that have been described above.

Stage 1: Identify Instructional Goals

What you want the learners to be able to do by the end of instruction.

Stage 2: Conduct Instructional Analysis

Determine what students are doing when they perform each goal. Determine the skills, knowledge, and attitudes, required for learners to have before beginning your course.

Stage 3: Analyse Learners and Contexts

Analyse the context in which the learners will acquire the skills and how they will use them.

Stage 4: Write Performance Objectives

Write the performance objectives on what the learner will be able to do when they complete the instruction.

Stage 5: Develop Assessment Instruments

Develop the assessments that are parallel and test each performance goal.

Stage 6: Develop Instructional Strategy

Identify strategies that will foster student learning, include pre-instructional activities, presentation of content, learner participation, assessment, and follow-through activities.

Stage 7: Develop and Select Instructional Materials

Produce the instruction using the identified strategies. Produce materials such as, guides, modules, presentations, media, and LMS site to upload the content (for online).

Stage 8: Develop and Conduct Formative Evaluation

Collect data to be used for improving instruction including one-to-one evaluation, small group evaluation, and field trial evaluation.

Step 9: Revise Instruction

Revise instruction according to feedback, this is a step in a repeat cycle, creating an iterative process in the design model.

Step 10: Design and Conduct Summative Evaluation

This step is usually not part of the design process. This step involves an independent evaluator and usually does not involve the designer. It is the culminating evaluation of the effectiveness of instruction. Below is a diagram showing these stages:

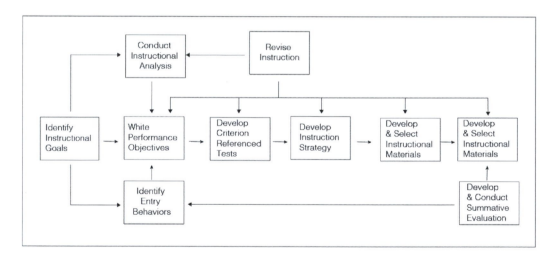

FIGURE 14.2. Dick and Carey Model

ASSURE Model

Developed by Robert Heinich and Michael Molenda decades ago, the ASSURE model gained popularity because of its use in a popular textbook for educators.

While focusing on the needs of learners, the model places emphasis on lesson planning and use of technology. The model contains the following steps:

- Analyse learners

- State objectives
- Select methods, media, and materials
- Utilise media and materials
- Require learner participation
- Evaluate and revise

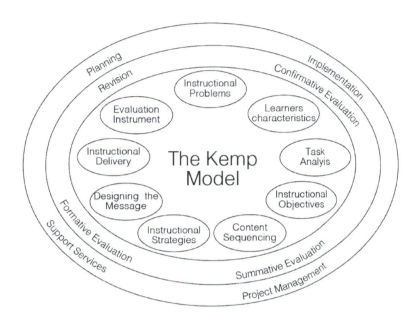

FIGURE 14.3. The Kemp model

The Kemp Model

The Kemp design model which has a circular structure conveys that the design process is a continuous cycle, therefore, it needs constant planning, design, and evaluation to ensure quality instruction.

This model includes 9 elements:

- Identify learning goals and instructional problems or obstacles that may hinder them
- Research the audience to identify learner's characteristics that you can use to create more relevant course material
- Identify the relevant subject content and analyse tasks to see whether they align with the defined goals
- Clarify the instructional objectives to the learners and how they will benefit from the instructional programs
- Make sure the content for each instructional unit is structured sequentially and logically to facilitate learning
- Design instructional strategies in such a way that will help learners to master the content

and learning outcomes
- Plan the instructional message and the mode of delivery
- Develop evaluation instruments to evaluate the progress of the learners towards achieving the objectives
- Select resources that will provide support for both teaching and learning activities.

These steps are illustrated in the diagram below:

The Common Model

This model by Smith and Ragan has three stages: Analysis, Strategy and Evaluation.

Analysis

The focus of the analysis phase is on the target learner, the context and environment in which the learning will take place, the identification of learning goals and objectives, and the learning tasks. A needs assessment is carried out in order to gather information for the analysis phase. Needs assessment takes into account the gaps between "what is" and "what should be." A needs assessment is a process for determining how to close a learning or performance gap by identifying the critical needs and determining the best way to meet them.

When these gaps have been established, the identified needs are then formulated into goals. Programs must target the needs of the target learners in order to be successful. Instructional and goal analysis is carried out to identify the required knowledge, skills, behaviors, and attitudes to meet them. These are further broken down into specific measurable and observable objectives.

The discrepancy model of needs assessment, which examines the gaps or differences, between individuals who perform desired behaviours and those who do not, is a particularly useful and relevant needs assessment approach. Each gap discovered during the analysis is categorized as a need. After the gaps have been identified, the causes of the gaps can be researched and quantified. This information is then used to shape the development of learning or intervention tasks aimed at achieving the intervention goals.

In the design of instruction, objectives serve several important functions. It guides the choice of activities and resources that promote effective learning. Objectives also serve as a framework for assessing and evaluating the extent to which learning is occurring, and they play an important role in guiding the learner by identifying the skills and knowledge to be mastered. The designer considers the environment and context in which learning will take place during the analysis phase. The environmental analysis approach is founded on three environmental domains: physical, social, and institutional.

Concerns about the physical environment in which the intervention will be used are referred to as physical concerns. The learners and their social connections and networks, including those that will influence the learning experience, are referred to as social concerns. Institutional considerations affect any institutional goals and influence program design decisions. Working closely with members of the targeted population early in the design and development process allows designers to fully consider the domain factors most relevant for the creation of programs that reflect and address the needs of learners while also aligning with the domains in which the programs will be used.

The next step in the ID process is task analysis, which is used to identify the actual tasks needed to achieve the goals identified in the needs analysis. This second analysis looks at the content needed to achieve the desired instructional outcome. The objectives and tasks are typically classified into three domains or categories: cognitive, psychomotor, and affective. The cognitive domain includes objectives and tasks related to information recall, conceptual knowledge development, knowledge application to problem solving, and other intellectual aspects of learning.

The psychomotor domain includes abilities and activities that necessitate the use of physical capabilities and activities, such as performing, manipulating, and constructing tasks. The affective domain includes goals that address attitudes, emotions, and values. Consideration of the learning experience, including the cognitive, psychomotor, and affective factors involved, increases the likelihood that learners will successfully develop the desired knowledge, skills, behaviors, or attitudes.

Strategy

The strategy phase of the ID process is informed by and draws on tested theories to guide the creation of instructional activities. Theories are drawn from a variety of disciplines, such as education and learning psychology, behavior change, and motivation. Cognitive learning, information processing, and multimedia learning are examples of widely used theories. Which learning theories are most applicable are influenced by the structure and type of learning required by each objective.

The analysis of the content clearly influences the selection of instructional strategies; that is, the determination of domain (whether the target is a behaviour, skill, knowledge, or attitude), as well as the analysis of the tasks that comprise the desired performance. Different types of learning tasks necessitate varying degrees of cognitive effort and learning environments.

The focus of this strategy phase of the ID process is on designing the learning activities that will best serve the specific group of learners for whom the program is being developed. Learning activities are learning experiences that include informational content and are designed to have learners act on content in specific ways. Each specific objective is considered, as well as how best to actively engage learners in the learning experiences in order to achieve the desired result. The development of instructional strategies is regarded as the most important step in the ID process; it is the step that can contribute the most to the success of instruction.

When deciding on instructional strategies, designers must also consider and choose the media and methods that will best deliver the desired experience. In the strategy phase, Smith and Ragan's model emphasizes three key categories: organization, delivery, and management. Organizational strategies are concerned with how instruction will be sequenced and delivered. The instructional media that will be used and how learners will be grouped are both concerns of delivery strategies.

Learners, for example, could be divided into groups based on their prior knowledge, attitudes toward the topic, skill abilities, and level of motivation. Developers should evaluate the motivational appeal and ability of each element to support learners in recalling prior knowledge, providing new learning stimuli, activating responses, providing feedback, and encouraging practice and transfer when selecting appropriate media elements used for learning activities (e.g., text, audio, graphics, and animation). Finally, management strategies concentrate on instructional scheduling and implementation.

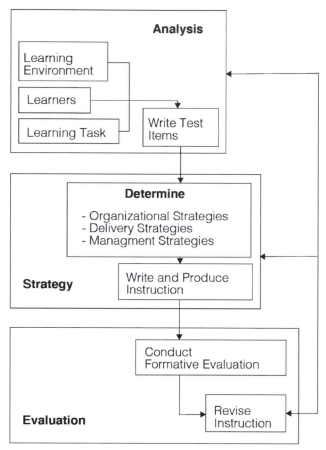

An Instructional Design Process Model

Smith and Ragan, Instructional Design, 1993

FIGURE 14.4. The Common Model of Instructional Design by Smith and Ragan (2005)

Evaluation

Formative evaluation refers to the iterative process of trying out and revising activities or content prior to implementation. The assumptions made during the analysis and strategy phases are put to the test during the evaluation phase. The goal of formative evaluation is to ensure that the instructional goals are met and to revise the program as needed before implementation. Formative evaluation necessitates a strategy for determining the extent to which learning is occurring. It entails attempting learning activities with members of the learning group. To assess the learner's mastery of the objectives, evaluation instruments are used.

Formative evaluation should take place at all stages of the identification process. During the early stages of the ID process, formative evaluation (even needs assessments) can be checked for fit and refined by stakeholders. This helps to avoid wasting valuable time and resources on ineffective components. Using a continuous formative evaluation approach and revising the program based on the findings allows developers to identify flaws that can be addressed before full-scale implementation. It also increases the likelihood that the program will produce the desired learning and performance outcomes when implemented. Failure to conduct formative evaluation at all stages of the ID process misses opportunities for problem identification and increases the likelihood that learners will not achieve the intended goals despite significant investment of resources.

Part Five

Global Perspectives of Curriculum Development Practice

With the understanding that a dysfunctional curriculum can threaten the survival of a nation, governments worldwide continue to invest huge sums of money and time in curriculum development. In practice, a great deal of curriculum development work throughout the world is concerned with updating and renewal of curricula as each society grapples with the same question - what knowledge is worthwhile? Curriculum development processes are fundamentally the same the world over but operationalised differently according to socio-political contexts. In this last part of the book, we present in chapter 15 the many faces of curriculum development in a few developed and developing countries taken from Africa, Asia, and Europe. Chapter 16 is devoted to current and future directions of curriculum planning for the twenty-first century.

15

Curriculum Development Activities in Africa and Beyond

With the coming of independence, the educational policy of many African countries changed from having a western orientation to meeting the needs of the African context. While there were individual country efforts towards this trend, there were also some concerted efforts that significantly affected curriculum development activities in different African countries. UNESCO for instance, has over the years contributed to educational views in Africa through its series of conferences, the most famous of which is the MINEDAF series (meetings of African Education ministers). The analysis that follows shows the extent to which curriculum issues have featured in these conferences. This will be discussed together with case studies of three African countries namely: Cameroon, Nigeria, and Kenya. In this chapter, we also present the faces of curriculum development in two non-African countries from which lessons may be learnt and extrapolated to local situations.

Meetings of African Education Ministers

The Addis Ababa Conference (1961)

The meeting created the first temporary plan on short and long-term educational development in Africa, providing a forum for African countries to decide on their primary educational needs and to promote economic and social development in Africa. There was a focus on school equipment and textbooks when assessing Africa's needs. Textbooks were expected to respect new curricula requirements and African countries and there was a need to train textbook writers to acquire skills for this demand. The report of the conference still called for new curriculum directions to meet the changing needs of African social and economic life.

Curriculum content (in 1961) was not in line with African conditions. Thus, the teaching of scientific and technical subjects had to be encouraged in order to provide training for highly qualified research personnel, engineers, science teachers, economists and more, to end the preference for teaching non-African history and to promote the synthesis of African and universal values in school curricula.

The conference of Addis-Ababa therefore set goals to be achieved in educational records over the following years, and mainly focused on educational planning and the mobilisation of resources to encourage universal primary education.

The Abidjan Conference of 1964 came in the wake of a series of meetings organised by UNESCO to assess the implementation within Member States of the Addis Ababa plan of action of 1961. This focused on exchange of experiences on efforts made since independence, to rethink the objectives, the structures, and the content of education.

The conference in Abidjan also discussed extensively the adaptation of secondary education contents to ensure that balanced persons are produced. They also recommended the establishment in African Member States, of curriculum development centres to which universities and centres of research should be associated. The participants agreed to expand the scope of the school curriculum to include language and natural sciences.

Between 1961 and 1964, efforts had been made in a number of African countries to adapt school textbooks to new curriculum demands. Ethiopia was reported to be particularly active in this regard. During the same period, UNESCO helped to create a didactic materials centre in Yaounde, Cameroon.

The Nairobi Conference (1968)

The discussions at this conference outlined objectives, content and method orientations for primary and secondary levels of education. There was some emphasis on the non-cognitive objectives of education, as the conference declared. For primary education, it was recommended that it should be given a rural orientation as a way of adapting it to its immediate environment. Without transforming the primary school into a purely agricultural or technical institution, learners should be imbued with respect for manual work.

With regard to the choice of language of education, each country was requested to review its peculiar linguistic structure and develop suitable policies for the use of primary education languages. The conference felt that the use of foreign languages in schools (like the teaching of foreign-oriented content) contributed to the psychological alienation of the child thus making learning more difficult. In addition to the language issue, science should be taught at primary level intensively.

In order to understand the world, the primary school leaver should acquire basic science and maths. Secondary school training was conceived in two phases with the first cycle focusing on scientific knowledge, observation and deduction skills and a sensitivity to environmental issues and basics of science and technology's daily applications. The upper secondary school should emphasise the application of scientific knowledge and should expose learners to practical life and work situations.

It was recommended that the curricula at this level should aim at inculcating an agreed set of cultural, social and aesthetic values. History and geography programmes should be revised to improve learners' understanding of history, culture, economics and the social problems of Africa.

General guidelines were given on re-structuring primary and secondary education, while specific attention was paid to mathematics, science and technology. Attention was drawn to the need for a balanced curriculum content, bringing together the scientific, the cultural, the social and the aesthetic disciplines.

The Lagos Conference (1976)

It was observed that African countries gave increasing prominence to science and mathematics in the school curriculum, while a good number of them had introduced technical and vocational subjects.

After reviewing the above advances in curriculum reform, the Lagos conference concluded that African education (the nature of institutions and the curriculum) was still suffering from serious shortcomings inherited from the colonial period. The school was still disconnected from its social environment. It therefore urged Africa to reconsider its education system, to fundamentally adjust it to the new requirements of its economic and social development. African Member States were therefore recommended to decolonise curricula for schools.

A very important recommendation of the Lagos conference (part of its Recommendation 15) was the one recommending the creation of an African Curriculum Organisation, for better regional cooperation in curriculum reform and renovation of school curricula. This organisation (ACO) was later to play a major role in building up African capacity in the field of systematic curriculum development.

The Harare Conference (1982)

The Harare conference of 1982 was convened by UNESCO to discuss problems of education in Africa, with special focus on the economic and social development of the region. It was observed that many countries had embarked on programmes of integrated science at the primary level and that there had been attempts to relate science curricula to the environment and to emphasise pre-vocational skills.

It was recommended that African Member States promote a policy of national mobilisation for science and technology involving at the basic education level: (a) integrated science and technology on a wide scale, (b) creating a favourable environment for curriculum development, and (c) training teachers to cope with science at the basic education level; in non-formal education, the establishment of community centres for the dissemination of scientific and technological knowledge; in upper secondary education, a diversified curriculum, emphasising (a) technical-vocational subjects in accordance with national development needs.

One inference that can be drawn from the report of the Harare conference is that the participants re-affirmed the commitments and re-iterated the recommendations of the four preceding conferences

The Dakar Conference (1991)

The Conference properly focused on promoting literacy and basic education. Experiences were shared during deliberations on promoting African languages, promoting science and technology, in order to make the curriculum more culturally relevant. It was therefore recommended that African States improve conditions for education and learning. Methods, content and teaching aids. In suggesting education strategies for the 1990s, the Dakar conference recommended improvement of the quality of basic education, with special emphasis on teacher training and learning outcomes. It also proposed greater interaction of learners with their environment and more effective participation in development through the acquisition of knowledge and the development of appropriate skills and attitudes.

The conference went on further to suggest (in the context of a long-term regional plan of action for basic education for all), the promotion of regional cooperation in the following curriculum related areas: capacity building for evaluating the quality of education; enhancing capacities for the production of and increasing the availability of teaching and learning materials for basic education, particularly in the African languages; the training and further training of teachers to enable them to provide high quality teaching suited to the needs of different types of learners (Recommendation No 2 of MINEDAF VI).

The African Curriculum Organisation (ACO) under the supervision of UNESCO was tasked with capacity building within African countries in systematic curriculum development and the promotion of inter-African and international cooperation in curriculum development.

This led to the revision of syllabuses and the creation of curriculum development centres in the 1970s. The ACO was also expected to support the translation of educational goals to operational objectives, develop content, materials and methods to achieve such objectives. From 1976-1984 the ACO carried out capacity building in the following areas:

- Techniques of data collection and analysis of curriculum development (Ibadan, Nigeria 1976)
- Techniques of Curriculum Development (Dar es Salam, Tanzania 1977)
- Curriculum material development (Banjul, Gambia 1978)
- Environmental curriculum in the African school curriculum (Lusaka, Zambia 1979)
- Curriculum for early childhood education (Nairobi, Kenya 1979)
- Curriculum for primary science (Maseru, Lesotho 1991)
- Curriculum material production (Ibadan, Nigeria 1983; Domasi, Malawi 1984)

The above efforts made through concerted efforts or organisations are inexhaustive. However, it is worthy of note that such efforts greatly impacted curriculum development activities in many countries in Africa.

Case Studies - Cameroon, Nigeria, Kenya, China and Scotland

Cameroon

The curriculum of schools at different levels of education have undergone revision, some of which are subtle and others significant. Like other African countries, significant reforms started only after independence. In this section curriculum development activities (without being exhaustive) are traced from the pre-colonial era to the post-independence era to present day in Cameroon.

A Historical Evolution of the Primary School Curriculum

The pre-colonial era was the era of the missionaries whose main mission was evangelism. The aim of education was to enable the indigenes to read the bible and so their focus was mainly on primary education. The curriculum emphasised reading and writing, arithmetic, and the study of the bible. The language of instruction during this period was English and vernacular languages like

Isubu, Duala and Mungaka were used at the lower levels of primary school. During the colonial era, the Germans overtook the British in the scramble for Africa and became the first colonial masters from 1884 to 1914. Their aim was to spread the German or Teutonic culture. School subjects included arithmetic, German history, Natural science, World Geography, moral principles, and behaviour. Later on, some vocation/technical education and teacher education emerged. Vocational schools included schools of agriculture and apprenticeship schools. The vocational school also prepared pupils for a secretarial career to cope with the growing demand of local administration for clerical staff as well as policemen, messengers, and domestic servants

More subjects were taught during the era of the British colonial masters. Generally, the syllabus was made up of handwriting, number, handicraft, nature study, religion, hygiene, drawing, and singing. These were taught in junior classes. In senior classes, history, citizenship, geography, and physical training were taught. Also, some effort was made in the area of technical education. The vernacular was used in the first 3 years of pupils' schooling because the use of English may have slowed down the students' progress.

The French colonial masters on their part also had a mission to spread the French language and culture. The curriculum emphasised the French language. The purpose of education was to educate the child physically, morally, intellectually to make her/him useful to her/himself and society. Teachers were mostly trained from France, Algeria and other French colonies. There were also trained and untrained indigenous teachers. The primary school had three levels and vocational education was provided in some advanced schools. In 1950, the curriculum of local primary schools were harmonised with that of France. The subjects included Moral instruction and Civics, Language, Hygiene and Practical Exercises, Recitation and singing, Manual work: sewing and drawing, History and Geography, Physical education, Recreation, Writing, Arithmetic, Nature study. Schools were categorised and those referred to as advanced primary schools trained teachers, nurses, postal service workers, clerical personnel etc. Secondary education started when the Yaoundé Advanced school was converted to classical and modern secondary schools with their curriculum the same as that of France. More technical and teacher training schools were also opened.

On January 1st, 1960, French-speaking Cameroon declared their independence from the French administered United Nations Trusteeship. French Cameroon was known as La Republique du Cameroun. British Southern Cameroons became independent in 1961. This gave rise to two sub-systems of education in Cameroon – The English and French sub-systems.

With the coming of independence, educational policy in Cameroon like in other countries in Africa began orienting education towards meeting the needs of national independence and development in all aspects of national life. Significant efforts towards qualitative improvements in education began in the 1980s.

Teacher education at the primary level came into focus. More teachers were trained since there was numerical expansion in schools. As a result, the government embarked on some reforms. One of them was the launch of the Institute of Rurally Applied Pedagogy (IPAR in its French acronym) geared towards training a new breed of teachers in pedagogy and community development skills. Owing to poor planning and conceptualisation, the IPAR project failed.

Also, the government with the aid of the United States Agency for International Development and the University of Southern Carolina launched a project to revise and improve initial and in-service teacher education in the under-scholarised parts of the country. Thus in 1989 the first national syllabus for nursery school was launched and the government organised a conference in an attempt to harmonise the school programmes of the two subsystems, but this failed. In 1993 the government created the General Certificate of Education, and the Baccalaureate examination Boards to take care of secondary graduation examinations that needed more credibility.

The National Forum on Education

This Forum took place in 1995 and it was a significant platform for curriculum reform. The forum made an assessment of the educational system in Cameroon. In the preparatory documents for the forum, some issues were identified amongst others, with respect to primary and secondary education. It was observed that important areas of learning such as democracy, peace, tolerance, human rights, and plastic arts were not offered in the syllabus. Thus, the syllabuses were outdated; there was no policy on the teaching of national languages apart from the two official languages. It is said that the 1995 Forum in Education marked a turning point in Cameroon's educational system.

The new policy orientations were addressed in the 1998 Law to Lay Down Guidelines on Education in Cameroon This led to more curriculum reforms to include subjects like Human Rights education, Moral education, Health education, National Culture (Arts and Crafts, music, drawing, drama) and Home economics for boys in both the English-speaking and the French-speaking systems. Also, the English-speaking system is now implementing a six-year instead of a seven –year curriculum that had been in place since the 1964/65 school year. In addition, Physical Education was going to be a compulsory subject assessed at the First School Leaving Certificate examination. National languages were to be promoted at the primary and secondary school levels. This has been introduced and is ongoing in identified pilot schools. Also, bilingualism (French and English) was to be enhanced as a factor of national unity and integration. Thus, the new primary school syllabuses prescribed the teaching and assessment of French from class one in the English-speaking schools and English from class one in the French-speaking schools.

With regard to teaching materials even though different types were suggested, the basic teaching materials remain the textbooks. Thus, in order to regulate and improve the quality of textbooks used in school, a textbook committee of 30 members comprising publishers, editors, examination board representatives, donor agencies and representatives of civil society was set up in 2000. The committee received training in the selection of textbooks based on defined criteria. Apart from textbooks it was resolved that other types of teaching materials (chalk, pens, paper, rulers etc) should be sent to individual schools by the beginning of each year. This strategy is referred to as a 'minimum package.'

In 2006, after a pilot experiment to curb the high rate of repetition of classes by primary school pupils, two teaching strategies were used from class 2 to class 6 for the teaching and learning of language (English and French) and Mathematics. These were compensatory teaching and the competency-based approach combined with automatic promotion and the New Pedagogic

Approach. Automatic promotion is conceived to be within a cycle. That is, from class I to II, class III to IV, or class V to VI or VII and not class II to III or IV to V since later promotion requires changing the cycle. Weak pupils who are automatically promoted are given remedial/compensatory education to reduce deficiencies in preparation for promotion (through normal examinations) to the next cycle. The pilot experiment on the reduction of class repetition in Cameroon showed that combining automatic promotion, compensatory education and competency-based teaching had a positive effect on performance. However, there are issues about the implementation of the policy of automatic promotion, ranging from inadequate human and material resources to no motivation on the part of teachers.

Based on issues regarding teacher education raised at the 1995 forum on education, some reforms were also carried out in the primary teacher training programmes. Teachers were going to be trained only for the Grade I certificate. The Grade II and Grade III certificates which were lower were scrapped. Also, the training programme now consisted of three essential components: theoretical component, bilingual training and the practical component.

In addition to the Cameroon initiatives in 1990, the World Conference on Education for All (EFA) which was held in Jomtien, Thailand, made a clarion call for universal quality primary education. During this conference, emphasis was laid on access, equity and quality primary education for all. In addition, the EFA conference also underscored that active and participatory approaches are particularly valuable in assuring learning acquisition and allowing learners to reach their fullest potentials. It was, therefore, necessary to define acceptable levels of learning acquisition for educational programmes and to improve and apply systems of assessing learning achievement. This in addition to the resolutions at the World Education Forum 2015 in Incheon, Korea propelled Cameroon to carry out major actions which included the writing of syllabuses on HIV/AIDS, on Human Rights and on ICTs. Furthermore, the revision of curricula to align with the provisions of the Incheon World Education Forum became imperative.

Faced with the problem of quality and the phasing out of the Cameroon Primary School Syllabuses for both subsystems, which date as far back as 2000, the building up of a new curriculum became a necessity and was developed.

The Current Primary School Curriculum in Cameroon

The vision of the new curriculum launched in 2018 falls in line with the SDG4 which seeks to ensure inclusive and equitable quality education and promote lifelong learning for all with focus on access, equity and inclusion, quality and learning outcomes within a lifelong learning approach. In addition, the vision of the Continental Education Strategy for Africa (CESA 2016-2025), reorienting "Africa's education and training systems to meet knowledge, competencies, skills, innovation and creativity required to nurture African core values and promote sustainable development at the national, sub-regional and continental levels" has carefully been addressed in this curriculum. This is in corroboration with the law to Lay Down Guidelines for Education (1998) which states in Article 4 that the general aim of education is to ensure the intellectual, physical, civic, and moral development of the child as well as its economic, socio-cultural, political, and moral integration in society.

Against this background, the current Cameroon primary education system outlines seven National Core Skills which should be acquired by the end of both nursery and primary cycles of education. They include:

Communication in the two official languages (English and French) and the use of at least one national language.

- Use of basic notions in Mathematics, Science and Technology
- Practice of Social and Citizenship Values (morality, good governance and budgetary transparency)
- Demonstration of the Spirit of Autonomy, a Sense of Initiative, Creativity, and Entrepreneurship
- Use of Basic Information and Communication Technology Concepts and Tools
- Practice of Lifelong Learning
- Practice of Physical, Sports and Artistic Activities

The Cameroon National Core Skills Framework comprises four broad-based competences as follows: intellectual, methodological, personal and interpersonal, and communication competencies.

Intellectual Competencies are mental skills. These include:

- exploiting information
- solving problems
- acquiring logical thinking and a sense of observation
- exercising critical judgement
- practising creative and innovative thinking

Examples of methodological competencies include:

- giving oneself efficient working methods
- exploiting information and communication technologies
- organising one's learning
- arousing the desire to learn each subject

Personal and interpersonal competencies enable the learner to:

- develop his/her personality
- acquire abilities in view of his/her socio-cultural integration and individual fulfilment
- cooperate with others

Communication competences enable the learner to:

- communicate in an appropriate manner in the two official languages
- communicate in at least one national language

The seven competences and four core skills have been weaved into learning areas as shown on table 15.1. The pedagogical orientation of the new curriculum is constructivist with focus on project based-learning and cooperative learning.

This organisation was done for the different levels. The curriculum is learner-centred and is based on the development of skills needed to meet the challenges of contemporary Cameroon in particular and the world at large. The syllabuses are presented in three levels: Level 1 (class 1 and 2), Level 2 (class 3 and 4) and Level 3 (class 5 and 6). In all, ten subjects have been identified from the five domains namely: English Language, Mathematics, Science and Technology, French, Social Studies, Vocational Studies, Arts, Physical Education and Sports, National Languages and Cultures, and Information and Communication Technologies (ICTs). In order to render the curriculum standard and to guarantee quality assurance, the following phases and procedures were followed:

- Writing and validating the Cameroon National Core Skills Framework
- Carrying out needs analysis
- Writing and validating the Curriculum Framework
- Training of 105 writers by consultants
- Writing the first draft
- Reading and evaluating the first draft by the scientific committee
- Integrating the recommendations and suggestions of the scientific committee
- Experimenting the curriculum in all the ten regions of Cameroon
- Integrating the recommendations and suggestions from the field
- Re-evaluating the curriculum by the scientific committee
- Integrating the recommendations and suggestions from the scientific committee
- Reviewing the curriculum by the consultants and the scientific committee
- Finalising and validating the curriculum

Table 15.1. Domains, Weighting, Competences to be Developed and Related Subjects

Domain/Weighting	Competences to be Developed	Subjects
Basic knowledge (60 percent)	• Communication in the two official languages (English and French) and the use of at least one national language • Use of basic notions in mathematics, science and technology • Practice of lifelong learning - The four broad-based competences	• English Language • Mathematics • Science and Technology • French
Communal life and national integration (5%)	Practice of social and citizenship values (Morality, good governance and budgetary transparency) • Practice of lifelong learning • The four broad-based competences	• Social Studies

Vocational and life skills (20%)	▪ Demonstration of the spirit of autonomy, a sense of initiative, creativity, and entrepreneurship ▪ Practice of physical, sports and artistic activities ▪ Practice of lifelong learning ▪ The four broad-based competences	Vocational Studies ▪ Arts ▪ Physical Education and Sports
Cultural identity (5%)	▪ Practice of lifelong learning ▪ The four broad-based competences	National Languages and Cultures
Digital Literacy (10%)	▪ Use basic information and communication technology concepts and tools ▪ Practice of lifelong learning ▪ The four broad-based competences	Information and Communication Technologies (ICTs)

Source: Ministry of Basic Education (2018). Cameroon Primary School Curriculum: English Subsystem Level I: Class 1 & Class 2.

In carrying out this curriculum development activity priority was given to national expertise by working with two renowned consultants representing the language of instruction of the two subsystems. This was done in strict respect of the specificities of the two subsystems of education. However, each subsystem has maintained its specificities with regards to learning strategies/methods, teaching-learning materials, and assessment strategies and tools.

The ADDIE Model guided the entire process of the curriculum development as follows:
- A for the Analysis phase; explains the situational analysis (teachers, learners, supervisors, education community)
- D for the Design phase; focuses on the structure of teaching-learning and assessment of learning outcomes
- D for the Development phase; is where the writing and rewriting of all the planned activities in the design phase are carried out
- I for the Implementation phase; covers the period of the experimentation. This period offers feedback for revision
- E for the Evaluation phase; is where plans for the evaluation of the entire curriculum are made as it is progressively being used.

Problem-based learning is the main method of teaching. Commitment to project-based learning enables the learner to solve many problems and makes the teaching-learning process more skill-based.

The following steps will enable the teacher to put his/her plan into action:
- Identify learning outcomes in function of the national core skills and as stated in the integrated monthly schemes of work.
- Based on the integrated learning theme of the month, identify a project and plan the activities

that will lead to its realisation.

- The different activities are planned chronologically (entry behaviour, simple to complex) in relation to the contents and contextualised through the ILT.
- Monitor the realisation of the project and ensure that all learners carry out their tasks.
- Organise culmination events, that is, presentation of projects and assessment every last Thursday and Friday of the four weeks. Depending on the level, the presentations and assessment should cover three forms: oral, written and practice. A checklist should be prepared depending on the stated learning outcomes in order to record learners' progress in the class broadsheet (this will constitute a gradual building of the information for pupils' report cards which are filled every term).
- Carry out remediation activities where necessary.
- Do an auto-evaluation of the process. Note should be taken that this is a cyclical process within each teacher's community of practice (the school).

Assessment in primary schools in Cameroon can take three forms (oral, written, practical). There are many ways through which information can be gathered about a learner's progress. This can be done through observation checklists, learner's self-assessment, daily practical assignments, samples of learner's work, learner's willingness to participate and contribute in projects/conferencing, oral and written quizzes, portfolios; willingness to be involved in class and school activities.

This curriculum is designed to guide the development of knowledge, skills and attitudes in the learners and to set the foundation for learning with emphasis on Science, Technology, Engineering and Mathematics (STEM). The curriculum therefore responds to one of the key missions assigned to the Ministry of Basic Education (MINEDUB). This new pedagogic tool replaces the one of 1987 for the nursery and that of 2000 for the primary.

Curriculum Development Activities at the Secondary Level

At the secondary school level, no organised or significant curriculum reform activities comparable to those occurring at the primary level were noticed. However, curriculum reform efforts in secondary education can be found in three decrees and were geared towards reorganising pre-service teacher training -École Normale Supérieure (ENS) Yaounde and its annex institution in Bambili. These decrees were issued in 1975, 1979 and 1988. A lot of dissatisfaction arose from these decrees, some of which included the fact that the criteria for selecting candidates into teacher training colleges was not objective; there was no systematic in-service training for teachers at the primary and secondary levels; no training facilities for nursery school teachers and more. These were discussed at the National Forum on Education.

The forum arrived at the recommendations: Selection for secondary school teacher training into the first cycle required a pass in the Advanced Level in at least 2 papers plus at least 4 Ordinary Level papers excluding Religion or the Baccalauréat (all series). For the second cycle, a Licence or bachelor's degree or equivalent was required. The secondary teacher training institutions have three major programmes: One which trains teachers for the first cycle and two others which train teachers for the second cycle of secondary education (high school) and that which trains teachers for primary teacher training colleges.

With regard to the secondary school curriculum itself, the new educational orientation from the 1995 forum on Education brought about a major pedagogic reform in Cameroon schools. This pedagogic reform was captioned "New Pedagogic Approach (NPA)" by its originator, the Ministry of National Education (MINEDUC). This reform effort intended to mobilise and encourage Cameroonian teachers to shun outmoded teaching strategies such as rote learning and a call for a shift from teacher-centred to learner-centred pedagogy. Therefore, NPA entailed approaches that use active methods of teaching and are learner-centred. These include integrated teaching, project pedagogy, discovery learning, cooperative learning, etc.

A few years after the NPA was instituted, another approach was introduced to replace the NPA. This was called the Objectives Based Approach (OBA). In this approach teachers conducted their lessons by stating objectives and using the teaching method that best suited the objectives. At the end they gave a general assessment of students from what they were taught. It must be noted that such an approach was more theoretical. An approach was needed that helped students in solving real life problems. Thus, the Competency-based Approach (CBA) was tested in Cameroon's secondary schools during the 2012 to 2013 academic year, and fully introduced in 2014 (Ndifor, 2014), with the purpose of moving from rote memorisation to a more experiential and practical approach in school. This is the approach currently used in secondary schools in Cameroon. However, it must be noted that there are several issues with the implementation of this approach.

With regard to revisions in the examinations syllabuses of the General Certificate of Education (GCE) the following revisions were made during a GCE Review Conference in Limbe, Cameroon which held from April 4-6, 2011.

The following subjects were reviewed either at Ordinary or Advanced Level or at both levels:

- **Citizenship Education**: This new subject is born to the GCE Board at the Ordinary Level. It treats current universal concepts such as human rights, democracy, child labour, terrorism, civic responsibilities, HIV/AIDS, etc., aimed at transforming a person into a complete responsible national and a universal person.

- **French Language**: It was recommended that, French should be taught in French at all times and not teaching French in English. That emphasis should be placed on Listening, Speaking, Reading and Written skills

- **Philosophy**: O-Level Logic was born, whose proposed course content is basically introductory. At the A-level, the hitherto overloaded syllabus content was reduced, giving rise to a more focused program.

- **Geography**: For O-Level, the geography of Cameroon is now a syllabus area emphasising human and physical aspects. This reinforces the need of learners to have better knowledge of the country and highlights the potentials for and challenges to the economic growth of the country; now introduced basic ideas of models in both physical and human geography in order to bridge the gap between the Ordinary and Advanced Levels; themes re-arranged into subject areas. Modification goes a long way to align the Ordinary and Advanced Level syllabuses. The new syllabus has equally put in place the impact of processes on man and the environments as well as their mitigation strategies. Also, more emphasis has been put on aspects such as global warming, desertification, internet communication and poverty spiral so as to stress on the Millennium Development Goals (MDGs). Hence the subject is made more applicable and relevant to society so as to make it more attractive.

Field work has been eliminated from Ordinary Level. Its elimination forestalls the school-based assessment which was highly subjective.

For A-Level, the 3-paper examination was maintained with the following modifications: Some aspects of former papers 2 and 3 were integrated with paper 2 now based on physical and human geography theories and concepts. Paper 3 now deals exclusively with Cameroon, Map work and Techniques. Formerly, only the human aspect of Cameroon was emphasised, but with the review, Cameroon is considered in its entirety. Case studies in Human Geography have been restricted in order to lighten the syllabus content. Also, the scheme of assessment is a novelty in the syllabus plan. Furthermore, to meet up with global trends and the realisation of MDGs such as Global warming, desertification, globalisation, food security, poverty spiral etc. have been given more emphasis.

English Language: A-Level English Language has been instituted and syllabus proposed. New syllabus structured into 2 parts: 1) School-based in the form of continuous assessment involving evaluation of school based projected and spoken English (2) Testing reading comprehension, grammar vocabulary, and summary and text reconstruction, composition and prescribed texts.

For O-Level English emphasis was placed on grammar and vocabulary. A major innovation was the inclusion of a school-based project and spoken English to be assessed on set down criteria to avoid subjectivity.

1. Physics: 780 – A-Level Physics: Options added to reviewed syllabus to enable candidates orient themselves towards a career. Content of each of the three papers modified as well as the weighting.

2. Computer Science and Information and communication Technology:

The main innovations at the Ordinary level include: A broad scope with 50% of the syllabus devoted to Computer Science and 50 percent to ICT and a change in name from *Computer Science* to *Foundations of Computer Science and Information Technology* to reflect the new content.

- Greater visibility of key foundation concepts and relevance of content to industry.
- Introduction of a section on electronic logic gates which form the foundation of computer hardware.
- Information and communication Technology at the Advanced Level: Clear and more precise specification of the practical content of the syllabus; greater emphasis on the internet as a tool for providing a range of services for the modern economy; introduction of concepts which facilitate an understanding of e-services such as e-banking, e-commerce, e-government, e-governance; need for candidates to develop skills in the use of multimedia; greater awareness of the predominance of Information Systems including Health Information Systems, Management Information Systems, Library Information Systems.

The main innovations of the Computer Science Advanced Level syllabus are: greater visibility of key concepts; awareness of recent evolutions in processor technology; awareness of novel operating system models; greater emphasis on web technology

- **Mathematics**: At the Ordinary Level, the 2 Mathematics were maintained – 570 Mathematics and 575 Additional Mathematics. For the 2 Mathematics, changes were effected in terms of the structure of the examinations and the content. For the structure, unlike in the past, now all questions are compulsory. Innovations were made to have a bridge between O-and A-Level by introducing certain new concepts.

All Advanced Level Mathematics maintained namely:

- 765 – Pure Maths with Mechanics (PMM)
- 770 – Pure Maths with Statistics (PMS)
- 775 –Further Maths

New topics introduced to adapt syllabuses to those of similar examination bodies and above all, new concepts such as logic and Boolean algebra have now been incorporated to enable candidates compete favourably for professional schools.

- Food Science and Home Economics: Changes effected to give a scientific background to better equip students for Food science and 740-Nutrition. Others who cannot further their education can be self-reliant. Changes made to take care of students who may not be able to continue after Ordinary levels, making them self-reliant.

Course content of other countries was compared to give the content a global view and then adapt it to suit our environment. Emphasis on the practical aspect was reinforced by introducing new topics and also on student-based assessment. Assessment Objectives were also restructured in line with Bloom's taxonomy level of evaluation to meet technological trends. The structure of the examination was slightly modified as well.

Curriculum Development Activities at the Tertiary Level

Regarding tertiary education, there was an effort to improve the quality between 1991-1993 and more universities were created. Enrolments in tertiary education increased. Universities have moved from one state university to 8 state universities, with many privately owned universities. A major reform that took place at this level was the professionalisation of education. The Bachelor's, Master's and PhD (BMP) is a reform in Higher Education (HE) which has as one of its goals, the professionalisation of education. The main aim of professionalising programs in HE is to train qualified national human resources. Professionalisation in HE came up because graduates from the University of Yaounde did not receive the type of education required by a demanding private sector. When public sector employment became saturated, graduates found themselves ill-equipped for employment in the private sector. Consequently, one of the key goals of the 1993 Higher Education reforms was the professionalisation of teaching programmes. In order to achieve this objective, universities were required to define, in consultation with other stakeholders, the local market needs, involve professionals in the conception of programmes, define professional programmes, and draw up the profiles of teaching staff to be recruited (Njeuma, et al. 1999). This was actually implemented in the 2007/2008 academic year.

Furthermore, the 2001 Higher Education Orientation Law and the Private Law ushered in some quality assurance strategies in Higher education. Part 1, Article 6 of this law has as mission: the quest for excellence in all domains of knowledge; the promotion of science, culture and social progress; the training and further training of senior staff; the deepening of ethics and national consciousness; the promotion of democracy and the development of a democratic culture amongst others.

Challenges

Even though many reforms have been instituted at all three levels of formal education, there are concerns about their implementation. These include:

- Inadequate human and material resources,
- Lack of funding,
- High enrolment
- Lack of motivation on the part of teachers,
- Unwillingness of government to go the extra mile,
- Resistance to change,
- Poor supervision of instruction.

Other curriculum development concerns in Cameroon include:

- Failure to harmonise the two systems of education in all sectors
- Developing more effective models of bilingual education
- Creation of National Curriculum development and research centres.

Nigeria

Before western imperialism in Nigeria, different parts of the country had their unique structures which they operated. The Northern parts had people whose religious belief was Islam and were deeply entrenched both in the religious belief and educational orientation of a uniform Qur'an education policy (Ozigi & Ocho, 1981), while in the Southern and Western parts, the ethnic groups each had their own traditional form of education based on their culture and tradition. However the aim was generally to inspire competence, develop knowledge and skills acquisition. This education was geared towards developing critical skills, character and culture but there was no formal curriculum. Teaching was informal through the apprenticeship system and the child learned basic life skills like craftmanship and farming for boys and domestic chores especially cooking for girls through imitation/modelling. Apart from modelling and imitation, other methods of teaching included direct instruction, storytelling, role-play and songs. This was the scenario until 1842 when the Christian missionaries arrived the South and introduced Western education. The aims of education were just to enable recipients to learn to read the Bible in English and the local language, gardening and agriculture as well as train Local schoolmasters, catechists and clergymen and so the emphasis was on the 3Rs.

In 1872, the British colonial government began to intervene in the educational system by donating to missionary societies in order to support education. The grant was increased in 1877 and remained so until 1882, when the government decided that the administration of the schools should not be entirely in the hands of missionary organisations. Therefore, colonial education in addition to spreading Christianity provided education to train indigenous people of Nigeria for positions that will propagate and establish the interest of the colonial masters like tax collectors, interpreters, local police and other administrative duties. Subsequently, in 1914 the people of different ethnic groups and faiths were brought together as one country, resulting in a pluralistic society that necessitated the adoption of a federal structure for Nigeria. Education made enormous progress as the colonial government also introduced the use of school inspectors, standardized the syllabuses being operated by both private and mission schools and also introduced external examinations.

Nigeria became an independent country on October 1, 1960 and became a full republic in 1963 and there was a need to revise the curriculum in order to enhance societal development. A team of curriculum experts was invited from Harvard University in the USA to examine Nigeria's educational system and school curriculum that were then in use and make appropriate recommendations. A curriculum revision was done and curriculum plans were revised from time to time as the need arose. Due to global growth and development in technology, Nigeria's educational planners called for a further revision of the curriculum. The response to this call resulted in the National curriculum Conference held in 1969. Subsequent to the 1969 conference, a seminar was organised on "A National Policy of Education" in 1973 attended by various bodies such as the Conference of Teacher Training Colleges, Nigerian Union of Teachers, Primary School Administrators, Officials, State and Federal Ministries of Education, UNESCO Team, etc., out of which came the National Policy on Education first published in 1977, which has been revised from time to time since then. This is what ushered in the educational system now referred to as the 6-3-3-4 system. The 6-3-3-4 system became operational in 1983. The new curriculum was diversified in nature. It focused on Science, Pre-Vocational and Performance based learning. In 1999, Universal Basic Education (UBE) was introduced in response to the Declaration on Education for All as recommended by the Jomtien Conference of 1990.

The focus of the UBE was free, compulsory education for the first nine years of primary and junior secondary schools. The inauguration of UBE ushered in the 9-3-4 curriculum in Nigeria. The UBE scheme was geared towards introducing new pedagogical methods in order to elicit high cognitive processes in students, including student-centred learning; consolidating cross-cutting themes in order to condense curriculum content and scope and making the curricular more flexible and adaptable to disenfranchised groups; including indigenous knowledge concepts across various disciplines; strengthening school-to-work linkages; including the introduction of entrepreneurial skills; Raising the awareness about diversity, tolerance, ethic and civic responsibility; raise awareness about emerging issues such as HIV/AIDs, environmental preservation, family life, sexuality and gender issues; keeping pace with the global changes and the demand on education. Another edition of the policy was published in 2004 as a result of some policy innovations and changes.

The then Nigerian Educational Research Council (NERC), now known as Nigerian Educational Research and Development Council (NERDC), as well as Comparative and Scientific Adaptation Centre (CESAC) were given the responsibility of implementing the recommendations of the US experts from Harvard University. CESAC at first was part of a centralised national curriculum strategy to identify and evolve a more suitable system of education that is continually adapted and responsive to the nation's economic and social aspirations. Curriculum development therefore became one of its main functions. Inadequate funds and shortage of personnel has forced the centre to restrict its activities to curriculum innovation and renewal and primarily in the sciences and mathematics for secondary schools.

CESAC developed a number of projects for use in Nigeria. It attempted to design syllabuses based on the relevance of the subject matter to the learner's environment. The centre has developed the Nigerian secondary schools project series in science (biology, chemistry and physics), Social Studies, Home Economics, Mathematics, Agriculture, Business Studies, Technology, English and Moral Education. The Nigerian Secondary School Project (NSSSP) developed between 1970 and 1972 was trial tested by 61 secondary schools in Nigeria before revision took place in 1978.

Problems within the Nigerian Education System

Curricular contents and educational policies have not enjoyed the same level of confidence and diligence in their implementation as in their design and conceptualisation. As a result, the education system is plagued by the following problems which are particularly related to the curriculum:

- There are hardly any funds available to buy materials and to expand the educational infrastructure;
- No school inspections are carried out to monitor curriculum implementation;
- Instructional materials are poorly developed and supplies are inadequate;
- Teacher morale is poor and their competence is insufficient to deliver the new curriculum;
- Low student achievement, especially in science subjects due to overloaded content, lack of teacher competence, an inadequate supply of teaching materials, and a faulty mechanism for assessment that creates an unfair reward system.

The following solutions have been suggested in order to address the problems experienced with the education system in general and the curriculum in particular: greater decentralisation of education in a true sense; increased funding of education so that educational plans may be achieved; and the creation of entry and exit points for older children flexible enough to accommodate those who missed enrolment at age 6 and yet are still young enough to benefit from basic education. To achieve these educational goals and policies it is essential that the country experiences social and political stability.

Kenya

Background

Kenya is a unitary state and an east African country that attained independence from British colonial rule in 1963. Before colonial rule, its 42 ethnic groups had cultural practices that promoted education for survival unique to each ethnic group. The imperialists established formal education albeit replacing it with colonial ideologies and Eurocentric practices while condemning African cultural practices and altering the curriculum for survival (Nganga and Kambutu, 2016). At independence, political freedom came with the desire to establish school curricula that serve national needs and interests, and relevant to context. Free primary education was instituted immediately after independence and secondary education grew rapidly. However, the curriculum was devoid of essential skills and local culture, having been fashioned after elitist educational system colonial curricula. The educational system prepared school leavers for white collar jobs only. At that time, the 8-4-4 structural framework of the curriculum was instituted (8 years primary education, 4 years of secondary education and four years of tertiary education).

Curriculum renewal efforts

By 1986, there was a high level of unemployment and a dire need for educational reforms to promote self-reliance and survival. Since then, there have been major curriculum reviews in 1992, 1995, 2002, 2010 and 2017, respectively. Reviews have addressed issues of content, overloads within and across contents, need for curricula that develop human capital by identifying talents and nurturing learners, among other emerging issues. In 2017, new curriculum frameworks were developed for basic and secondary education, with competency- based pedagogical orientations. This was done in response to the report of the task force commissioned in 2012 to align curriculum content and the goals of Vision 2030.

The Kenya institute of education (KIE) has been concerned with the curriculum development in the country since its creation in 1968. It was succeeded by the Kenya institute of curriculum development (KICD) in 2013. Among other functions, the institute has the responsibility to develop, review, and approve programs, curricula, and support materials, and carry out educational research to inform curriculum policy. The KICD uses internationally recognised components or processes of curriculum development by adopting a cyclical eight stage model in their reform efforts (KICD, 2021) as shown in figure 15.1.

- Needs assessment
- Conception and policy formulation
- Curriculum design
- Development of syllabuses and curriculum support materials
- Preparation of curriculum implementers
- Piloting and phasing-in
- National implementation
- Monitoring and evaluation.

Curriculum structure

Curriculum development work has resulted in a new curriculum structure 2-6-3-3 to replace the 8-4-4. Presently, the primary school curriculum content comprises English, Kiswahili, mother tongue, mathematics, science, social studies, religious education, creative arts, physical education, and life skills education as subjects. Secondary school subjects are English, Kiswahili, maths, biology, chemistry, geography, history, religious knowledge and applied practical subjects and cultural subjects. A total of thirty subjects are grouped in six learning domains. There is a system of compulsory and elective subjects.

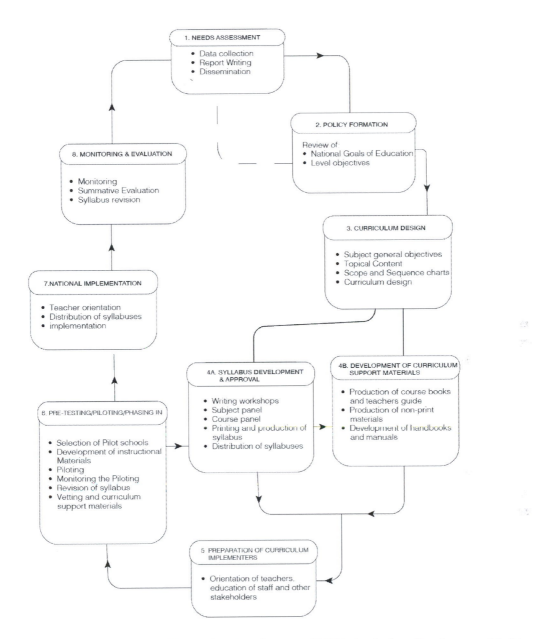

FIGURE 15.1. Kenya Institute for Curriculum Development (KICD) Curriculum Development Model

Challenges and Future Directions

To proceed effectively and efficiently in curriculum development, Otunga and Nyandusi (2009) suggested that political factors, socioeconomic context, cultural context, ICTs, legal context of curriculum development and linkages should be factored adequately into curriculum development processes and activities in Kenya. Other critics hold that the most recent well-intentioned curriculum reforms have not considered deep systemic challenges in the country ranging from infrastructural, institutional, and cultural issues. In addition, changes in curriculum content have been addressed without corresponding reforms in teacher education to effectively implement the new orientations requiring student-centred and constructivist pedagogies (Klune, 2019). As the new curriculum is rolled out and still unfolding, a stock taking national curriculum conference was organised in August 2019.

China

Background

With a population of 1.4 billion people, making up one fifth of the world's population, China is a 21st century economic power still considered as a developing country. Over the years, she has used education to design and promote her vision for the future. Literacy rates have increased from 20%in 1950 to 97% in 2018 (Data world bank.org, 2021). After repudiation of the cultural revolution under Mao Tse-Tung between 1966 and 1976, a new leadership in China opted for modernisation policies emphasising agriculture, industry, technology, and defence. In 1978, education was re-designed based on a centralised curriculum with little opportunities for local variations (Wiles &Bondi, 2011).

Curriculum renewal efforts

In 1988, governments began encouraging diverse interpretations of educational programmes by producing different textbooks based on the same curriculum. In 2001, a new curriculum framework encouraging diversification was produced. The new framework saw a shift from centralisation to joint efforts between central government, local authorities, and schools. A new version of the curriculum framework produced in 2011 offered greater flexibility (OECD, 2016) for curriculum work.

Presently, China develops curricula at three levels: national, provincial, and school levels. The ministry of education produces plans for primary and secondary education at the national level. These are general plans that set standards, lesson hours and general guidelines on curriculum management. At the provincial level, educational authorities develop an implementation plan whereby they interpret the intents and purposes of the national curriculum. They translate it into a curriculum that fits the local context. The plan is forwarded to the ministry of education before implementation. Schools organise their teachers to develop their courses according to the provincial plan. The local educational bureau guides and supervises schools' curriculum work, providing feedback to the provincial authorities about implementation.

The government encourages and supports the development of diverse and high-quality textbooks for primary and secondary education according to set standards. There is a national centre for school curriculum and textbook development. The national and provincial textbook commissions review and approve textbooks at their respective levels before use in schools. There is a national examinations authority that focuses on examinations and the national institute for education whose mission is educational research.

Curriculum structure

China operates nine years of compulsory education covering six years of primary school and three years of junior secondary school. According to the new curriculum, primary school has subjects such as Chinese language, mathematics, moral studies, natural science, physical education, art, music, and comprehensive practical activities. Chinese language and mathematics make up 60% of class time. At the secondary school, subjects include Chinese, mathematics, foreign language, science, history and geography, physical and health education, art, and comprehensive practical activities. There are compulsory and elective subjects at the senior secondary level. Comprehensive practical activity at both primary and secondary school levels is a broad-field comprising information technology, community service, research, and social practice. Its overall goal is to promote student creativity and a sense of social responsibility through practical experiences.

Characteristic features

Generally, the Chinese curriculum stresses teamwork, love for country, selflessness, in addition to basic skills acquisition. The secret to rapid development and high-quality programs is thought to result from 1) a rigorous examination system with quality controls in desired areas like mathematics and technology 2) key schools that receive superior resources and recruit superior students 3) study abroad policies that offer students opportunities for specialised academic training in developed countries (Wiles and Bondi, 2011).

Scotland

Background

With a population of 5.46 million inhabitants, Scotland is one of the four countries that make up the sovereign state of the United Kingdom. By the Scottish Act of 1696, Scotland established the first national system of education in the world, giving the nation a very long history of public education. Compulsory education for children between 5 and thirteen began as far back 1872. Today literacy rates stand at 99%. There are public and private schools. State schools are owned and operated by local education authorities.

There was radical change and expansion of Scottish education in the 20th century. Roman Catholic schools joined the system but retained their distinct religious character. The upper age limit for compulsory schooling was raised to 14 in 1901 and further to 16 in 1973. As a result, secondary education was the major area of growth in the inter-war period, particularly for girls. New qualifications were developed to cope with changing aspirations and economics, with the Leaving Certificate being replaced by the Scottish Certificate of Education Ordinary Grade (O-Grade) and Higher Grade (Higher) qualifications in 1962, which became the basic entry qualification for university.

Curriculum renewal efforts

In the 1960s, secondary grammar schools were phased out bringing in comprehensive schools. A national debate on education was held in 2002 to define curriculum, establish principles for curriculum design and define curriculum levels. In 2003, work began on national curriculum reform. Developments in education and the economy, both locally and globally, provided powerful drivers for change in curriculum design leading to the introduction of a new curriculum framework in the 2010/11 academic year. Curriculum for Excellence (CfE) as it is known, is one of the most ambitious programmes of educational change ever undertaken in Scotland (Scottish government, 2008a p.8). Curriculum for Excellence places a high premium on learner-centred education. At its centre are four fundamental capacities that reflect and recognise the lifelong nature of education and learning. These four capacities are expected to help children and young people to become:

- Successful learners
- Confident individuals
- Responsible citizens
- Effective contributors (www.CurriculumForExcellenceScotland.gov.uk).

Curriculum for Excellence aims at achieving a transformation in Scottish education by providing a coherent, more flexible, and enriched curriculum from 3 to 18, firmly focused on the needs of the child and young person and designed to enable them to develop the four capacities. According to recommendations spelt out in the curriculum framework documents, Curriculum planning should utilise seven principles for curriculum design: 1) challenge and enjoyment 2) breadth 3) progression 4) depth 5) personalisation and choice 6) coherence 7) relevance. Learning should be made available in a range of ways including interdisciplinary learning and a range of opportunities which ensure a broad approach, enabling, for example, a coherent understanding of environmental issues.

In addition, the framework focuses on experiences that contribute to student learning, rather than detailed definitions of content or prescribed hours of study. The intention is to avoid rushing learners through the levels as fast as possible. This arrangement of experiences and outcomes is intended to give teachers the flexibility and latitude to follow issues through and to provide personalised and varying programmes of learning so that the learner is secure at a level before moving on. The experiences and outcomes can be packaged in different ways appropriate to the individual learner.

To help learners gain the knowledge, skills and attributes needed for life in the 21st century, a refreshed narrative on Scotland's curriculum of excellence within the current context was published in September 2019. Each year, there is a national learning festival to stimulate new thinking about schooling.

Curriculum structure

The curriculum is coherent from ages three to eighteen. Preschool begins at age 3 and lasts for two years but it is not compulsory. From age 5, there is P1-P7 implying seven years of primary education and S1-S6 which is six years of secondary education. Education is compulsory from P1 to S3. This is known as general education. General education consists of well-planned experiences and outcomes across all the curriculum areas from early years through to S3. This includes understanding the world, Scotland's place in it and the environment, referred to as Learning for Sustainability. Students of S4 to S6 study for qualifications that help them gain entry to college based on interest and abilities. Besides, they are availed of opportunities for developing skills for learning, skills for life and skills for work; opportunities to maximise their individual potential, benefitting from appropriate personal support and challenge; and support to help them move into positive and sustained destinations beyond school. Overall, the curriculum has five levels as indicated on table 15.2.

Table 15.2. Structure of Curriculum for Excellence (CFe)

S/N	Level	Duration	Corresponding school grade
1	Early	3 years	preschool to P1
2	Level one	3years	P2-P4
3	Level two	3 years	P5-P7
4	Level 3&4	3years	S1-S3
5	Senior	3years	S4-S6

There are eight curriculum content areas:
- Expressive arts (arts & design, drama, music, dance)
- Health and wellbeing (health and physical education)
- Languages (including English, Gadhelic, and modern languages)
- Mathematics (emphasis on numeracy)
- Religious and moral education (Christianity and other world religions)
- Sciences experiences in biological, chemical, physical andEnvironmental Science
- Social science experiences in historical, geographical, social, political, and business contexts
- Technologies include creative, practical and work-related experiences and outcomes in craft, design, engineering, graphics, food, textile, and information technologies.

These content areas are not school subjects to be put on the school timetable but a repertoire from which desired learning experiences can be drawn. Throughout this broad curriculum, emphasis is expected on Scottish contexts, Scottish cultures and Scotland's history and place in the world. Government sets guidelines for curriculum development and gives schools flexibility and freedom to curriculum implementers to make decisions. The national curriculum framework is less detailed and less prescriptive. There is therefore no national curriculum as such but mechanisms have been put in place for quality assurance and control.

There are three national organizations responsible for quality assurance namely: the Care Inspectorate, Her Majesty's Inspectorate of Education and the Quality Assurance Agency for Higher Education. The Care Inspectorate inspects care standards in pre-school provision. Her Majesty's Inspectorate of Education within Education Scotland is responsible for the inspection of pre-school, primary, secondary, further education, community learning and development while The Quality Assurance Agency for Higher Education (QAA Scotland) is responsible for higher education inspection.

Qualifications at the secondary school and post-secondary (further education) level are provided by the Scottish Qualifications Authority, which is the national awarding and accrediting body in Scotland, and delivered through various schools, colleges and other learning centres, including those in the community learning and voluntary sectors.

Characteristic features

The curriculum is broad and rigorous. It is characterised by interdisciplinary learning, opportunities for individual achievement, and consideration of school ethos and life of the school as a community.

Landmark developments in Scottish curriculum development include:

Student-centred approaches to instruction

Teachers as professional curriculum developers and change implementers

Flexible and local planning

Challenges and future directions

Although the CfE has so far been successful, Priestley, Minty and Eager (2014) argue that the nature and extent of innovation in schools is dependent on two teacher factors: 1) teachers lack the ability to make sense of a complex and confusing curriculum policy that characterises the CfE and 2) teachers within each school do not articulate a clear vision about what such policy means for them. They also point out three limitations of the curriculum model which underpin the CfE. Firstly, attempting to fuse the process and product models of curriculum development creates problems for schools seeking to innovate. Secondly, CfE is light on specification of knowledge. It maintains the existing framework of school subjects within the content areas, but hollows out the substantive content, leading to a view that content does not matter. Important knowledge may thus be removed. While the specification of subjects should not be the starting point for curriculum planning, what has been called the accumulated wisdom of the ages is important. Thirdly, CfE is not specific on pedagogical orientations. For example, active learning is being promoted as stated in documents but there is little clarity about what this means.

16

Curriculum Planning for The Twenty-First Century

For the past two decades, there have been clarion calls for a paradigm shift in curriculum planning at global and national levels, to best meet current and future challenges of the twenty-first century (see Obanya, 2004; Henderson et al, 2017; Marope, 2017; Opertti, 2017). A term originally coined by Thomas Kuhn, *paradigm shift* generally means a major change in approach or underlying assumptions of how something works. In the field of education, it involves the adoption of a new outlook on the part of researchers and others as a means of thinking about change in education.

Because the twenty-first century is a period where the only constant thing is rapid and unpredictable change, curricula must not only adapt to change but must lead change and be constructive contributors to change. This has set curriculum scholars to work, bringing out to the limelight, far reaching implications and recommendations for the future of curriculum theory and practice. Various drivers of change in the century have been identified, new conceptions of curriculum are emerging, and new strategies to cope with change are being proposed and employed. This chapter discusses these trends and prospects and engages the reader in reflections on how best to plan and implement appropriate curricula for this spectacular century.

Key Drivers of Educational Change in the Twenty-First Century

Information and Communications Technology Revolution

In 1955, there were only 250 computers worldwide, and by 2010 there were 377 million personal computers, laptops, tablets, and mobile phones of all types, and 435 million by 2016 (Statista, 2016). The internet and these related technologies have not only increased access to information but now form a major source of information to anyone who can afford the service. The volume of information available to learners is simply overwhelming. Students are developing intellectually along new lines because these technologies do not only provide information but have the power to influence and educate. The implication of this rapid growth of ICTs for education is that learners will require skills to use them to i) extract information, ii) be able to critically evaluate information from diverse sources and iii) use them as media for learning.

This is also time to rethink the role of curriculum developers, teachers, and learners whose role has been compiling vital information, teaching it, learning, and assessing it. Many questions loom on the horizon. Would students still need textbooks? Will some curriculum content be scrapped off the formal curriculum? Whose information is more authentic? Who determines what information is made available to students? Curriculum leaders have the daunting task of sorting out, organising, and reorganising the huge volume of information now available to learners.

New ways of working and new tools for working

With the growth and availability of new technologies, 21st century workplaces require new working tools and new ways of working, which stimulate a demand for new competences for effective and efficient performance at work. Workers will need diverse competencies to access a wide range of established, emerging, and unknown tools to create solutions for addressing complex problems. What is the role of the school, particularly the curriculum in equipping 21st century workers who are today's students with the needed skills? Workers will need to be trained and retrained in latest technologies, technical reading and writing among others.

The world is becoming more connected and outsourcing services across borders becoming the norm, as globalisation accelerates. People require competences to collaborate across national and virtual boundaries to share information and emerging knowledge. Employees who wish to be highly rewarded in the workforce of the future need to be adept at using a wide range of communication technologies such as teleconferencing, text messaging and social media, where virtual teams collaborate in virtual environments daily.

New demands of work and workplaces

Curricula that prepare people for the 21st century workplace need to ensure high mastery of subject matter that forms a foundation for diverse specialisations. 21st century workplaces demand in-depth knowledge and high mastery of subject matters required for specialised work such as engineering, medicine, agriculture, teaching and others. However, technical skills are necessary but insufficient for success at work and in the 21st century workplaces. Soft skills, or 21st century skills like creativity, communication, collaboration, critical thinking, popularly known as the 4cs as well as problem solving, positive attitudes, technology savvy are needed to harness technical knowledge into effective competences. School curricula need to select content and instructional strategies that are embedded with soft skills for employability.

Climate change

As human livelihoods are persistently disrupted while widening and deepening vulnerabilities due to climate change, communities must seek solutions from different perspectives, including education. Climate change drives the need for education for sustainable development and for the educational grooming of new global citizens with sustainable lifestyles and exemplary environmental custodianship. This implies the inclusion of certain competencies in the 21st century curricula at all levels of schooling. This could take the form of new subjects introduced into the written curricula and co-curricular activities and community outreach.

Covid-19 and other emerging diseases

Untold hardships caused by malaria, Ebola, HIV/AIDS notwithstanding, the SARS COV-2 virus with its constantly changing variants nearly brought the world to a standstill from late 2019 to early 2020. The impact of covid-19 on human activities including education has been tremendous. Temporary closure of schools and ill adapted distance learning strategies have been disrupting curriculum implementation. Implications for educational and curriculum reform include:

- Health education programmes for all, focusing on prevention and control of diseases.
- Revisiting the content of health-related disciplines for professionals.
- Considering blended learning mode as the standard for curriculum delivery.
- Professional training of teachers in the use of digital technologies, distance learning pedagogies.

Social and political instability

In addition to climate change and disease, vulnerabilities are deepening due to injustice, inequity, oppression, social and political instability. Wars and terrorism may be concentrated in a few countries, but their impact is both local and global. The impact is dramatically changing foreign policy, international relations, and shared responsibilities. In 2015, nearly 60 million people were displaced due to violence, either refugees, internally displaced, or seeking asylum. In Cameroon, there is a rising increase of an ugly phenomenon of violence in schools where students stab to death their peers and teachers for trivialities and incomprehensible reasons.

These occurrences are igniting a new local and global discourse on the prevention of violent extremism through education, introducing another dimension to citizenship education that can nurture peaceful and reconciled 21st century citizens. Debates have highlighted the importance of culture and the humanities in future curricula. For example, there are more concerns now for multiculturalism, inter-religious dialogue, peace education, human rights education, and ethics interface with technology around issues of cyber criminality, security, and peace.

Advances in learning theory

Learning research is also giving a fresh emphasis to concepts such as emotion and action in learning. It emphasises learning through enactment. For example, neuroscience research suggests that complex sensorimotor networks store the information in an extended way. This renders knowledge representation stable leading to enhanced learning. Neuroscience is progressively shedding light on deep learning and by implication, on deep pedagogies. It is also providing insight into how emotion can bias a learner's attention, revealing the mechanisms by which rewarding environments can support learning and by which fearfulness and anxiety can obstruct it (Howard-Jones and Jay, 2016 cited in Marope, 2017). Through understanding the processes by which emotional stimulation and activity can engage and support the learner, the sciences of mind and brain offer a scientific basis for developing and implementing micro or classroom level curriculum. This is critical because curriculum implementation at the micro level is what gives effect to curriculum statements made at the supra, macro, and meso levels.

The broadening concept of development

The concept of development has evolved from the predominantly economistic views of the 20th and even early 21st century. Development is a "more complex and holistic concept that includes economic growth, peace, political stability, social equity, sustainability, human capabilities and conditions, human rights and freedoms, culture, politics, ethics, morals, religion, knowledge, and technology among others" (Marope et al., 2015).

Beyond growth, countries expect their education systems to support holistic, inclusive, equitable, just, and sustainable development. The expanded view of development must be visible in curricula. Curricula are not of good quality if they do not promote justice, equity, and inclusion (IBE-UNESCO 2008). Concerns for peace, justice, rights, ethics, equity, inclusion, climate, and sustainability have led to curricula for global citizenship education. Specifically, there are growing concerns for global security, peace, and stability leading to a resurgence of Delors' "learning to live together" across curricula. Other emerging international curriculum frameworks are geared towards attainment of the Sustainable Development Goals (SDGs).

Internationally agreed goals for development

The millennium development goals of 2000 and more recently the seventeen sustainable development goals stipulated by the United Nations in 2015 under agenda 2030 are significant drivers of educational change. SDG 4 addresses quality education, gender equity and life-long learning. SDG 4 can be used to achieve all other SDGs. This necessitates change in curricula and pedagogy. However, the 2020 UNESCO report on implementation of the SDGs notes that progress has been made in some areas but there is little or no evidence of significant changes in educational trends. In 2020, school closures kept 90% of students out of school (1.57 billion) over the world, causing approximately 370 million children to miss out on essential learning experiences due to the covid -19 pandemic. Many people were unable to learn remotely because they do not have access to computers or the internet at home. During March and April, about 70 nations reported moderate to severe disruptions or a complete cessation of children vaccination services. Children in impoverished and disadvantaged communities were at a considerably higher risk of child labour, child marriage, and child trafficking as more families fall into extreme poverty. This is evidence that points new directions to curriculum planning.

Industry 4.0

This is a name given to the fourth industrial revolution that describes the ongoing automation of traditional manufacturing and industrial practices using modern smart technology. This means people can analyse and diagnose issues without the need for human intervention. It should be recalled that the first industrial revolution was based on the mechanisation of production using water and steam. The second saw mass production using electricity. The third industrial revolution witnessed the use of computers and technology automation. With Industry 4.0, there is digitization of manufacturing. Artificial intelligence, robotics and biotechnology are growing at an exponential rate.

Industry 4.0 will disrupt patterns of demand for competences in the labour market, in work and in life, though the details and directions are unknown at this time. Because of the pace and intensity of change, Industry 4.0 also necessitates more foresight and capacity of curricula if they are to sustain relevance. For instance, some current jobs may disappear, and unknown ones will emerge. Tools and ways of working will transform into unknown directions. Industry 4.0 is not only about the economy and production technologies but also about the disruptive effect of technology in all facets of life. People will therefore need new competences not just for jobs and work, but more importantly for life. Are education and learning systems, and more specifically curricula preparing learners for the unknown future?

Reconceptualising and Repositioning Curriculum

In the face of such rapid changes that would affect curricula in no small measure, there are wake up calls for reconceptualising the curriculum of the 21st century. William Pinar an iconic proponent of Reconceptualist curriculum theory, held as far back as four decades ago that "what is necessary is a fundamental reconceptualization of the curriculum, how it functions and how it might function in emancipatory ways" (Pinar, 1978, p.211). Recently, Marope (2017) argued that curriculum must be reconceptualised because current conceptions confine it to learning experiences in primary and secondary education, often ignoring tertiary education, informal and non-formal learning systems. Such fragmentation of curriculum may not facilitate integration and transfer of learning which is needed if we view the challenges of the 21st century from a systems perspective. She offers a new inclusive conceptual definition of curriculum:

> "a dynamic and transformative articulation of collective expectations of the purpose, quality and relevance of education and learning to holistic, inclusive, just, peaceful, and sustainable development and to the wellbeing and fulfilment of current generations" (p.10)

The new paradigm reconceptualises curriculum along eight dimensions.
- curriculum is the first operational tool for ensuring the sustained development relevance of education and learning systems,
- it should be a catalyst for innovation, disruption, and social transformation,
- a force for social equity, justice, cohesion, stability, and peace,
- an integrative core of education systems,
- an enabler of lifelong learning,
- a determinant of the quality of education and learning,
- a determinant of key cost drivers of education and learning systems and
- a lifelong learning system.

The new paradigm also places curriculum at the centre of national development instead of the current situation where it occupies the margins or peripheries.

Re-Thinking Curricula in Africa in the Twenty-First Century

Since the Dakar and United Nations millennium summits held in 2000, access to basic education improved significantly in sub-Saharan Africa countries (SSA) with substantial increase in primary school enrolment. Reform focus began shifting to secondary education with a view to raising the quality of teaching and learning and aligning curriculum with the needs of the labour market. With the emergence of a new United Nations development agenda that produced the Sustainable Development Goals (SDGs) there was added impetus to curriculum reform efforts. SDG 4 talks about "achieving inclusive and quality education for all", namely that all girls and boys complete free primary and secondary schooling by 2030. It also aims to provide equal access to affordable vocational training; to eliminate gender and wealth disparities; and to achieve universal access to a quality higher education. Education is also seen as a means towards achieving other goals, like gender equity (SDG 5), healthy lives (SDG 3), addressing climate change (SDG 13) and promoting inclusive economic growth (SDG 8).

Apart from these global reform directives, other initiatives that have informed curriculum development and renewal in Africa include the Africa Union's Agenda 2063: The Africa We Want, and the Continental Education Strategy for Africa (CESA) 2016-2025. Many curriculum reforms have thus taken place in different African countries in response to the 21st century change factors earlier identified.

Empirical Evidence of reform efforts

Fleisch et al (2019) carried out a comprehensive study designed to update knowledge about secondary school reforms in sub-Saharan Africa (SSA) since the World Bank report in 2007. After reviewing several related published and unpublished research reports on curriculum reforms and visiting sites of case studies, the investigators reported their findings around 8 key questions. Some of the major findings organised around four themes will be presented in this section.

What kinds of curriculum reform have occurred in SSA since 2007?

Reforms that have taken place fall in two categories.

Big idea reforms. They are the dominant type of curriculum reforms often ambitious and associated with international movements, such as outcomes-based, competency-based or, most recently, 21st century skills. They require substantive and comprehensive redesign of the curriculum, particularly a shift away from the emphasis on the acquisition of knowledge towards the acquisition of skills. These so-called big idea reforms usually transform all subjects across all levels with new ways of organising the teaching programmes. Of the 25 countries reviewed, 13 adopted Competence Based Education reforms. These are Cameroon, Ethiopia, Gabon, Kenya, Madagascar, Mali, Mauritania, Nigeria, Rwanda, Senegal, Swaziland, and Tanzania.

Reforms associated with the vocationalization of the curriculum. These are subject-specific curriculum reform proposals that attempt to introduce technical, vocational and/or occupational courses and streams within the secondary school curriculum. Occurring mostly in the areas of Science, Mathematics, Languages, Geography and commercial subjects, the examples that stand out are Geography and Life Skills in Lesotho, Entrepreneurship learning in Rwanda and Life Orientation and Mathematics in South Africa.

How successful has the practical implementation of new curricula been?

A review of the research suggested that many of the "big idea" curriculum reforms have been less than successful. While the likely reasons for the lack of success are many and varied, the research can be categorised into those related to pragmatic (often implementation) challenges and those that claim the idea of competence-based educational reform is conceptually faulty. Competence based education and competency-based pedagogy have been largely unsuccessful because of under-resourced educational environment, limited language proficiency among implementers, low teacher morale and large class sizes (Esongo, 2017; Yessoufou, 2014; Komba & Mawandaji, 2015 cited in Freisch et al, 2019).

To what extent has new curriculum content promoted 21st century skills?

Twenty first century skills are communication, creativity, collaboration, critical thinking, and problem solving. Findings indicate little evidence across the continent to answer this question. Much of the school subject curriculum appears to be based on traditional assumptions about learning, which emphasise literacy and numeracy and conventional school subjects. However, 21st century skills, like critical thinking, can and have been incorporated into conventional subjects and formal examinations in South Africa.

How successful have assessments been?

Many post-colonial education systems have modified their examination systems, but old colonial examination systems continue to exist side by side with the new ones. For example, the new and the old systems can be found in Zimbabwe, where the Cambridge Ordinary and Advanced level examinations co-exist with the local ZIMSEC examination systems. The authors of this research reported paucity of literature on national or regional qualifications framework, which made it difficult to ascertain implementation, success, or failure in achieving goals. Only South Africa had the South Africa qualifications framework (SAQA) which is modelled after that of England and Australia.

Conclusions

While acknowledging the criticisms, failures and challenges facing curriculum reform efforts in the period reviewed, Fleisch et al (2019) conclude by identifying curriculum trade -offs or compromises for curriculum planners in SSA to consider for future action. They are:

- Trade-off 1: System-wide curriculum transformation vs. incremental curriculum change
- Trade-off 2: Academic curriculum vs. diversification
- Trade-off 3: Introducing new subjects vs. infusing new knowledge into existing subjects
- Trade-off 4: Curriculum depth vs. breadth
- Trade-off 5: Comprehensive schools vs. specialised schools
- Trade-off 6: Western vs. indigenous knowledge systems

- Trade-off 7: International vs. national assessment
- Trade-off 8: School-based continuous assessment vs. high stakes public examinations
- Trade-off 9: National Qualifications Frameworks

The way forward

Continuous iterations in a seemingly unending process are the very essence of curriculum development. We conclude the discussions about curriculum development in this book with acknowledgement of Udo Bude's assertion that Curriculum Development is a permanent search for qualitative improvement of the relevance and feasibility of the curriculum, in response to changes in society (Bude, 2000). Educationists will not cease to seek solutions to educational problems even after the 21st century. We also see the curriculum field in a dynamic state. The paradigm that saw education and schooling as synonymous and focused on knowledge acquisition that was predetermined and organised, is gradually giving way to a broader conceptualisation of the relationship between the two; with a focus on knowledge application thereby changing the conceptions of the curriculum. Curriculum theory and indeed the curriculum field will keep on evolving as educators devise new frameworks to understand and cope with changes around us.

Appendix A

Excerpts of the Vision Statement for Cameroon Primary School Curriculum

The vision of the new curriculum falls in line with the SDG4 which seeks to ensure inclusive and equitable quality education and promote lifelong learning for all with focus on access, equity and inclusion, quality and learning outcomes within a lifelong learning approach. This is in line with the vision of the Education Forum which states that by 2030, all girls and boys should be able to complete free, equitable and quality primary and secondary education leading to relevant and effective learning outcomes. Access to quality early childhood development, care and pre-primary education should be granted so that children are ready for primary education. By the same token, all men and women should have affordable and quality technical, vocational and tertiary education, including university; and the number of youths and adults who have relevant skills, including technical and vocational skills, for employment, decent jobs and entrepreneurship should be substantially increased. In addition, the vision of the Continental Education Strategy for Africa (CESA 2016-2025), reorienting "Africa's education and training systems to meet knowledge, competencies, skills, innovation and creativity required to nurture African core values and promote sustainable development at the national, sub-regional and continental levels" has carefully been addressed in this curriculum. The present curricular reform, taking its cue from these instruments, is an attempt to respond to current trends so as to provide an education, from early childhood that would address the needs of each child through the development of their mind-set. This is in corroboration with the law to Lay Down Guidelines for Education (1998) which states in Article 4 that the general aim of education is to ensure the intellectual, physical, civic and moral development of the child as well as its economic, socio-cultural, political and moral integration in the society.

APPENDIX B

Appendix B

I. Scheme of work for Biology form three

Family of life situations	Example of competencies expected	Sequence	Unit	Week	Lesson	Teaching-learning activities	Didactic materials	evaluation	remarks
	Biology - related - curiosity and sense of observation meal planning -making appropriate choices in meal consumption **Psychosocial** -team spirit and cooperation -healthy living	3	Promoting good health	15	7. What is a balanced diet? Examples of balanced diet	Identify common meals and say if they are balanced or not	Different meals in the locality		Health and nutrition experts can be consulted
					8 identifying nutritional and calorific requirements of males and females	Explaining variations in nutritional and caloric requirements between men and women	Food specimens, charts and models		
					9. determining the reference intake (R)or guideline daily (GDA) amount for men and women	Explanations on importance of GDA. Group work on calorific values of some packaged foods	Charts showing these values; packaged foods	Diagnostic, formative and summative evaluation	

Source: Adapted from **The Biology pedagogic office/ NASTA/TRC (2016 p.34)**. *Schemes of work for first cycle secondary general education*. **Bamenda, Cameroon**

II. Template for scheme of work used in the new competency- based curriculum in Kenya

Week	Lesson	Strand	Sub strand	Learning outcome	Inquiry question	Learning experience	Learning resource	Assessment	reflection
1									
2									
3									

Source: KICD, 2020

An extract from the primary school schemes of work

Week	Lesson	Strand	Sub strand	Learning outcome	Inquiry question	Learning experience	Learning resource	Assessment	reflection
1	1	Personal Hygiene	Use of toilets and latrines	The learner should be able to identify a toilet/latrine and urinal in the school	Why should we use the toilet/latrine and urinal appropriately?	Learners identify a toilet/latrine using charts, pictures, video clips	Charts Realia	1.Observation 2. Oral questions	
2									
3									

Source : adapted from Kenyayote.com

APPENDIX C

REPUBLIC OF CAMEROON
Peace-Work-Fatherland
****
THE UNIVERSITY OF BAMENDA
****

REPUBLIQUE DU CAMEROUN
Paix – Travail – Patrie
****
UNIVERSITE DE BAMENDA
****

COURSE OUTLINE

FACULTY/SCHOOL: HTTC Bambili
DEPARTMENT: Science of Education
SEMESTER: First 2016/2017 academic year
COURSE TITLE: Educational Technology
COURSE CODE: EDU 511
CREDIT VALUE: 3

Course Description

The course begins by introducing student teachers to facts and concepts related to educational technology as an academic discipline. General principles guiding the use of technological processes and resources in solving educational problems are presented. Major topics treated include the production, use and management of basic, traditional, modern and advanced instructional media and resources within the Cameroon context. Instructional design processes and their applications are also dealt with.

Learning Objectives

By the end of the course, the student should be able to:
- Apply appropriate technological processes, products and media to teaching, learning, counseling and administration in secondary grammar schools.
- Manage effectively technological resources for teaching and learning
- Produce and collect teaching and learning materials for teaching in different subject areas
- Design lessons using scientific principles to make instruction more effective, efficient and appealing
- Identify and analyze the strengths and limitations of modern/advanced educational media
- Facilitate distance learning using advanced technological media

Outcome

Competence in the use, management and production (where possible) of basic and advanced technological tools and processes to solve educational problems within the Cameroon school context.

Method of Teaching

Direct, indirect and interactive teaching strategies will be used with emphasis on experiential learning and independent study.

S/N	Activity	Contact hours
1	Lectures	39
2	Practicals	00
3	Tutorials	06
Total		45hrs

Assessment

S/N		Marks
1	Class presentations/ group work	15
2	Written assignment	10
3	Attendance	5
4	Semester examination	70
Total		**100**

Course Instructors

S/N	Course	Tel	Email
1	Dr. Zama Martha	677 738 321	m_zama@yahoo.com
2	Mr. Djibie	675 345 291	

Recommended Texts and References

Inyang-Abia, M.E. (1988). *Essentials of Educational technology: A handbook for educators and media practitioners.* Uyo: Legacy (Nig) Ltd.

Yogendra K. Shouma, (2002). *Fundamental aspects of Educational Technology.* New Delhi: Kanishka,

Tambo, L.I. (2012). *Principles and methods of teaching.* Limbe: Anucam.

Christian Depover, Thierry Kansenti, Banilis Komes, (2007*). Enseigner avec les Technologies. Favolifer les apprentissages, Dêveloper des Compétences,* Quebec: Presse de l'université du Quebec.

Marshall, Jones(n.d.) *What is Educational Technology?* Available at http//www.Coe.winthrop.edu > PRES_FULL_EdTech

Stôsić, L. (2015) "The importance of Educational Technology in Teaching". *International Journal of Cognitive Research In Science, Engineering And Education. volume 3 No. 1* Available at ijcrsee.com>ijcrsee>article-download.

TEACHING PLAN

Wk	SLOT		Topics	Delivery Mode			
	Day	Time		L	T	P	%
1.	Fri	7:00-10:00 (Group 1) 10:00-13:00 (Group 2)	**UNDERSTANDING BASIC CONCEPTS** -Technology, Educational Technology, - Benefits of Technology in Education -Challenges of Educational Technology Practice in Cameroon secondary schools				
2.	Fri	7:00-10:00 (Group 1) 10:00-13:00 (Group 2)	**TECHNOLOGICAL PROCESSES IN EDUCATION** _ Systems thinking and educational technology -Instructional Systems; Instructional Systems Design - ASSURE Model				

3.	Fri	7:00-10:00 (Group 1) 10:00-13:00 (Group 2)	**TECHNOLOGICAL RESOURCES IN EDUCATION** -Educational media: Types, classification, Factors affecting selection and production -ICTs and classroom communication				
4.	Fri	7:00-10:00 (Group 1) 10:00-13:00 (Group 2)	**Visual display media** Using Boards and Projectors effectively. Producing and using charts				
5.	Fri	7:00-10:00 (Group 1) 10:00-13:00 (Group 2)	**Visual Media and print media** Major features of pictures, models, real objects and Textbooks, magazines, newspapers. Uses, management, advantages and disadvantages				
6.	Fri	7:00-10:00 (Group 1) 10:00-13:00 (Group 2)	**Audio- and Audio-Visual Media** _ Effective use of radio, tapes, CDs, microphone, television for instruction. - Multimedia: smart phones, iPods, tablets				
7.	Fri	7:00-10:00 (Group 1) 10:00-13:00 (Group 2)	**The Computer System and Related Technologies** - Hardware and Software. -The Internet as a learning resource				
8.	Fri	7:00-10:00 (Group 1) 10:00-13:00 (Group 2)	**Computer Assisted Instruction** -Computer Tutorials, simulation, drill etc. -Using computers to teach learners with special needs				
9.	Fri	7:00-10:00 (Group 1) 10:00-13:00 (Group 2)	**Using Computer Programs to Support Teaching and Learning** Practice on how to use MS Word, MS Excel, MS PowerPoint.				
10.	Fri	7:00-10:00 (Group 1) 10:00-13:00 (Group 2)	**Computer Managed Instruction** Using computers to manage teaching activities: scoring and grading, attendance lists.				
11.	Fri	7:00-10:00 (Group 1) 10:00-13:00 (Group 2)	**Technologies in Distance Learning** -teleconferencing, e-learning, webinars, virtual learning environments, MOOC etc.				
12.	Fri	7:00-10:00 (Group 1) 10:00-12:00 (Group 2)	Using computers and other electronic devices for **Educational Administration and Counseling.**				
13.	Fri	7:00-10:00 (Group 1) 10:00-13:00 (Group 2)	**Other resources** -The live teacher: Similarities and differences between the live teacher and other media in teaching -Using community and other resources for learning: zoos, museums, monuments, libraries etc				
14.	Fri	7:00-10:00 (Group 1) 10:00-13:00 (Group 2)	Revision				

15.	Fri	7:00-10:00 (Group 1) 10:00-13:00 (Group 2)	Revision				

Dr. Zama Martha   Mr. Djibie   Prof. Kongnyuy P.
Course Master   **Co-Instructor**   **Head of Department**

GLOSSARY

Achievement test

A measuring tool that determines the extent to which a student has acquired knowledge or skill in a content area after instruction.

Adaptation (of curriculum)

Adjusting a new curriculum to meet the diverse needs of students and local realities.

Adoption

It is the formal acceptance of a new curriculum. Adoption may take the form of an official ceremony presided over by educational authorities.

Affective domain

One of the major areas of learning identified by Benjamin Bloom and associates in their taxonomy of educational objectives. It describes a hierarchy of six learning states that emphasise feelings, emotions, attitudes, and values.

Aptitude test

It is a cognitive measure used to predict how well an individual is likely to perform specific tasks and react to a range of situations in the future.

Articulation

A principle of curriculum design whereby elements of the curriculum show coherence over time or across content.

Assessment

The process of finding out the quantity or quality of a thing against set criteria. In curriculum studies,

Assessment of learning deals with how well a student or group of students have learned a particular set of skills or kind of knowledge using various measuring techniques. 2) It is also called testing.

Attitude

Attitude is an internal state that affects personal choices and actions over an object, person, or event.

Balance

A principle of curriculum design that seeks to ensure that there is neither too little nor too much of some elements in the curriculum.

Basic education

According to the International Standard Classification of Education, basic education comprises primary education and lower secondary education. In Cameroon basic education is limited to nursery and primary education.

Behaviourism

It is a school of psychological thought, which assumes that new behaviour is learned through conditioning. To the behaviorists, learning therefore occurs as people continually respond to stimuli in their environment.

Bilingual education

1) It is the utilization of two languages as means of instruction for students and considered part of or the entire school curriculum,

2) It includes the teaching of academic content in two languages, in a native and second language. Varying amounts of each language are used depending on the outcome goal of the model.

Bilingualism

It is the ability of someone to speak two languages. In Cameroon, this often refers to the ability to speak the two official languages, English and French.

Broad field

A broad learning area that combines several subjects, for example, science in junior secondary schools is a broad field comprising physics, chemistry, biology, and geology.

Class

1) A group of students taking a course at a given time, for example a form 4 class

2) A lesson on a specified subject, for example a physics class.

Co-curriculum

The co-curriculum comprises non-academic activities that fall outside the realm of the written curriculum although the activities are official and recommended.

Cognitive constructivism

A branch of learning psychology that believes knowledge is constructed by learners based on their existing mental structures.

Cognitive domain

This is one of the broad areas of learning identified by Benjamin Bloom and associates in his taxonomy of educational objectives. The domain describes a hierarchy of six mental skills: remembering, understanding, applying, analysing, evaluating and creating.

Cognitive strategy

A type of intellectual skill for learning and thinking. Learning strategies include rehearsal (verbally repeating, underlining, or copying materials), elaboration (associate new information with the existing one through paraphrasing, summarizing, note-taking, and questions and answers), and organizing (arranging material in an organized and meaningful order through outlining, concept mapping, advance organizer, etc.).

Cognitivism

A school of psychological thought which believes that learning occurs through mental processes, senses, and experience. Cognitivists assert that that an individual's thought processes (internal factors) contribute to outward manifestation of behaviour. Behaviour is therefore not limited to factors in the environment.

Compensatory education

It refers to programs designed to help learners that are disadvantaged in one way or the other.

Compensatory teaching

Also called remedial teaching, this is meant to help learners with identified learning difficulties.

Competence

It is a state of possessing a cluster of abilities to use knowledge skills and attitudes appropriately in a specified context. For example, an effective teacher has teaching competence

Competency- based approach

An approach to curriculum, teaching or education that emphasises learning outcomes in terms of what learners can do with what they know.

Competency

It is a statement about the knowledge and skills required to show success.

Constructivism

Constructivism is a combination of learning theory and epistemology. Constructivist learning theories hold that learners' understanding, and knowledge of the world is based on how they make meaning of their life experiences.

Continuity

It is a principle of curriculum design that allows the repetition or re iteration of curriculum elements over time.

Core curriculum

A set of learning experiences that all learners are required to have

Course

A set of lessons offered to learners for a specified duration and it leads to the award of a grade after assessment of learning.

Criterion referenced test

This kind of test is designed to show how well a student performs a task or skill or how well the student understands a concept in relation to a predetermined criterion or standard.

Cultural diversity

It is the state of having a variety of cultural or ethnic groups within a community or society.

Culture

The way of life of a people that is defined by their language, customs, beliefs, artefacts, and traditions.

Curriculum

1) All the planned and unplanned content and activities implemented in the classroom as well as other activities outside the classroom which directly or indirectly enrich learners' experiences.

2) A curriculum may be viewed as representing a practical plan for achieving the educational goals of a nation.

Curriculum aim/goal

A broad description of purposes or ends stated in general terms without criteria of achievement or mastery. Curriculum aims relate to educational aims and philosophy.

Curriculum change

Curriculum change is the process of altering some practices in the curriculum and bringing in new ones. It incorporates the concepts of innovation, reform, development, renewal, and improvement of a curriculum.

Curriculum content

It is the subject matter that students are expected to learn, expressed in the form of topics, themes, facts, concepts, rules, and principles. 2) A list of subjects indicated on a curriculum guide for study.

Curriculum decision-making

Curriculum decision -making is the process of making choices for curriculum action, requiring curriculum workers to select content, learning activities, assessment strategies and other learning opportunities from a range of alternatives.

Curriculum design

Curriculum design refers to the ways in

which curriculum components are arranged to form a unified and meaningful whole. It is also called curriculum organisation.

Curriculum development

A purposeful, progressive, and systematic process to create positive improvements in the courses and programs of an educational system.

Curriculum development process

A complex and comprehensive value -laden process that comprises situation analysis, design, development of materials, implementation, and evaluation of programs and courses.

Curriculum evaluation

Curriculum evaluation is the process of collecting, analyzing, and interpreting data to find out the extent to which curriculum goals and objective have been attained. Evaluation helps us judge the worth of a programme.

Curriculum experiences

It describes a component of curriculum that is provided to students through instructional strategies, activities, and materials. It is sometimes referred to as learning experience.

Curriculum foundations

Curriculum foundations are ideas, activities and background forces that shape the minds of curriculum developers as they determine the structure and content of a curriculum.

Curriculum guide

A curriculum guide is a document containing a broad description of educational goals and content with an underlying philosophy.

Curriculum ideology

Curriculum ideologies are personal beliefs about what educational institutions should teach, for what ends, and for what reasons

Curriculum implementation

1) It is the process of interaction between the curriculum developers and teachers, ranging from field trials to professional development and teaching. The final stage of implementation takes place within the school and the teacher occupies a central position. It includes all the activities associated with teaching and learning including evaluation.

Curriculum material

Curriculum materials are tangible resources that guide teacher planning and implementation of lessons. They include curriculum guides, syllabuses, schemes of work, lesson plans, textbooks, and audio-visual aids.

Curriculum matrix

A table or graphical illustration made when designing a curriculum to visualise the relationships between learning outcomes with what is taught and how it is taught.

Curriculum model

A model specifies or describes a procedure to be used based on theory or philosophical orientation.

Curriculum planning

A process of deciding the learning opportunities to be offered to leaners, leading to the creation of plans and materials.

Curriculum studies

A field of study in Education that deals with

the meaning of curriculum, its methods of inquiry and how curricula are developed and maintained.

Curriculum support material

Curriculum support materials are those resources that direct the teacher and student how to better exploit the conventional materials. These include teachers' guides, handbooks, student workbooks, manuals, and school timetables.

Curriculum theorising

Theorising is a process that may lead to development of curriculum theory. Whereas theory is a noun denoting the existence of a complete end-product, theorizing is a verb denoting ongoing reflections.

Curriculum theory

Curriculum theory is a coherent and systematic body of ideas used to give meaning to curriculum phenomena and problems to guide people on deciding on appropriate justifiable actions.

Development tryout

This is one on one evaluation carried out with individual learners when trying out new curriculum material.

Diagnostic evaluation

The type of evaluation made at the beginning of a lesson or a program to identify the status of the learner or prerequisites of the program.

Diffusion and Dissemination

Both processes concern spreading information to stakeholders about a new curriculum. While diffusion refers to general spread of information, dissemination involves conscious efforts to let information about a curriculum innovation to reach targeted audiences.

Education

The acquisition of knowledge, skills and attitudes that prepare individuals to fit into their roles as members of a society. It can be formal, informal, or non-formal.

Elementary school

It is an institution where children (usually between the ages of 5-12 years receive the first stage of education. It is also called primary school.

Empiricism

It is the perception that experience, especially of the senses, is the only source of knowledge.

Epistemology

It is the study of the nature of knowledge and the process of knowing. Typical epistemological questions include: "what is knowledge?" and "how do we know something?"

Essentialism

It is a common core curriculum that is based on the essential knowledge to be transmitted to students in a systematic and disciplined way, in order to preserve intellectual and moral values and standards

Deconstructionism

It is the view that education is a tool for the reconstitution of the society and the implementation of social reforms

Evaluation

Evaluation is a process that yields information about the worthiness, goodness, the appropriateness, or validity of something for which a reliable measurement or assessment has been made.

Existentialism

It is an educational philosophy which believes in the importance of individuals making choices in the school curriculum.

Expert review

This happens when educational experts give their opinions on the suitability of newly developed curriculum materials.

Field trial

In this initial phase of curriculum implementation, curriculum plans, and materials are used in the real world for a period and evaluated before their formal acceptance or revision.

Formal education

Structured and systematic form of teaching and learning. It typically takes place in schools and training institutions.

Formative evaluation

It is the kind of evaluation that is made to improve or modify a program, a course or a lesson, a textbook or any curriculum system

Hidden curriculum

It is the kind of curriculum that is neither stated anywhere nor intended by curriculum planners, consisting of invisible but influential learning experiences in the school life of learners. For example, lessons on punctuality or honesty may not be stated anywhere but students may learn these values in school.

Historical foundation

These are foundations of the curriculum that focus on how the ideas of scholars influenced the curriculum at different points in time and how these ideas have changed or evolved. Curriculum history is a useful tool to the curriculum developer/teacher as it gives them a deeper awareness about curricular changes over time.

Horizontal organisation

It is the organisation of curriculum elements in a way that recognises and determines relationships across subject matter.

Human growth and development

The process of physical, mental, moral, emotional, and social changes occurring in humans as they age and move to the end of their life spans.

Humanism

A school of psychological thought. According to humanists, the behaviour of individuals is determined by how they perceive themselves. 'Self' is the central concept in humanistic psychology. As far as learning is concerned, humanist psychologists hold that human needs and values are important influences on the learning process.

ICTs

It is an abbreviation of Information and Communication Technologies. A term used to describe diverse communication technologies and resources, including the internet, wireless networks, cell phones, computer hardware and software.

Idealism

It is a philosophy that holds the view that it is the mind that is central in understanding the world and nothing gives a greater sense of reality than the activity the mind engages in, trying to understand its world.

Individual differences

A term used to describe natural variations among humans.

Individualised instruction

A teaching approach designed to meet the needs of an individual learner.

Instruction

1) It is a process that deliberately assists someone to learn with or without the help of a human being 2) Teaching

Instructional design

1) It is the systematic planning of instruction. A process that leads to creation of specifications for plans, products and materials that are used for face to face or distance delivery of instruction.

2) It is a branch of knowledge dealing with research and theory about instructional strategies, and the procedure for developing, implementing, and evaluating these strategies.

Instructional evaluation

It deals with gathering of empirical evidence on how learners are performing or achieving the objectives of a course, unit, or lesson. Comprises teacher made tests, examination, quizzes, (written and oral).

Instructional system

It is a set of interacting parts functioning together to facilitate learning for a particular purpose. Examples of instructional systems include the curriculum, syllabus, a course, module, a lesson, a form 4 physics class, a training workshop, an educational website, web blog.

Instructional systems design (ISD)

ISD is the process by which learning products

and experiences are designed, developed, and delivered. These learning products include online courses, instructional manuals, video tutorials, learning simulations. The terms instructional design (ID), instructional technology, learning experience (LX) design, curriculum design, and instructional systems design (ISD), are sometimes used interchangeably.

Instructional theory

The body of knowledge that provides guidance on how to better help people learn and develop abilities.

Integration

It is a design principle that relates curriculum content and activities across the program. This may be achieved by identifying thematic units and integrative threads for use across subject matter.

Intellectual skills

Intellectual skills incorporate procedural knowledge (how to do things). Intellectual skills are subdivided into different levels of learning: discrimination, concrete concept, defined concept.

Kindergarten

A word commonly used in Germany and other countries to describe early childhood education that typically lasts for two years. It is called nursery school in Cameroon

Law of effect

It is one of Edward Thorndike's laws, which states that the strength of a response increases or decreases when results are satisfying.

Law of exercise

One of Edward Thorndike's laws, which states that connections between stimuli and responses are strengthened by practice and weakened when practice diminished.

Law of readiness

It is one of Edward Thorndike's laws, which states that a satisfying state of affairs results from a learner's readiness to learn. This facilitates the stimulus-response bond.

Learned curriculum

It represents what a learner internalises or acquires from exposure to school.

Learner

Also called a pupil or student, a learner is anyone enrolled in a school or a training institution.

Learner-centred design

It is a way of arranging curriculum elements such that the focus of instruction shifts from teacher to the student, with the aim of developing the independence of the learner. Students' interests and needs influence the choice of content, activities, materials, and pace of learning.

Learning

1) The process through which behaviour is changed or modified through training or experience 2) The process of constructing meaning.

Learning experiences

A wide variety of interactions among learners and different contexts and settings which transform their perceptions, facilitate understanding, and nurture the acquisition of knowledge, skills, and attitudes.

Learning objective

A statement about specific and measurable student behaviour that will indicate that learning has taken place after engaging in a learning activity.

Learning outcome

A statement of student performance after engaging in a learning activity. It could result from the attainment of a set of related learning objectives.

Learning theory

An organized set of ideas explaining how individuals acquire, retain, and recall knowledge

Lesson plan

A lesson plan is a schedule that guides the teachers on what to do in a specific time to specific group of learners. It is a kind of roadmap for every lesson. Lesson plans ensure teachers have a logical, systematic process which maximizes student learning.

Materials evaluation

This is the process of evaluating materials that a curriculum team has produced or is producing.

Maturation

It is the ability to do certain tasks at certain stages of life due to growth and development of physical and cognitive structures.

Measurement

Measurement is the assignment of numerals to objects and events according to rules (Kerlinger, 1973).

Metaphysics

It refers to an idea, doctrine or posited reality outside of human sense perception. Simply put, metaphysics refers to the studies of what cannot be reached through objective studies of material reality.

Module

In education, a module refers to an instructional unit that focuses on a particular topic. It contains information about the topic and teaching-learning activities.

Monitoring

It involves gathering information on how the implementation process is progressing. Such information facilitates the process. It is a type of formative evaluation. Monitoring is done by Heads of departments, principals, and pedagogic inspectors.

Motor skills

These are sequences of motor responses or movements, which are combined into complex performances. For example: dancing, jumping, writing, playing

Multicultural education

Learning opportunities that reflect the diverse cultures and groups within a society and within the classrooms.

Needs assessment

A systematic process for determining and addressing needs, or gaps between current conditions and desired conditions. Needs assessment also called situation analysis is an important step in curriculum planning.

Norm referenced test

A test is said to be a norm-referenced test when a student's performance score is compared with that of peers.

Null curriculum

The learning opportunities and experiences that are not taught to learners in school.

Peer group

Peer groups are social networks of children of about the same age and social stratus. These are usually classmates and playmates making them intimate to one another.

Perennialism

Perennialism in education is the idea that school curricula should focus on what is everlasting. The goal of a perennialist educator is to teach students to think rationally and develop minds that can think critically.

Philosophical foundation

Those elements of philosophy which have a bearing on choices made regarding the purposes and contents of the school. Comprises ideas originating from what people believe about the nature of knowledge and what knowledge is worthwhile for learners.

Pilot trial

This is the trial phase of implementation of curriculum plans and materials. They are usually tried with a smaller population before full implementation. Trial is done in a few schools called pilot schools.

Placement evaluation

It is the type of evaluation used to place students according to prior achievement or personal characteristics at the most appropriate point in an instructional sequence. (Madaus and Airasian,1972).

Primary education

Primary education is the first stage of formal education, coming after nursery school (pre-school or kindergarten) and before secondary school.

Process evaluation

It happens when evaluators review the whole process of curriculum making to find out how well each of the stages or phases of the curriculum process was carried out.

Program

A series of related courses whose completion leads to the award of a certificate. For example, a typical teacher education program would have courses in pedagogy, a teaching subject, among others.

Program evaluation

The systematic process of assessing and judging the effectiveness and efficiency of a program by examining its parameters, needs, components, and outcomes.

Psychological foundation

Consists of ideas emanating from psychology that form the basis of curriculum decisions. They relate to learning processes, learners' development, and their needs.

Psychomotor domain

One of the major areas of learning identified by Benjamin Bloom and associates in their taxonomy of educational objectives. It deals with making movements according to hierarchical levels.

Quadrivium

This includes music, arithmetic, geometry, and astronomy (scientific arts). After learning the basic skills of the Trivium (Grammer, Logic and Rhetoric), which are applicable to all other studies, the scientific arts known as the Quadrivium are studied. The Quadrivium is the "place where four roads meet" (arithmetic, geometry, music, and astronomy).

Readiness

Readiness to learn occurs when a child has achieved cumulative learning of component sub-skills and the developmental maturity necessary to integrate these sub-skills into the desired skill.

Reliability

The degree of consistency of results.

Scaffolding

First introduced within education by Vygotsky, this term describes the kind of support that a teacher or someone who is more knowledgeable offers to a learner.

Scheme of work

A scheme of work is an outline of teaching units that are sequentially arranged to facilitate teaching in a particular subject across a term or an academic year. Irrespective of the format used, schemes generally include topics, duration, objectives, activities, resources, and evaluation strategies.

School based curriculum development

School-based curriculum development can be seen as an endeavour aimed at diminishing dependency on central or national curricula and increasing the school's autonomy.

School time-table

A timetable is a schedule of events that guides school activities throughout the day, week, term, or year. It is a four-dimensional table that considers the teacher, the student (class), classroom and time slot (period).

Schooling

The act of receiving education or training in a specialised institution called a school.

Scope

Scope describes the amount of subject matter and learning experiences to be covered by the school or class at any one time. It concerns the breadth and depth of curriculum content.

Secondary education

A level of schooling after primary education. In some countries it is divided into junior and senior secondary sections.

Self-actualisation

Self-actualization is the full realization of one's creative, intellectual, and social potential through internal drive or intrinsic motivation.

Sequence

Sequence represents the order in which that which is to be taught will occur over time.

Situation analysis

Situation analysis is the process of examining factors that exist in the environment or society where the curriculum and instruction are going to be implemented

Social diversity

This is a phenomenon whereby a group, community or larger society consists of people belonging to subcultures, different religious inclinations, different age brackets and who may display many other differences in their characteristics.

Socialisation

A term used to describe the acquisition process of all behaviours expected of members of a society

Society centred design

The society-centred curriculum is also called the problem-centred curriculum. This design emphasizes real world experiences, group problem solving and understanding citizenship.

Sociological foundations

These are factors which intervene in the curriculum development process due to cultural beliefs, societal expectations, values, norms, and traditions of a society

Special education

It is a purposeful intervention designed to overcome or eliminate the obstacles that keep children with disabilities from learning

Spiral curriculum

It refers to a curriculum design in which key concepts are presented repeatedly throughout the curriculum, but with deepening layers of complexity, or in different applications. This concept is widely attributed to Jerome Bruner.

Subject-centred design

It is a curriculum structure where content is centred around various subjects or disciplines

Summative evaluation

It is the kind of evaluation that comes at the end of a curriculum project or a segment of instruction.

Syllabus

A detailed and operational document for teaching and learning derived from curriculum goals and focused on one subject or one theme. A syllabus indicates goals and objectives, content, and strategies for teaching, learning and evaluation according to subject areas or themes.

Systems thinking

It is a process of understanding how things influence one another as a whole. It is an approach to solving problems by focusing on the whole that often tends to be bigger than the sum of its parts.

Task analysis

Task analysis is the systematic study of the processes needed to complete tasks in order to achieve specific goals or objectives. This knowledge ensures that products and services are designed to efficiently and appropriately respond to the goals.

Taught curriculum

It describes all knowledge skills and attitudes that a teacher deliberately makes the learner to acquire.

Teacher education

1) Professional preparation for careers in teaching for nursery, primary and secondary schools.

Policies and procedures designed to equip prospective teachers with the knowledge, attitudes, behaviours, and skills they require to perform their tasks effectively in the classroom, school, and wider community.

Teaching

1) A set of activities carried out by a human being to facilitate learning.

2) A profession

Teaching strategy

A general way of approaching teaching. For example, the direct teaching strategy

Technical education

It is a kind of education which equips learners with skills that involve the use of practical approaches and physical instruments in executing projects.

Tertiary education

A level of learning after secondary education, often taking place at a university. It is also called higher education.

Test

A test is a tool, a method or an instrument intended to measure the level of student knowledge or skill.

Tested curriculum

The tested curriculum describes all the learning experiences learners are tested on.

Textbook

A textbook is an organised body of written material useful for the formal study of a subject area. Written material may be presented in print or electronic form. Textbooks are schoolbooks.

Theory

A set of related statements that are arranged

to give functional meaning to a series of events.

Verbal information

Verbal information declarative knowledge (e.g., facts, information, names, places, etc.).

Vertical organisation

This concerns organisation of curriculum elements to show their relationships over time. This is done to produce continuous and cumulative learning through the entire duration of the curriculum.

Vocational education

The kind of education that prepares learners for jobs related to a specific trade, craft, or occupation.

Written curriculum

The written curriculum consists of explicitly stated learning opportunities offered to learners in any given school system. Such statements are contained in documents like curriculum guides, syllabuses, schemes of work, timetables, textbooks, and course manuals.

Zone of proximal development

The zone of proximal development refers to the difference between what a learner can do without help and what he or she can achieve with guidance and encouragement from a skilled partner.

Bibliography

Abebe, T. (2014). The Practices and Challenges of School-Based Supervision in Government Secondary Schools of Kamashi Zone of Benshangul Gumuz Regional State. Department of Educational Planning and Management. M.A., Jimma University.

Ahmadi, A. A. (2015). Issues and prospects of effective implementation of new secondary school curriculum in Nigeria. *Journal of Education and Practice,* 6(34), 29-39.

Ahmadi, A., & Lukman, A.A. (2015). Issues and Prospects of Effective Implementation of New Secondary School Curriculum in Nigeria. *Journal of Education and Practice,* 6, 29-39.

Ajani, T. B. (2001). Educational administration and supervision: The challenges of the 21st century. *Journal of Curriculum Studies,* 2 (3), 16-31.

Amadioha, W.S (2016). Curriculum Development Practices in Nigeria: Definition, Aims and Brief History of The Comparative Education and Adaptation Centre (Cesac) *Australian Journal of Arts and Scientific Research,* 21 (2), 87-89

American Psychological Association, (2015). *APA Dictionary of psychology* (2nd ed.), Washington DC: American Psychological Association.

Amin, M. E. (2005). *Social science research: Conception, methodology and analysis.* Kampala: Makerere University Press.

Anderson, L. W. and Krathwohl, D.R. (2001). *A taxonomy for learning, teaching and assessing: A revision of Bloom's taxonomy of educational objectives.* Addison Wesley: Longman.

Anja, S. N. & Fonche, P. (2001). *A synoptic view of curriculum evolution and practices.* Bamenda, Cameroon: The Fonab Polytechnic.

Armstrong, D.G. (1989). *Developing and documenting the curriculum.* Boston: Allyn and Bacon

ASSURE Model. Retrieved from https://www.instructionaldesign.org/models/assure/

Awoniyi, T.A (1975). The Yoruba Language and the Formal School System: A Study of Colonial Language Policy in Nigeria, 1882-1952. *The International Journal of African Historical Studies,* 8 (1), 63-80

Aziz, S., Mahmood, M. & Rehman, Z. (2018). Implementation of CIPP model for quality evaluation at school level: A case study. *Journal of Education and Educational development,* 5(1), 185-206.

Beauchamp, G. (1977). Basic components of a curriculum theory. In A. Bellack & H. Kliebard (Eds.), *Curriculum and evaluation.* Berkeley: McCutchan.

Bel, R. (1971). Curriculum Definition Collection. Retrieved from http://www.homeofbob.com/pedagogy/plan/curDev/defList.htm

Bessong, F.E and Ojong, F. (2008). Supervision as an Instrument of Teaching – Learning Effectiveness: Challenge for the Nigerian Practice. *Global Journal of Educational Research* 7, (1&2), 15-20

Bestor, A. (1955). *The Restoration of Learning.* New York: Alfred A. Knopf.

Biehler, R. F., Snowman, J. & McCrown, R. (2012). *Psychology applied to teaching.* (13th edition). Belmont, CA: Wadsworth

Billings, D.M. & Halstead, J.A. (2009). *Teaching in nursing: A guide for faculty.* (3rd ed.), St Louis: Saunders Elsevier.

Bipoupout, J. (2007). *The Contribution of the Competency-based Approach to Education for All in Cameroon. Prospects*, 37, 205-221.

Bloom, B. S. (1956). *Taxonomy of educational objectives, Handbook I: The cognitive domain.* New York: David McKay C. Inc.

Bloom, B. S., Hastings, J. T. & Madaus, G. F. (1971). *Handbook on formative and summative evaluation of student learning.* New York: McGraw hill

Bobbit, F. (1918). *The Curriculum.* Boston, MA: Houghton Mifflin.

Borg, W. R. and Gall, M. D. (1989). *Educational research: An introduction* (5th ed.). White plains, NY: Longman.

Brindley, G. (1989). The role of needs analysis in adult ESL program design. In R. Johnson (ed.). *The second language curriculum.* (pp 43-78). Cambridge: Cambridge University Press.

British Council, (2008). Teaching English TKT- Essentials: Module 2- Lesson plan components. Retrieved from http://site.iugaza.edu.ps/nmasri/files/2012/02/2.2-Participant-worksheets.pdf

Brown, A. H. & Green, T. D. (2016). *The essentials of instructional design: Connecting fundamental principles with process and practice.* New York: Routledge.

Brown, B. & Shumba, A. (2011). Managing Africa's multiculturalism: Bringing the "Madiba Magic" into the African school curriculum. In, Therese M. S. Tchombe and A. B. Nsamenang (Eds.). *Handbook of African theories and practices: A generative teacher education curriculum.* (pp.531-548) Bamenda, Cameroon: HDRC.

Brown, D. F. (2006). *It's the curriculum, stupid: There's something wrong with it.* Phi Delta Kappan, 87 (10), 777–783.

Bruner, J. (1966). *Toward a theory of instruction.* Cambridge: Harvard University Press.

Bude, U. (2000). *Curriculum conferences: New directions in curriculum development in Africa.* DSE_Zed Texts: Bonn: DSE.

Cameroon (1998). Law no. 98/004 of April 1998 to lay down guidelines for education in Cameroon. Yaounde, Cameroon: MINEDUC.

Cameroon, Ministry of Basic Education (2018). *Cameroon primary school curriculum: English sub system.* Yaoundé: MINEDUB.

Cameroon, Ministry of Secondary Education. (2014). Mathematics Teaching syllabus. Yaounde: MINESEC.

Caswell, H. L & Campbell, D. S. (1935). *Curriculum development.* New York: American Book Company.

Centre for Educational Innovation. Constructivism. University of Buffalo. Retrieved from http://www.buffalo.edu/ubcei/enhance/learning/constructivism.html#title_134653 4865

Characteristics of Good Instructional Leadership. Retrieved from https://work.chron.com/characteristics-good-instructional-leadership-29287.html

Chesterton, D & Chesterton, S. (2019). School curriculum management: Who is responsible. Retrieved from https://www.researchgate.net/

publication/336375828_School_curriculum_management_Who_is_responsible/citation/download

Chikumbi, N. & Makamure, T. (2005). Training testers for quality education in Europe. *European Journal of Teacher Education*, 25(1), 11-17.

African Development Bank Group (2016). Continental Education Strategy for Africa 2016-2025. Retrieved from https://www.inclusive-education-in-action.org/resources/continental-education-strategy-africa-cesa-2016-2025#

Coolidge, A. (2014). The 5 Rules of textbook development. Available at open.bccampus.ca/2014/06/10/the-5-rules-of-textbook-development/

Cornelli, E.M. (2012). *A critical Analysis of Nyerere's Ujamaa: An Investigation of its Foundations and Values*. PhD Thesis: University of Birmingham.

Cristina, M. (2016, November 26). *Unit 4: Social and historical foundations of curriculum*. Education. htpp//www.slideshare.net

Cronbach, L. J. (1982). *Designing evaluations of educational and social programs*. San Francisco: Jossey-Bass.

Curriculum Definition Collections. Retrieved from http://www.homeofbob.com/pedagogy/plan/curDev/defList.htm#:~:text=Ralph%20Tyler%20(1957)%3A%20The,to%20attain%20its%20educational%20goals.

Curriculum Theory and Practice. Retrieved from https://nou.edu.ng/sites/default/files/201806/EDU%20731%20Curriculum%20Development%20THEORY%20%26%20PRACTICE.pdf

Curriculum Theory. Retrieved from https://www.andrews.edu/~burton/classes/edci730/BeauchampBook/chapter%204%20Curriculum%20Theory.pdf

Dasen, P. (2011). Culture, cognition, and learning. In, Therese M. S. Tchombe and A. B. Nsamenang (Eds). *Handbook of African theories and practices: A generative teacher education curriculum*. (pp. 159-174) Bamenda, Cameroon: HDRC.

Dawes, A. & Biersteker, L. (2011). Early Childhood Development. In, Therese M. S. Tchombe and A. B. Nsamenang (Eds). *Handbook of African theories and practices: A generative teacher curriculum*. (pp.111-122). Bamenda, Cameroon: HDRC.

Dewey, J. (1902). *The child and the curriculum*. Chicago: University of Chicago Press.

Dewey, J. (1933). *How We Think*. Boston: Houghton Mifflin

Dick, W., Carey, L., & Carey, J. O. (2011). *The systematic design of instruction*. Columbus, Ohio: Allyn & Bacon.

Doll, R. (1970). Retrieved from Curriculum Definition Collection. Retrieved from http://www.homeofbob.com/pedagogy/plan/curDev/defList.htm

Doll, R. C. (1978). *Curriculum improvement: Decision making process* (4th ed.). Boston: Allyn & Bacon.

Doll, W. (1970). Schools Are Killing Vital Learning Force Natural to Every Child. The Phi Delta Kappan, 51(7). Retrieved November 5, 2010, from http://www.jstor.org/stable/20372683

Duncan, J and Frymier, J. (1967). Explorations in the Systematic Study of Curriculum. *Theories into Practice*, 6, 180-199.

Eight Elements of an Effective Change Management Process. Retrieved from https://www.smartsheet.com/8-elements-effective-change-management-process

Eisner, E. W. (1979). *The educational imagination: On the design and evaluation of school programs*. New York: Macmillan.

Elmore, R. & Sykes, G. (1992). Curriculum policy. In P. W. Jackson (ed), *Handbook of research in curriculum*. New York: McMillan.

Eya, P., & Chukwu, L.C. (2012). Effective Supervision of Instruction in Nigerian Secondary Schools: Issues in Quality Assurance. Retrieved from https://www.semanticscholar.org/paper/EFFECTIVE-SUPERVISION-OF-INSTRUCTION-IN-NIGERIAN-IN-Eya-Chukwu/8529d460bd59fb216693f2b615e23a48a551fbc9

Fonkeng, G. E. (2007). *The history of education in Cameroon: 1884-2004*. Lewiston: Edwin Mellen Press.

Fonkeng, G.E. (n.d). Strategies to Reduce Repetition in Cameroon Primary Schools. Retrieved from https://www.saga.cornell.edu/saga/educconf/fonkeng.pdf

Foshay, W. and Foshay, A. (1980). The relationship of curriculum development and instructional development. *Educational leadership*, 38(8), 621-626

Fleisch, B., Gultig, J., Allais, S., & Maringe, F. (2019). *Background paper on secondary education in Africa: Curriculum reform, assessment and national qualifications frameworks*.

Fritz, C & Miller, G. (2003). Supervisory Options for Instructional Leaders in Education. *Journal of Leadership Education*, 2(2), 13-27

Gagne, R. M., Wager, W. W., Golas, K., & Keller, J. M. (2005). *Principles of instructional design* (5th Ed.). Belmont, California: Thompson Wadsworth.

Gagne, R. (1967). Curriculum research and the promotion of learning. In R. Tyler, R. Gagné, & M. Scriven (Eds.), Perspectives of curriculum evaluation (AERA monographs series on curriculum evaluation, 1, 19-38. Chicago, Illinois: Rand McNally.

Garcia, M., Virata, G. & Dunkelberg, E. (2008). The state of young children in Sub-Saharan Africa. In M. Garcia, A. Pence, and J. L. Evans (Eds.). *Africa's future, Africa's challenge: Early childhood, and development in Sub-Saharan Africa* (pp. 11-28). Washington DC: The World Bank.

Gatawa, B.S.M. (1990). *The politics of the social curriculum: An introduction*. Harare, Zimbabwe: Jongwe Press.

Gay, G. (1985). Curriculum development. In T. Husen and N. Postlethwaite (Eds.). The *International or Encyclopedia of Education*. pp.1170-9. Oxford: Pergamon Press.

Gay, L. R. (1985). *Educational evaluation and measurement: Competencies for analysis and application*. Columbus: C.E. Merrill publishing co.

Glatthorn, A. A, Boschee, F., Whitehead, B. M. & Boschee, (2008). *Curriculum Leadership: Strategies for development and implementation* (2nd ed.). Thousand Oaks, CA: Sage publications Inc.

Glatthorn, A. A, Boschee, F., Whitehead, B. M. & Boschee, (2019). *Curriculum leadership: Strategies for development and implementation*. (5th ed.). Thousand Oaks, CA: Sage publications Inc

Glatthorn, A. A. (1987). *Curriculum renewal*. Alexandria, VA: Association for Supervision and Curriculum Development (ASCD).

Glatthorn, A. A. (2004). *Developing a quality curriculum*. (1st ed.). Long Grove, Illinois: Waveland Press.

Glickman C.D., Gordon, S.P., Ross-Gordon, J.M. (2004). *Supervision and instructional leadership: A developmental approach* (6th ed.). New York: Pearson Education Inc.

Glickman, C. D., Gordon, S. P., & Ross-Gordon, J. M. (2001). *Supervision and instructional leadership* (5th ed.). Needham Heights, Massachusetts: Allyn & Bacon.

Goodlad, J. (1979). *Curriculum inquiry: the study of curriculum practice*. New York: McGraw-Hill.

Greenough, R. (1961). Africa calls development of education, the needs and problems. UNESCO

Gronlund, N. (1990). *Measurement and evaluation in teaching*. Robert Linn: Macmillan.

Guba, E. G. & Lincoln, V. S. (1981). *Effective evaluation: improving the usefulness of evaluation results through responsive and naturalistic approaches*. San Francisco: Jossey Bass.

Guggisberg, F. G. (1922). The Goal of the Gold Coast. *Journal of the Royal African Society,* 21(82), 81–91.

Gutek, G. L. (1988). *Philosophical and ideological perspectives on education*. Englewood Cliffs, NJ: Prentice-Hall.

Hailu, M. A. (2018). The Roles and Challenges of School Curriculum Committee in the Implementation and Improvement of Curriculum in the General Secondary Schools of Habru District North Wollo. *Research on Humanities and Social Sciences,* 8 (17), 1-16

Hass, G. (1987). *Curriculum planning: A new approach* (5th ed.). Boston: Allyn & Bacon.

Hawes, H. (1979). *Curriculum and reality in African primary schools*. Harlow, Essex UK: Longman group.

Hazi, T. Y. (2004). *Theory and practice of educational administration: A new approach*. Boston, MA: Orientate and Co

Heinz, Kimmerle. (2006). *Ubuntu and Communalism in African Philosophy and Art*. http://rozenbergquarterly.com Accessed 11/2/2020.

Hewitt, T. W. (2006). *Understanding and shaping curriculum: What we teach and why*. London: Sage.

Hopkins, L. T. (1941). *Interaction: The democratic process*. Boston: D. C. Heath

School curriculum and qualifications. Retrieved from https://www.Curriculumforexcellencescotland.gov.uk

Ikhianosime, F. (n d). The Problem of definition in Curriculum development and Theories. Retrieved from https://www.academia.edu/8486877/The_Problem_of_definition_in_Curriculum_development_and_Theories

Huebner, D. (1966). Curriculum Language and Classroom Meanings. In J.B. Macdonald and R.R. Leeper (eds.). *Language and Meaning*. Washington, D.C.: Association for Supervision and Curriculum Development

Huebner, D. E. (1975). The tasks of curriculum theorist. In Vikki Hillis (Ed.). *The Lure of The Transcendent: Collected Essays by Dwayne Huebner*, (pp. 212-230). Mahwah, New Jersey: Lawrence Erlbaum Associates, Publishers.

Huenecke, D. (1982). What is curriculum theorizing? What are its implications for practice?

Educational Leadership, 39 (4), 290-294.

Hunt, T. (2006). Five case histories of textbook development. In C. Braslavsky and K. Halil (eds), *Textbooks and quality learning for all: Some lessons learned from international experiences.* Geneva, Switzerland: UNESCO International Bureau of Education.

Inyang -Abia, M. E. (1988). *Essentials of educational technology: A handbook for teachers and media practitioners.* Uyo, Nigeria: Legacy (Nig.) Ltd.

Inyang-Abia, M. E. (2004). *Essentials of education technology: A handbook for teachers and media practitioners. (3rd ed.).* Calabar, Nigeria: MIFAM services Ltd.

Jackson, EP. W. (1968). *Life in classrooms.* New York: Teachers College Press.

Jansen, J. (1989). *Curriculum Reconstruction in Post-colonial Africa: A review of Literature.* UNESCO

Johnson, H. T. (1968). *Foundations of curriculum.* Columbus, OH: Charles E. Merrill.

Judd, A. S. (1917). Native Education in the Northern Provinces of Nigeria. *Journal of the Royal African Society,* 17(65), 1–10.

Kanjee, A., Sayed Y & Rodriguez, D. (2010). Curriculum planning and reform in sub-Saharan Africa. *Southern African Review of Education,* 16(1), 83-96

Kemp Design Model. Retrieved from https://www.instructionaldesign.org/models/kemp_model/

Kenya Institute of Curriculum Development KICD (2011). https//kicd.ac.ke.

Kerlinger, F. N. (1973). *Foundations of behavioral research.* (2nd ed.). New York: Holt, Rhinehart, Winston.

Kerlinger, F. N. (1986). *Foundations of behavioral research.* (3rd ed). New York: Holt, Rinehart, and Winston.

Klume, C. (2019). A look at Kenya's new curriculum implementation. Available at aka.edu/news/pages/News Details.aspx? nid=NEWS_a

Kobola, M.W. (2007) The Role of the School Principal in the Implementation of the Revised National Curriculum Statement: A Case Study. Retrieved from http://uir.unisa.ac.za/bitstream/handle/10500/1811/dissertation.pdf.txt?sequence=2

Kwabena, O 2006. The British and curriculum development in West Africa: A historical discourse. *Review of Education,* 52, 409-423.

Longstreet, W. S. & Shane, H. G. (1993). *Curriculum for a new millennium.* Boston, MA: Allyn and Bacon.

Lungwangwa, G. (2011). *An investigation into the ideology of Zambian humanism as a basis of education in Zambia.* A thesis submitted for award of M. Ed in 1980 at the University of Zambia.

Maccia, E. (1966). *Educational Theorizing and Curriculum Change.* Retrieved from https://files.eric.ed.gov/fulltext/ED018308.pdf

Macdonald, J. (1965). *A Philosophy of Education.* Glenview, Illinois: Scott, Foresman, and Company.

Maddaus, G. F. & Airasian, P. W. (1972). Functional Types of Student Evaluation. *Measurement and Evaluation in Guidance.* 4(4),221-233

Mager, R. F. (1989). *Making instructions work or skill bloomers: A step-by-step guide to designing and developing instruction that works* (2nd ed.). Atlanta, Georgia: Centre for Effective

Performance.

Major Approaches and Models of Curriculum Change. Retrieved from https://www.cleverism.com/major-approaches-models-of-change-management/

Managing the Curriculum. Retrieved from https://pdf4pro.com/view/chapter-3-managing-the-curriculum-3-1-df8e.html

Marope, M. (2017). *Reconceptualizing and repositioning curriculum in the 21st century: A global paradigm shift*. Geneva: UNESCO-IBE.

Marope, P.T.M., Chakroum, B., & Holmes, K.P. (2015). *Unleashing the potential: transforming technical and vocational education and training*. Education on the move series. Paris: UNESCO

Marsh, J.C. (1997). *Perspectives: Key concepts for understanding curriculum*. Hove, East Sussex, United Kingdom. Psychology Press.

Marsh, D. D. (1992). Enhancing Instructional Leadership: Lessons from the California School Leadership Academy. *Education and Urban Society, 24*(3), 386–409. https://doi.org/10.1177/0013124592024003006

Marzanno, R & Kendall, J. (1996). Critical Issue: Integrating Standards in the Curriculum. At: www.ncrel . Org /.../ cu 300. Htm

Marzooghi, R. (2016). Curriculum typology. *International Journal of English Linguistics, 6* (7), 166- 170.

Mager, R. (1988). *Making instruction work*. Belmont. CA: Lake Publishing Co

Mbigi, L. & Maree, J. (2005). *Ubuntu: the spirit of African transformation management*. Johannesburg: Knowledge Resources.

Mbiti, J. S. (1990). *African religions and philosophy*. Oxford: Heinemann.

McKay, D. O. (2018). *Diversity: understanding and teaching diverse students*. Retrieved from education.byu.edu.

McNamara, C. (n.d) Basic Guide to Program Evaluation (Including Outcomes Evaluation). Retrieved from https://managementhelp.org/evaluation/program-evaluation-guide.htm

McNeil, J. D. (2006). *Contemporary curriculum in thought and action*. (6th ed.). Hoboken, NJ: John Wiley & sons Inc.

McNeil, R.C., (2011). A Program Evaluation Model: Using Bloom's Taxonomy to Identify Outcome Indicators in Outcomes-Based Program Evaluations. *Journal of Adult Education, 40*(2), 24-29.

Middlewood, D. (2010). Leadership of the Curriculum: Setting the Vision. In Middlewood, D., & Burton, N. (Eds.). *Managing the curriculum*. SAGE Publications Ltd.

Miller, J. P., & Seller, W. (1990). *Curriculum: Perspectives and practice*. Toronto: Copp Clark Pitman

Mkpa, M. A. (2005). Challenges of implementing the school curriculum in Nigeria, *Journal of Curriculum studies, 12*(1), 9-17.

Moloketi, G.R. (2009). Towards a common understanding of corruption in Africa. *Public Policy and Administration, 24*(3), 331-338.

Morrison, G. R., Ross, S. M., & Kemp, J. E. (2006). *Designing effective instruction* (5th ed). New York: John Wiley and sons.

Mosweunyane, D. (2013). The African Educational Evolution: From Traditional Training to Formal

Education. *Higher Education Studies*, 3 (4), 50-59.

Moumouni, A. (1968). *Education in Africa*. London: Andre Deutsch

Mpka, M. A. (2007). *Curriculum development*. Owerri: Nyins Totan Publishers.

Mugumbate, J. & Nyanguru, A. (2013). Exploring African Philosophy: The Value of Ubuntu in Social Work. *African Journal of Social Work* 3, (1), 82-100

Mukhungulu, M.J., Kimathi, V.A and Odhiambo, A.K. (2017). African Philosophy of Education: Analysis of the Neglected Ideals of Nyerere's Ujamaa, *Journal of Education and Practice*, 178-186.

Musgrave, P.W. (1979). *Sociology of Education*. (3rd ed.). London: Methuen.

Musingafi, M. C. C., Mhute, I., Zebron, S., & Kaseke, K. E. (2015). Planning to Teach: Integrating the link among curricula, theory schemes and lesson plans in the teaching process. *Journal of Educational Practice*, 6(9), 54-60.

Nabuike, E.K., Aneke, M.C., and Otegbulu, I.T. (2016). Curriculum Implementation and Teacher Issues, Challenges and the Way Forward, *International Journal of Commerce, IT and Social Sciences*, 3 (6),41-46

Neary, M. (2003). Curriculum concepts and research. In curriculum studies in post compulsory and adult education: A teacher's and student teacher's study guide, (pp 33-56). Cheltenham, UK: Nelson Thorne's Ltd.

New Pedagogic Approach: Concepts, Advantages and Implementation. Retrieved from on 26/2/2021 from https://www.studymode.com/essays/New-Pedagogic-Approach-Concepts-Advantages-And-Implementation.

Ngalim, V. B. (2014). Harmonization of the educational subsystem of Cameroon: A multicultural perspective for democratic education. *Creative education,* 5(5), 334-346.

Ngalim, V. B. (2017a). Revisiting the political will in educational development: The case of Cameroon. *International Journal of Case studies*, 6(5), 5-18.

Ngalim, V. B. (2017b). Breaking the walls of pedagogic discrepancies in Cameroon secondary schools. *European Journal of Education Studies* 3(5) ISSN 25011111 available at https://oapub.org/edu/index.php/article/view/751/2130 accessed 14/2/

Nganga, L. & Kambutu, J. (2010). Curriculum development in Kenya. In J. D. Kirylo and A. K. Nauman (Eds.). *Curriculum development perspectives from around the world*. Olney, MD: Association for childhood education international.

Ngaujah, D.E. (2003). An Eco-cultural and Social Paradigm for Understanding Human Development: A (West African) Context. Retrieved from http://www.unige.ch/fapse/SSE/teachers/dasen/Dorris%20on%20Bame%27s%20Theorypdf

Njeuma,D., Endeley, H., Mbuntum, F., Lyonga, N and Nkweteyim, D. (1999). 'Reforming a National System of Higher Education: The Case of Cameroon,' A Report of the ADEA Working Group on Higher Education. World Bank. Retrieved on August 5th, 2013 from http://www.adeanet.org/pubadea/publications/pdf/he_cameroon_en.pdf

Nsamenang, A. B. (1992b). *Human Development in Cultural Context: A Third World Perspective*. Newbury Park, California: SAGE Publications.

Nsamenang, A. B. (1995). The force of beliefs: How the parental values of the Nso of Northwest Cameroon shape children's progress toward adult models, *Journal of Applied Developmental Psychology*, 16, (4), 613-627

Nsamenang, A. B. (2000). Indigenous approaches to developmental research. In J. G. Miller, Indigenous approaches to developmental research: An overview (pp. 1– 4). *International Society for the Study of Behavioural Development Newsletter*, 1, 37.

Nsamenang, A. B. (2004). *Cultures of human development and education: Challenge to growing up in Africa*. New York: Nova Publishers.

Nsamenang, A. B. (2006). Human ontogenesis: An indigenous African view on development and intelligence. *International Journal of Psychology*, 41 (4), 293–297.

Nsamenang, A. B. (2008). Mis(understanding) Early childhood in Africa: the force of local and global motives. In M. Garcia, A. Pence, and J. L. Evans (Eds.). *Africa's future, Africa's challenge: Early childhood, and development in Sub-Saharan Africa*. (pp. 135-150) Washington DC: The World Bank.

Nsamenang, A. B. (2015). Ecocultural Theories of Development. In Wright, J.D (Ed), *International Encyclopedia of the Social & Behavioral Sciences* (2nd ed.). pp. 838-844). Elsevier. https://doi.org/10.1016/B978-0-08-097086-8.23205-4.

Nsamenang, A.B. (2006a). One voice from Africa on the role of the ISSBD in the developing countries. Discussion paper on "Role of ISSBD in Developing Countries," 19th ISSBD Biennial Meetings, Melbourne, Australia, July.

Obanya, P. (1994). *Curriculum Reform for Educational Development in Africa: The Role of UNESCO*. Dakar Regional Office (BREDA): UNESCO

Obanya, Pai (2004). *The Dilemma of Education in Africa. Nigeria*: Heinemann Educational Books.

Ocholla, D. N. (2000). Curriculum Response to a Changing National and International Information Environment: Theoretical and Methodological Paradigms on Review and Revision. *Education for Information*, 19(2001), 143–167.

Ocitti, J. (1994). *African indigenous education: As practiced by the Acholi of Uganda*. Nairobi: East African Literature Bureau.

O.E.C.D. (2016). *Education in China: A snapshot*. Paris: O.E.C.D (Organisation for Economic Cooperation and Development.

Oliva, P. (1997). *The Curriculum: Theoretical dimensions*. New York: Longman.

Oliva, P. (2008). *Developing the Curriculum* (7th ed.). Boston, Massachusetts: Allyn & Bacon.

Oliva, P. F. (2004). *Developing the Curriculum*. Boston: Pearson.

Oluniyi. O. & Olajumoke, A.C. (2013). Curriculum Development in Nigeria; Historical Perspectives. *Journal of Educational and Social Research*, 3 (1), 73-80

Opertti, R. (2008). Competency-based approaches and the implementation of curriculum change in Latin American region: Current processes and pending challenges. In Ph. Jonnaert, R. Opertti and M Moussadak (eds.) *Competencies, logic, and curriculum development: Debates, perspectives and alternatives*. (pp.79-100.) Brussels: De Broek.

Ornstein, A.C., & Hunkins, F.P. (2018). *Curriculum foundations, principles, and issues* (7th ed.).

Pearson Education limited.

Otunga, R. N. and Nyandusi, C. (2009). *The context of curriculum development in Kenya*. Available at http://kerd.ku.ac.ke/123456789/218 .

Patton, M. Q. (1987). *How to use qualitative methods in evaluation*. Newsbury Park, London: Sage publications.

Patton, M. Q. (1997). *Utilization-focused evaluation: The new century text*. Thousand Oaks, California: Sage.

Pinar, W.F. (1978) The Reconceptualisation of Curriculum Studies. *Journal of Curriculum Studies*, 10 (3), 205-214.

Popham, W. J. (2007). Instructional insensitivity of tests: Accountability's dire drawback. Phi Delta Kappan, 89(2), 146–147

Popham, W. J., & Baker, E. I. (1970). *Systematic instruction*. Englewood Cliffs, NJ: Prentice Hall.

Posner, G. J. and Rudnitsky, A. N. (1994). *Course design: A guide to curriculum development for teachers*. (4th Ed.). White Plains: New York: Longman

Posner, G. J. Rudnitsky, A.N. (2006). *Course design: A guide to curriculum development for teachers* (7th ed.). Boston. Pearson.

Pratt, D. (1980). *Curriculum, Design and Development*. New York. Harcourt Brace Jovanovich

Priestley, M., Minty, S. & Eager, M. (2014). School-based curriculum development in Scotland: Curriculum policy and enactment. *Pedagogy, Culture and Society*, 22 (2), pp. 189-211.

Print, M. (2020). *Curriculum development and design*. (2nd ed.). New York: Routledge.

Rado, E. R. (1972). The Relevance of Education for Employment. *Journal of Modern African Studies*, 10(3), 459–475.

Ragan, W.B. (1960). *Modern Elementary Curriculum*. New York. Henry Holt.

Reiguluth, C. M. (1999a). What is instructional design theory and how is it changing? In C.M. Reiguluth (ed.). *Instructional design theories and models: A new paradigm of instructional theory Vol. II*. (pp.5-29) NJ: Lawrence Erlbaum Associates publishers.

Reynolds, P. (1997). *Traditional healers and leaders in Zimbabwe*. Athens Ohio: Ohio University Press.

Romiszowski, A.J. (1988). The Selection and Use of Instructional Media: For Improved Classroom Teaching and for Interactive, Individualized Instruction. (2nd ed.). New York: Kegan Page.

Rossett, A. (1995). Needs assessment. In, G. Anglin (Ed). *Instructional technology: past, present, and future*, (2nd ed.) (pp 138-196). Englewood, CO: Libraries unlimited.

Rwelamila, P. D., Talukhaba, A. A.& Ngowi, A. B. (1999) Tracing the African failure syndrome: the significance of 'ubuntu'. *Engineering, Construction and Architectural Management*, 6(4), 335-346.

Rwelamila, P.D., Talukhaba, A.A. and Ngowi, A.B. (1999) Tracing the African Project Failure Syndrome: The Significance of "Ubuntu". *Engineering, Construction and Architectural Management*, 6, 335-346.

Samkange,S and Samkange,TM. (1980). *Hunhuism or ubuntuism: A Zimbabwean indigenous political philosophy*. Harare: Graham Publishing

Santrock, J. W. (2011). *Educational psychology* (5th ed.). New York: McGraw-Hill Education.

Saylor, J. G., Alexander, W. M., & Lewis, A. J. (1981). *Curriculum planning for better teaching and learning* (4th ed.). New York: Holt, Rinehart & Winston.

Schubert, W. H. (1986). *Curriculum: Perspective, paradigm, and possibility.* New York: Macmillan

Schubert, W. H. (2010). Curriculum venues. In Craig Kridel (ed.) *Encyclopedia of Curriculum studies* (p. 272). Sage Publications, Inc.

Schweitzer, Karen. (2020, October 29). Curriculum Design: Definition, Purpose and Types. Retrieved from https://www.thoughtco.com/curriculum-design-definition-4154176

Sergiovanni, T. J., & Starratt, R. J. (2002). *Supervision*: (7th ed.). New York: McGraw-Hill Companies Inc.

Serpell, R. (2011). Peer group cooperation as a resource for promoting socially responsible intelligence: Ku-gwirizana ndi anzache. In Therese M. S. Tchombe and A. B. Nsamenang (Eds). *Handbook of African theories and practices: A generative teacher curriculum.* (pp. 195-204) Bamenda, Cameroon: HDRC.

Shiro, M. S. (2013). *Curriculum Theory: Confliction visions and enduring concerns.* California: Sage Publications, Inc.

Silva, E. (2009). *Measuring skills for 21st-century learning.* Phi Delta Kappan, 90(9), 630.

Silva, J., Delleman, P., & Phesia, A. (2013). Preparing English language learners for complex reading. *Educational Leadership*, 71(3), 52–56.

Sitwe, M. B. (2010). *The importance of situational analysis and needs assessment in the initial stages of curriculum development.* Retrieved from https://sitwe.wordpress.com/2010/10/29/the-importance-of-situational-analysis-and-needs-assessment-in-the-initial-stages-of-curriculum-development

Skilbeck, M. (1984). *School-based curriculum development and teacher education.* London: Harper & Row.

Smith, B.O. & Orlovsky, D.E. (1978). *Curriculum development: Issues and ideas.* Chicago: Rand McNally

Smith, B.O. Stanley, W.W. & Shores, J. H. (1957). *Fundamentals of curriculum development.* Yonkers, NY: World book company.

Smith, P. L. & Ragan, T. L. (1999). *Instructional design.* Columbus, Ohio: Merrill.

Smith, P.L & Ragan, T.J. (2005). *Instructional Design* (3rd ed.). Wiley and Sons, Inc

Smith, W & Andrews, R. (1989). *Instructional leadership: How principals make a difference.* Alexandria, Virginia: Association for Supervision and Curriculum Development.

Smith. P. L. & Ragan, T. L. (2005). *Principles of curriculum and instructional development.* Columbus, Ohio: Merrill.

Snowman, J. and Biehler, R. F. (2006). *Psychology applied to teaching* (11th ed.). Boston, MA: Houghton Mifflin.

Social and Historical Foundations of Curriculum. www. slideshare.net/MarilynCristina2/unit-4-cristina-gudio.

Soliman, I. (ed), (1981). *A model of school-based curriculum planning.* Canberra: Curriculum

Development Centre.

Srivastava, D.S. *Curriculum and Instruction*. Delhi-110033: Isha Books

Stabback, P. (2007). Guidelines for Constructing a Curriculum Framework for Basic Education. Presented at the Regional Workshop "What basic education for Africa?" Kigali, Rwanda – 25-28 September 2007 UNESCO-IBE. http://www.ibe.unesco.org/fileadmin/user_upload/COPs/News_documents/2007/0709Kigali/Curriculum_Framework_Guidelines.pdf

Statista (2016). Shipment forecast of laptops, desktop PCs and tablets worldwide from 2010 to 2021 (in million units). Statista: The Statistics Portal. https://www.statista.com/statistics/272595/global-shipmentsforecast-for-tablets-laptops-and-desktop-pcs/

Stufflebeam D.L. (2003) The CIPP Model for Evaluation. In Kellaghan T., Stufflebeam D.L. (eds.) International Handbook of Educational Evaluation. Kluwer International Handbooks of Education, vol 9. Springer, Dordrecht. https://doi.org/10.1007/978-94-010-0309-4_4.

Supervision of Instruction: The History of Supervision, Roles and Responsibilities of Supervisors, Issues Trends and Controversies. Retrieved from https://education.stateuniversity.com/pages/2472/Supervision-Instruction.html

Syomwene, A. (2020). Curriculum theory: Characteristics and functions. *European Journal of Education studies*, 7(1), 326-337.

Szostak, R. (2003). Comprehensive Curricular Reform: Providing Students with a Map of the Scholarly Enterprise. *Journal of General Education*, 52(1), 27–49.

Taba, H. (1962). *Curriculum development: Theory and practice*. New York, NY: Harcourt Brace.

Tambo, L. I. (2012). *Principles and methods of teaching*. Limbe, Cameroon: ANUCAM

Tanner, D., & Tanner, L. (1995). *Curriculum development: Theory and practice* (3rd ed.). New York: Merrill

Taylor, (2005). Background paper prepared for E and A Global printing report. The quality imperative.

Taylor, C. S. & Nolen, S. B. (2008). *Classroom assessment: Supporting teaching and learning in real classrooms*. (2nd ed.). Upper Saddle River: NJ: Pearson.

Taylor, P. (2004). How can participating processes of curriculum development impact on the quality of teaching and learning in developing countries? Available at unesdoc.unesco.org/ark/48223/pf0000146686

Tchombe, T. M. S. (1999). Structural reforms in education. Available at https://www.educationdev.net/educationdev/Docs/Ca

Tchombe, T. M. S. (2011). Cultural Strategies for Cognitive enrichment in learning among the Bamileke of the West Region of Cameroon. In, Therese M. S. Tchombe and A. B. Nsamenang (Eds). *Handbook of African theories and practices: A generative teacher curriculum*. (pp. 205-216) Bamenda, Cameroon: HDRC.

Tchombe, T. M. S. (2011). Theories of learning. In, Therese M. S. Tchombe and A. B. Nsamenang (Eds). *Handbook of African theories and practices: A generative teacher curriculum*. (pp. 175-194). Bamenda, Cameroon: HDRC.

The Academic Senate for California Community Colleges (1996). The Curriculum Committee: Role, Structure, Duties, and Standards of Good Practice. Retrieved from https://asccc.org/sites/

default/files/publications/Curriculum_0.pdf

The African Ubuntu Philosophy. University of Pretoria. Retrieved from https://repository.up.ac.za/bitstream/handle/2263/28706/04chapter4.pdf?sequence=5

The Nature of the Curriculum. Retrieved from https://www.sagepub.com/sites/default/files/upm-binaries/44334_1.pdf

Tinder, G. (1991). *Political thinking: The perennial questions*. (5th edition). New York: Harper Collins.

Tutu, D.M., (2004). *God has a dream: A vision of hope for our time*, London: Rider

Tyler, R. W. (1949). *Basic principles of curriculum and instruction*. Chicago, IL: University of Chicago Press.

Tyler, R. W. (1957). The curriculum then and now. In Proceedings of the 1956 Invitational Conference on Testing Problems. Princeton, NJ: Educational Testing Service.

Tyler, R. W. (1994). *Basic principles of curriculum and instruction*. Chicago, IL: University of Chicago Press.

Tylor, E.B. (1920). *Primitive cultures*. NY: J.P. Putnam's sons.

UNSESCO-IBE (2019). Glossary of curriculum terminology. Geneva: UNESCO International Bureau of Education (IBE)

Urevbu, A. O. (1985). *Curriculum studies*. Harlow, Essex (UK): Longman group.

Vygotsky, L. S. (1978). *Mind in society. The development of high psychological processes*. Massachusetts: Harvard University Press.

Wanzare Z (2012). Instructional supervision in public secondary schools in Kenya. Educ. Manage. Adm. Leadership. 40(2):188-216

Watkins, W. H. (1993). Black curriculum orientations: A preliminary inquiry. *Harvard Education Review*, 63(3), 321-338.

Wheeler, D. K. (1967). *Curriculum process*. London: University of London press.

Wichtner-Zoia, Y. (2012). "Ubuntu" is powerful thinking. Retrieved from http://msue.anr.msu.edu/news/ubuntu_is_powerful_thinking

Wiles, J. W. & Bondi, J.C. (2011). *Curriculum development. A guide to practice*. (8th ed.). University of North Florida: Pearson.

Wilson, L.O. (2020). Types of curriculum. Available at thesecondprinciple.com/instructional design

Witkin, B. C. & Altschuld, J. N. (1995). *Planning and conducting needs assessment: A practical guide*. Thousand Oaks, California: Sage Publications.

Worthen, B. R., & Sanders, J. R. (1987). *Educational evaluation: Alternative approaches and practical guidelines*. New York, NY: Longman press.

Wright, D. R. (1981). Africa in the School Geography Curriculum, 1820–1970. *African Affairs,* 80 (321), 551–557.

Yates, R., 2000. Curriculum overview. Retrieved from http://www.multiage-education.com/russportfolio/curriculumtopics/curoverview.html

Yendork, J.S. (2017). PSYC 335 Developmental Psychology I. Retrieved from https://godsonug.files.wordpress.com/2017/09/session-slides-4_psyc-335.pdf

Zais, R. S. (1976). *Curriculum: Principles and foundations*. New York: Harper & Row.

Index

Made in the USA
Middletown, DE
24 August 2021